web 2.0
new tools, new schools

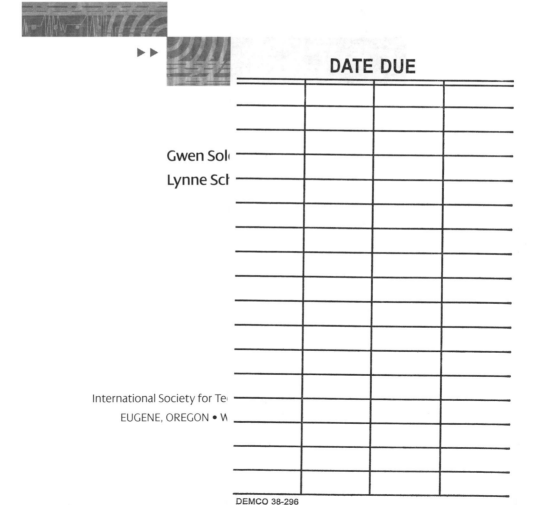

Gwen Sol

Lynne Sch

International Society for Te

EUGENE, OREGON • W

web 2.0 • new tools, new schools

Gwen Solomon and Lynne Schrum

Director of Publications: *Courtney Burkholder*
Production Editor: *Lynda Gansel*
Production Coordinator: *Maddelyn High*
Graphic Designer: *Signe Landin*
Rights and Permissions Administrator: *Diane Durrett*
Copy Editor: *Lynne Ertle*
Cover Design, Book Design, and Production: *Kim McGovern*

Library of Congress Cataloging-in-Publication Data

Solomon, Gwen, 1944-
   Web 2.0 : new tools, new schools / Gwen Solomon, Lynne Schrum. — 1st ed.
      p. cm.
   Includes bibliographical references.
   ISBN-13: 978-1-56484-234-3 (pbk.)
   1. Educational technology. 2. Web sites—Authoring programs. 3. Open source software.   I. Schrum, Lynne. II. Title.
   LB1028.3.S6195 2007
   371.33'4678—dc22

                                                                2007028802

First Edition
ISBN: 978-1-56484-234-3

Printed in the United States of America

International Society for Technology in Education (ISTE)
Washington, DC, Office:
   1710 Rhode Island Ave. NW, Suite 900, Washington, DC 20036-3132
Eugene, Oregon, Office:
   175 West Broadway, Suite 300, Eugene, OR 97401-3003
Order Desk: 1.800.336.5191
Order Fax: 1.541.302.3778
Customer Service: orders@iste.org
Book Publishing: books@iste.org
Rights and Permissions: permissions@iste.org
Web: www.iste.org

About ISTE

The International Society for Technology in Education (ISTE) is the trusted source for professional development, knowledge generation, advocacy, and leadership for innovation. A nonprofit membership association, ISTE provides leadership and service to improve teaching, learning, and school leadership by advancing the effective use of technology in PK–12 and teacher education.

Home of the National Educational Technology Standards (NETS), the Center for Applied Research in Educational Technology (CARET), and the National Educational Computing Conference (NECC), ISTE represents more than 85,000 professionals worldwide. We support our members with information, networking opportunities, and guidance as they face the challenge of transforming education. To find out more about these and other ISTE initiatives, visit our Web site at **www.iste.org**.

As part of our mission, ISTE Book Publishing works with experienced educators to develop and produce practical resources for classroom teachers, teacher educators, and technology leaders. Every manuscript we select for publication is carefully peer-reviewed and professionally edited. We look for content that emphasizes the effective use of technology where it can make a difference—increasing the productivity of teachers and administrators; helping students with unique learning styles, abilities, or backgrounds; collecting and using data for decision making at the school and district levels; and creating dynamic, project-based learning environments that engage 21st-century learners. We value your feedback on this book and other ISTE products. E-mail us at **books@iste.org**.

About the Authors

Gwen Solomon is director of techLEARNING.com, the award-winning Web site of *Technology & Learning* magazine. She is also a contributing editor to the publication. Prior to this work, Gwen was senior analyst in the U.S. Department of Education's Office of Educational Technology. Gwen also served New York City Public Schools as coordinator of instructional technology planning and as founding director of New York City's School of the Future. Before that, Gwen was a teacher and computer coordinator.

Gwen writes extensively about educational technology. Her latest book, *Connect Online: Web Learning Adventures*, written with Lynne Schrum, was published in May 2003. She also co-edited *Toward Digital Equity: Bridging the Divide in Education*, which was published in October 2003. Her other books and software are about using technology to teach writing skills. Her articles, columns, and reviews about educational technology have appeared in many publications. Some have won significant recognition and awards. Gwen also consults with educational technology companies on Web and marketing strategies. Gwen was chair of the Consortium for School Networking (CoSN) and a board member of ISTE.

Lynne Schrum is a professor and coordinator of elementary education in the College of Education at George Mason University. Prior to that, she served as chair of the Department of Teaching and Learning at the University of Utah. Her research and teaching focuses on teacher preparation, appropriate uses of information technology, and online and distance learning. She has written three books and numerous articles on these subjects. Lynne is the past-president of ISTE and currently is the editor of the *Journal of Research on Technology in Education* (JRTE).

Acknowledgments

Writing this book was a fascinating experience, the best part of which was working with other people who held parts of the puzzle we were trying to solve. We want to thank everyone we encountered along the way.

To start with, we thank the Web 2.0 Wisdom sidebar authors for providing us with such great examples of the ways they are using the tools. These people include (in alphabetical order) Helen Barrett, Steven Burt, Terry Freedman, Christine Greenhow, Tom Hammond, David Jakes, Christopher Johnson, Rich Kaestner, Scott McLeod, Robert Tinker, Harry Tuttle, Jeff Utecht, and David Warlick.

We also thank those who contributed major pieces. They include Barbara Bray and David Warlick for tutorials and Stan Solomon for compiling appendix B, Web 2.0 Tools.

The people who helped us edit our work deserve our gratitude as well. They include Mike Van Mantgem, our editor at ISTE, for his review and encouragement, and Cristin Frodella at Google for her help with the Google tools tutorials. Thanks also to Nancy Holincheck, a doctoral student at George Mason University, for assisting us in gathering information, checking for permissions, and providing other support.

We also are grateful to our families for their understanding and encouragement and to the many others whose work provided inspiration and support. They include Jo-Ann McDevitt and the staff of *Technology & Learning* magazine, home of techLEARNING.com; educators in addition to those mentioned above, such as Victoria Davis, Cheryl Oakes, Miguel Guhlin, and Tim Lauer; and the techLEARNING bloggers, whose words inspire us daily to believe that new tools will lead the way to new schools.

Contents

4 new tools in schools...77

5 professional development 99

6 leadership and new tools.........................117

introduction

let's start with a pop quiz

 YES OR NO:
Have you ever blogged, podcasted, wikied,
showed photos, or commented online?

If you said *yes* and reside in the United States, you're among 48 million people who have tried these new tools (Horrigan, 2006). If you said *no* but are still reading this, you obviously are curious about these latest technological innovations.

Welcome to the New Web, most often called Web 2.0. It is all about the free new tools such as blogs, wikis, photo and video sharing, and social networking that people are talking about and that many are using already.

What do they mean for education? These tools are changing how people, including our students, interact with the world. The changing nature of information and the new ways our students understand and make sense of the world signal that we need new strategies and new tools for teaching and learning. The challenges of the new millennium require that students be adaptable and analytical, and that they have the skills to identify and use the best tools in a rapidly changing environment.

Why should you care about these new tools and methods? After all, in spite of all the hype, technology has not yet changed schools very much. So why now—in an era of No Child Left Behind and high-stakes testing—should we care?

As you will see, the world has changed; our students have changed, and traditional schools are no longer up to the task of educating young people for the future.

You may say that the Web as we have known it is good enough, that these new tools are uncontrollable and students are venturing into uncharted territory. What was so bad about last year's tools?

With Web 1.0, students could find information online and use it (with proper citations, of course) to write reports using a word processor or PowerPoint. They could show their work to peers in class and parents at home and store it in portfolios on the school server. Sometimes they could even create Web pages that the district might allow to be posted.

Now they can write directly online in a blog and get immediate feedback from peers and others who could be anywhere. They can collaborate with peers near and far—in a wiki, also directly online. They can post photos, videos, podcasts, and other items online. The difference is that they can do the posting. They control the tools of production and publication. There are no more gatekeepers.

With these tools, people are changing the way that the real world works—business practices as well as social activities. Why not use them to change schools?

So welcome to this book, which is all about harnessing these new tools for learning. Since so much else is changing, will these tools help schools to change? Will these new technologies make the difference? We hope so. We wrote this book to help educators and policymakers understand what's at stake and why these tools are so important. We also take a look at ideas for the future of new tools in education.

We know that the world has changed. If we think back to life 20 years ago, we remember that several things we take for granted today were not in wide use, starting with cell phones, laptops, and handheld computers.

We know that technology is changing rapidly and the Web is providing new opportunities for learning, earning, and living. People no longer just search for information. Now they provide information,too. These people include our students.

We know that students are different today from students 20 years ago, mostly because of technology. To illustrate the latest versions of "the dog ate my homework" excuse, we count down Scott McNealy's (2006) top 10 reasons why students can't turn in their homework:

- ⑩ Tech support for my PC was outsourced offshore.
- ⑨ I had to delete it to make room for my iTunes.
- ⑧ I'm still handwriting it. The MS Office license was too expensive.
- ⑦ I e-mailed it … didn't you get it?
- ⑥ I couldn't afford the HP ink cartridge.

⑤ It took too long to type on a regular keyboard. Can I text it to you instead?

④ The cut and paste keys on my keyboard are worn out (Google, cut, paste).

③ I plan on "open sourcing" from the kid next to me.

② I had a visit from the Blue Screen of Death.

① The dog chewed up my laptop.

Have schools changed? Some have and more are adopting new practices. These are the new schools we mean in the title. There is no shortage of models—charter, restructured, private, public, and more. What we suggest is that to be a truly new school, it has to model new ways of teaching and learning, and of using new tools. It has to have at its core an interest in helping its students to be successful in the 21st century—in work and in play, and in all other aspects of living in a world that promises only change as the norm.

To begin with, the world is wired and that has an effect on today's students. In chapter 1, we look at how we already live in a world in which jobs are changing and requirements for workers are shifting so much that the most important skill for the future is adaptability. Part of this change is adapting to and using these new tools, and being flexible enough to learn to use the next set of tools to be able to address the next set of challenges.

Now that businesses are requiring employees to have new skills and are using new tools to run their businesses, young people need to be prepared—technologically and intellectually—partly because many countries are working hard to get their workers and students ready for globalization.

Luckily, students are off to a good start, technologically at least. Today's young people have grown up with technology, use it as a matter of course, and never knew a world without it. Chapter 2 explores these developments. We already know that certain types of pedagogy lend themselves to helping students develop 21st-century skills. Now it is time to put these methods together with new tools.

There is no shortage of tools. In chapter 3 we look at new Web-based applications that are enticing people to create, communicate, and share online. These tools are growing increasingly robust, supported by a community of creators. For the most part, our students know how to use these tools for their own purposes. Schools must help them to use the tools to learn as well as to satisfy intellectual curiosity. In addition, we are beginning to see the development and collection of another category of tools—free Web-based educational applications.

These are still early days in bringing together education and Web 2.0, yet there are models—both of learning and technology use—that point us in the right direction. We will see teachers who have guided their students to create a collaborative math solutions manual, an independent literature circle project, a collaborative guidebook about online security, and more. The educators you will meet in chapter 4 are pioneers who are an inspiration to us all.

For there to be widespread acceptance, today's educators and future educators need to be prepared. Chapter 5 looks at past models for professional development for technology integration and presents new models for both practicing and preservice teachers. The chapter examines the benefits of a community of practice approach to assisting everyone in understanding and using new ways of teaching and learning.

In addition to preparing educators, districts and schools face administrative challenges that demand new forms of leadership. Chapter 6 describes some of the complex issues facing education leaders and their strategies for coping. One solution relies on open-source infrastructure and software.

Keeping students and data safe and secure in an online environment is one of the more challenging problems today, and no more so than in schools. Chapter 7 outlines online safety and security issues. They are often difficult to resolve, but solutions and models are there for districts to implement.

Technology alone will not solve every educational problem. Some issues are intractable, but adding technology into the mix just might help, and in unexpected ways. Chapter 8 shows instances in which using new tools is having a positive effect or is showing potential to help solve complex educational issues.

Sounds pretty straightforward, doesn't it?

Of course, if you're involved with education, you already know that nothing is simple. In fact, a Public Broadcasting Service (PBS; 2006) Web site about the Story of American Public Education begins, "From the landing at Plymouth Rock to today, educators and community members have debated over the best way that government should fulfill its responsibility to educate citizens. Underlying these debates are central questions" (n.p.). The first question, according to PBS: "What is the purpose of a public education?"

It is almost 400 years later, and all we know is that there is no simple answer. At least we're still talking—and arguing. For example, the National Council of Teachers of Mathematics recommended in 2006 that we change how we teach mathematics, switching from an emphasis on what is called "fuzzy math" and returning to "the basics" (Lewin, 1999). In science education, one writer claimed, "The [science] curriculum is fragmented into tiny pieces that render the important connections invisible" (Anderson, 2006, n.p.). It sometimes seems that educational theory and practice are determined by a pendulum's swing.

In the U.S. we ask, "Does the United States work its students too hard, or not hard enough?" (Gewirtz, 1998, n.p.) We don't know if teachers give too much or too little homework or if homework makes any difference. We aren't even sure how to create effective teachers. Two 2006 reports highlighted the inadequacies of teacher preparation programs in higher education and asked if we know whether professional development in school districts is effective (Honawar, 2006; The Noyce Foundation, 2006).

We may not agree on the purpose of education or know what works in all cases, but at least we can sound a promising note about technology's use in schools. A growing body of evidence supports technology's important role in educating today's young people. Indeed, a recent report by the Metiri group stated that although its potential is still largely untapped, evidence suggests that technology can result in higher levels of learning. This review outlined trend data about technological innovations that experts and research say are working—and stated the potential of these innovations (Fadel & Lemke, 2006).

What is that potential? What will the future be? While there is no crystal ball, chapter 9 takes a look at promising ideas and chapter 10 offers a few tutorials to help you get started using some of the tools. Appendix A puts the time frame of Web 2.0 development into perspective, and appendix B lists many popular Web 2.0 tools. Utilizing Web 2.0 tools during a typical school day for students, teachers, and administrators is the topic of appendix C.

Of course, underlying all the positive implications for new tools in new schools, there is a dark side too. Web 2.0 sites and services are examples of disruptive technologies. According to Miguel Guhlin (2006e), "Social networking tools like MySpace (or Facebook and Bebo) and YouTube grant freedom of speech and assembly to the masses in a way that the American Revolution never could. For this reason, disruptive technologies are the greatest threat to the powerful who have traditionally controlled the means of publication…and that includes our schools" (n.p.).

If you care about the future of teaching and learning, this book is for you. We hope that classroom teachers will find the possibilities exciting and the examples inspiring. We hope that technology directors and coordinators will find that the explanations can help them persuade their colleagues. We hope that administrators will see how important these new tools are in educating students for their future rather than for our past. We hope that teacher educators will mine the ideas to help their students prepare. And we hope that policymakers will understand that there are solutions that will keep the education system working as well for future generations as it has for previous ones.

We believe that new solutions can improve education and prepare students for the future. Technology now provides the means to do many things that will make a real difference. Web 2.0 involves us all.

Let's take a look at where we are in the process.

1

new world,
new web, new skills

Think back to when you were in school; consider how different everything was then. There was a simpler, clearly defined path to the future, or so it seems in retrospect. While that may or may not have been true for all of us back then, no one today would view the world or the path to the future as being simple.

▶ ▶ ▶ ▶ ▶

new world

We live in a wired, globalized world in which communication and collaboration are possible 24/7. Corporations have become multinational and their workers can be anyplace and work at any time. Fast connections and standardized software link these corporations with workers wherever they are, and some members of this workforce live in parts of the world where salaries are low and benefits are unheard of. Technology is the driving force that created this environment. Technology makes people in remote locations viable employees who are eager to have the jobs.

Companies use technology to become lean and efficient. They can track their goods and services from point of origin to delivery and at every step along the way. They know what they need at any moment and can make adjustments to the supply flow in real time using technology from a distance. They trim expenses, including worker costs. When workers in Asia are as well educated as Western graduates, are just as well versed in using new tools, and require significantly smaller salaries, it is clear where the jobs will go.

> By the early 2000s, the notion of interactivity went from linking and clicking to creating and sharing. Now individuals not only find and read information but also create and share their own in real time. It is a new Web, known as Web 2.0.

The Web is changing too. It has morphed from static HTML pages where readers could find and copy information to interactive services, where visitors can create and post information. The transition from using desktop-based applications to new online tools means that we can work differently. We no longer just find and use information; the Web is now a participatory, interactive place where we create information collaboratively and share the results. Everyone can participate thanks to social networking and collaborative tools and the abundance of Web sites that allow us to post journals, photos, movies, and more. The Web is no longer a one-way street where someone controls the content. Anyone can control content in a Web 2.0 world.

So what does this mean for teaching and learning? As educational leaders, we should understand changes in the Web and how they reflect changes in the world around us. We should provide these new tools to our students so that they are prepared for new challenges.

Young people in the developed parts of the globe are very aware of the new tools at their disposal and many of them spend hours online using these tools. Because these new technologies and new capabilities engage and motivate students, we can use them to educate. If you're reading these pages, you're among the first wave of people who will move schools and educational technology forward by harnessing these new tools and new models of learning. Of course, young people may be ahead of us in using tools, but leaders like you will help them use the tools in educationally appropriate ways.

economics 102

While we debate the purpose of education in America, we have to accept that in part it is to ensure that citizens are ready to be intelligent employees. We may want to think in terms of a well-rounded education for its own sake, but that education has to include a focus on the skills and abilities that students will need if the next generation is to remain competitive in a changing world. *New York Times* columnist and Pulitzer Prize–winning author Thomas Friedman says the world is flat; the advantages the West used to have are disappearing; new dynamics are changing economics and society, and the East is gaining ground. A convergence of factors makes this a time of great change.

Friedman identifies three world "flatteners." First are the new technologies and the new processes made possible or enhanced by these technologies. Second are new ways of working and a new playing field for doing business. Third is a whole new set of people who have emerged onto the playing field and want to work. Because they have access to new technologies, they can "plug and play" their way into being competitive (Friedman, 2005).

The impact on businesses is clear. According to *BusinessWeek*, "Competition keeps intensifying around the world. For one thing, after decades of rising power, Asian companies are starting to run circles around American and European rivals across a wide variety of industries" (Hof, 2006, pp. 80–81).

For many companies, being competitive means spreading jobs throughout the world. For example, one out of every 10 jobs in the U.S. computer, software, and information technology industry will move overseas in the next two years, and one in four IT jobs will be sent offshore by 2010. The impact in dollars is as great as on employment. Daniel Pink (2006) in *A Whole New Mind* says, "At least 3.3 million white collar jobs and $136 billion in wages will shift from the U.S. to low-cost countries like India, China and Russia by 2015" (p. 39).

Competition takes place all over the globe. For example, Uruguay partners with the Indian outsourcing company Tata. "When Tata's Indian employees in Mumbai are asleep, its 650 Uruguayan engineers and programmers now pick up the work and help run the computers and backroom operations for the likes of American Express, Procter & Gamble and some major U.S. banks—all from Montevideo" (Friedman, 2006, n.p.).

Soon "technology will literally transform every aspect of business, every aspect of life, and every aspect of society." The world is changing from a primarily vertical "command and control" universe to a horizontal "connect and collaborate" one (Friedman, 2005, pp. 233–234).

The Web is key in this transformation; the democratization of information and technologies that is taking place online is a world-changing phenomenon. "These digital, mobile, personal, and virtual technologies; file changing and instant messaging; VoIP; videoconferencing; computer graphics, and new wireless technologies make all the other changes happen faster, better, and smarter" (Friedman, 2005, p. 51).

> In the future, *how* we educate our children may prove to be more important than *how much* we educate them (Binder, cited in Friedman, 2005, p. 302).

If companies in the developed world are to continue to excel at efficiency and innovation and survive against the competition, employees must acquire new skills such as having "ongoing relationships rather than executing transactions, tackling novel challenges instead of solving routine problems, and synthesizing the big picture rather than analyzing a single component" (Pink, 2006, p. 40).

Some people in the developed world will be left behind. Barbara Ehrenreich, whose books show how hard life is for the millions of people in the U.S. with low-end jobs and the problems of laid-off white-collar workers, "has started an organization called United Professionals to help white-collar workers, be they unemployed, uninsured, downsized, stressed out or merely anxious" (Greenhouse, 2006, n.p.).

Education at U.S. universities has traditionally been seen as valuable. Many students who want to reach the top have traveled there to learn. Friedman (2005) cites data from the Institute of International Education that shows in the 2004–2005 school year, 80,466 of the foreign students enrolled at colleges and universities in the U.S. were from India, 62,523 were from China, and 53,358 were from South Korea. Their enormous hunger to get ahead drives them to "outlearn the competition" (p. 214).

Now these countries are changing their precollegiate education systems to prepare the next generation. Starting in 2006 in Shanghai, according to Joseph Kahn (2006) of *The New York Times*, China is refocusing history textbooks from "wars, dynasties and revolutions to economics, technology, social customs and globalization" (n.p.). One author of the new textbooks says that the alterations "reflect a sea change in thinking about what students need to know.... The goal of our work ... is to make the study of history more mainstream and prepare our students for a new era" (n.p.).

The South Korean government is adopting open-source software for K–12 in a nationwide project to help create a national computing infrastructure and bring their national education system into the 21st century (Mereness, 2006).

"Eighteen of India's 28 states either are using Linux or have pilot projects for its use in various government departments and schools" (Lakshman, 2006, p. 40). Computer science classes based on Linux software will be mandatory in some of the states' high schools.

> It is important to ask: Who will be prepared for the new world? Who will have the technological and thinking skills needed for the 21st century? And how can we help them prepare?

"It is clear that the U.S. and other rich nations will have to transform their educational systems so as to produce workers for the jobs that will actually exist in their societies. ... In the future, *how* we educate our children may prove to be more important than *how much* we educate them" (Binder, cited in Friedman, 2005, p. 302).

Thus, it is important to ask: Who will be prepared for the new world? Who will have the technological and thinking skills needed for the 21st century? And how can we help them prepare?

Change is not based on technology alone. For example, Japan is "remaking its vaunted education system to foster greater creativity, artistry, and play. The Education Ministry has been pushing students to reflect on the meaning and mission of their lives, encouraging what it calls 'education of the heart'" (Pink, 2006, p. 53).

Intel's World Ahead Program will help emerging nations to become competitive. It will invest more than a billion dollars globally over the next five years, beginning in the Amazon rain forest, where it installed networking infrastructure and computer labs and has trained teachers. The project plans to extend wireless PC access to millions of citizens in Latin America and train more than a million teachers about the effective use of technology in the classroom. From there, project plans include such installations in other isolated communities in Africa, Asia, and the Middle East (Davis, 2006).

The United States recognizes the need to improve education. In the fall of 2006, the Business Roundtable urged Congress to pass legislation that promotes U.S. competitiveness and helps maintain the United States' science and technology leadership. Among its suggestions were to strengthen K–12 math and science education and expand undergraduate and graduate science and engineering programs.

Universal access to broadband is very important. South Korea leads all countries with 83% broadband penetration, followed by Hong Kong with 80.98%, Iceland at 74%, Israel at 69.08%, and Taiwan at 64.65%. The U.S. is in 20th place at 44.45% (WebSiteOptimization.com, 2006).

At the home and school levels, students have to take advantage of the new tools available on the Web, and teachers have to guide them with new ways of learning. Let's take a step back to see how we arrived at this technological crossroads.

new web

What we know today as the Internet (and the visual component of the World Wide Web) evolved from military to academic to commercial interests. In the 1970s, the U.S. Department of Defense wanted a secure communications system that could survive disasters. In the 1980s, the National Science Foundation (NSF) funded a network so that scientists at major universities could communicate and share research. In 1990, NSF announced a plan for privatization.

Browser software and commercialization changed the text-based Internet into the graphical World Wide Web that has become so familiar. People with access could create pages and show relationships among items; they could lead readers to follow their links. By the early 2000s, the notion of interactivity went from linking and clicking to creating and sharing. Now individuals not only find and read information but also create and share their own in real time. It is a new Web, known as Web 2.0.

Web 2.0 is an invented term, coined in 2004. (See appendix A, Web Timeline.) It encompasses the growing collection of new and emerging Web-based tools. Many are similar in function to desktop applications, with people using their browsers for access rather than installing the software on computers. Many tools are free and available to all, a change from applications that are purchased or licensed annually. Others are social in nature and promote self-expression, such as the community networks, blogs, wikis, and photo and video sharing sites.

As part of the open-source movement, programmers freely provide their source code for the sheer enjoyment of seeing their creation used. Others often add to it, improve it, and customize it. Much of this programming is built on Ajax, which stands for Asynchronous JavaScript and XML. Unlike traditional sharing on mainframe computers, today's programmers can work from any location. No one is tied to a specific workplace anymore.

Intellectually, Web 2.0 signals a transition from isolation to interconnectedness—not just for programmers but, more important, for end users. The tools allow multiple users to participate: editing, commenting, and polishing a document collaboratively rather than working alone. In some ways, both the software and the products created with it can be considered works in progress, available for anyone to contribute to, ad infinitum. Imagine a book that the author updates monthly, that others add to, edit, and correct, and that readers routinely receive a new version of each time changes occur.

Wired magazine writer Kevin Kelly (2005) sees the Web 2.0 era as one in which:

> People have come to realize that it's not the software that enables the Web that matters so much as the services that are delivered over the Web. … The net has replaced the PC as the platform that matters, just as the PC replaced the mainframe and minicomputer … and the key to success in this stage of the Web's evolution is leveraging collective intelligence. (n.p.)

These tools are effective for business success as well as for personal enjoyment. Let's take a brief look at some of the tools and then see how they've become effective for forward-looking businesses that are tapping into the technologies and strategies to succeed.

The new Web is open and democratic. There are no gatekeepers; most content is available without charge, and anyone may add to its volume of knowledge. The best example is Wikipedia. Developed by Jimmy Wales, Wikipedia is a collaborative encyclopedia that includes more entries on more subjects than the *Encyclopedia Britannica* (with about as good an accuracy rate), and the entries are created and updated by more people than you can imagine.

The United States has become a nation of bloggers, expressing ourselves as never before. According to a 2006 Pew Internet & American Life Project national phone survey, almost 40% of the approximately 147 million adult Internet users in the U.S. say they read blogs. Eight percent write blogs too. "The majority of bloggers cite an interest in sharing stories and expressing creativity. Just half say they are trying to influence the way other people think" (Pew Internet & American Life Project, 2006, p. iii). Table 1.1 shows the results of the survey.

Bloggers often have an effect on their readers. They often write about their lives, and their personal stories are compelling and bring return visitors. However, bloggers also discuss politics, media, government, and technology and some have distinguished themselves as a force for honesty and political action. Malcolm Gladwell (2002) in his analysis of change, *The Tipping Point*, identifies "connectors," people who spread the word as they see it to others. That message spreads "virally" through readership and syndication. Bloggers are connectors.

During the 2004 American presidential campaign, bloggers took on fund-raising as well as consciousness-raising roles for the Democratic primary-election candidate Howard Dean. Later, in the general election campaign, bloggers questioned the authenticity of documents offered by CBS News anchor Dan Rather, causing embarrassment for both that network and for Democratic presidential nominee John Kerry. In August 2006, bloggers "outed" a Lebanese photographer working for Reuters whose doctored photographs made events seem worse than they really were.

Table 1.1 | BLOGGER SURVEY RESULTS

The reason you personally blog	Major reason	Minor reason	Not a reason
To express yourself creatively	52%	25%	23%
To document your personal experiences or share them with others	50%	26%	24%
To stay in touch with friends and family	37%	22%	40%
To share practical knowledge or skills with others	34%	30%	35%
To motivate other people to action	29%	32%	38%
To entertain people	28%	33%	39%
To store resources or information that is important to you	28%	21%	52%
To influence the way other people think	27%	24%	49%
To network or to meet new people	16%	34%	50%
To make money	7%	8%	85%

▶ Source: Pew Internet & American Life Project Blogger Callback Survey, July 2005–February 2006. N=233. Margin of error is ± 7%.

Bloggers are quick to state their likes and dislikes about products and services too, and companies are watching consumer-written product reviews carefully. According to a report from Jupiter Research, "The growing phenomenon of consumer-generated content has become disruptive to online businesses, but many are studying the reviews and finding ways to use the content to their advantage. The research found 77 percent of online shoppers read consumer product reviews and ratings and are increasingly loyal to the stores that feature product feedback" (Sullivan, 2006, n.p.). This is a force to be reckoned with.

On the new Web, people can select from among a seemingly endless supply of content that addresses their needs instead of having information or entertainment delivered that someone else has picked for them. They can search for content online, read it, analyze it to decide what's important, interact with the author, and post the resulting knowledge. The work they post online could have as much impact as the work of any known author or expert on the topic, and the potential audience may be large and international. This is power that was unheard of before.

Given that the Web is democratic, and because Web 2.0 tools are free and available to anyone with a browser and Internet connection, everyone can have access to the sophisticated tools they need for almost any task. Because the tools themselves are adaptable, the programmers among us will rework and refine them and offer newer and even more improved models.

As broadband becomes cheaper and local communities set up wireless access from parks and other gathering places, everyone with a laptop will have access to the same sophisticated tools that professionals use. A browser is the only software needed.

new corporations

Businesses are adjusting to new realities.

For all its appeal to the young and the wired, Web 2.0 may end up having its greatest impact on business. And that could usher in more changes in corporations, already in the throes of such tech-driven transformations as globalization and outsourcing. Indeed, "what some are calling Enterprise 2.0 could flatten a raft of organizational boundaries—between managers and employees and between the company and its partners and customers" (Hof, 2006, n.p.).

Nimble corporations use technology and Web-traffic information to track customers and commodities, but there are even greater advantages from Web 2.0 tools and services. Some companies use wikis, or group-editable Web pages, for collaboration. Others use them instead of e-mail to create meeting agendas and post training videos. Some corporate executives even post on their own blogs to communicate directly with customers.

Some firms are using social-networking services. According to Rachael King (2006) of *BusinessWeek:*

> Recruiters at Microsoft and Starbucks, for instance, troll online networks such as LinkedIn for potential job candidates. Goldman Sachs and Deloitte run their own online alumni networks for hiring

back former workers and strengthening bonds with alumni-cum-possible clients. And companies such as Intuit and MINI USA have created customer networks to build brand loyalty. (n.p.)

Social network mapping helps business leaders to understand and harness the dynamics of their own workplace. "Managers are mapping informal collaborative relationships that foster creativity. Accenture created a graphic Web of social networks within client companies to analyze management. Seimans made a social network chart to show how its global software development team would work" (Jana, 2006, p. 4).

New tools are also being used to solve technology problems. For example, "companies struggle to overcome problems with current online communications, whether it's e-mail spam or the costs of maintaining company intranets that few employees use. So they're now starting to experiment with collaborative services, such as wikis" (Hof, 2006, n.p.).

As businesses and employees adopt new practices, their expectations for the next generation of employees will evolve into an assumption about technology skills and collaboration and communication skills that the new Web tools embody. Will our students be ready?

21st-century skills

As society and the world of work change, the skills that students need to live and thrive in it also change. The competition will be fierce and can come from anywhere in this flat world. In some ways, students today are ahead of their elders. Technology is second nature to them and they accept and use it without question. Schools lag behind.

The Partnership for 21st Century Skills (2004), a group that represents business and education in the United States, makes the case:

> ▶ Education is changing. We can no longer claim that the U.S. educational results are unparalleled. Students around the world outperform American students on assessments that measure 21st-century skills. Today's teachers need better tools to address this growing problem.

▶ Competition is changing internationally. Innovation and creativity no longer set U.S. education apart. Innovators around the world rival Americans in breakthroughs that fuel economic competitiveness.

▶ The workplace, jobs, and skill demands are changing. Today, *every* student, whether he/she plans to go directly into the workforce or on to a 4-year college or trade school, requires 21st-century skills to succeed. We need to ensure that *all* students are qualified to succeed in work and life in this new global economy. (p. 1)

> Using collaboration and communication tools with educational methods that also promote these skills—such as project-based learning—will help students acquire the abilities they need for the future.

The Partnership for 21st Century Skills (2006) also points out that:

▶ Standards that reflect content mastery alone do not enable accountability and measurement of 21st-century skills.

▶ An expanded approach to assessment, involving measurements that assess 21st-century skills, is necessary to ensure accountability of schools in the 21st century.

▶ Students cannot master 21st-century skills unless their teachers are well trained and supported in this type of instruction.

▶ Information and communications technology (ICT) literacy is the ability to use technology to develop 21st-century content, knowledge, and skills.

▶ Twenty-first century content areas like global awareness, financial literacy, civic literacy, and health awareness are critical to student success in communities and workplaces, and these should be taught.

▶ Targeted, sustained investment in research and development initiatives is required to promote 21st-century skills and craft teaching practices and assessment approaches that more closely convey and measure what students need to excel in the 21st century. (n.p.)

The North Central Regional Educational Laboratory (NCREL; 2003) has identified the following four categories of skills:

DIGITAL-AGE LITERACY

▶ Basic, scientific, economic, and technological literacies

▶ Visual and information literacies

▶ Multicultural literacy and global awareness

INVENTIVE THINKING

▶ Adaptability and managing complexity

▶ Self-direction

▶ Curiosity, creativity, and risk taking

▶ Higher-order thinking and sound reasoning

EFFECTIVE COMMUNICATION

▶ Teaming, collaboration, and interpersonal skills

▶ Personal, social, and civic responsibility

▶ Interactive communication

HIGH PRODUCTIVITY

▶ Prioritizing, planning, and managing for results

▶ Effective use of real-world tools

▶ Ability to produce relevant, high-quality products

The Partnership's 2004 report *Learning for the 21st Century* identifies six key elements of 21st-century learning: "emphasize core subjects; emphasize learning skills; use 21st-century tools to develop learning skills; teach and learn in a 21st-century context; teach and learn 21st-century content, and use 21st-century assessments that measure 21st-century skills" (p. 6).

Further, it reports, "Today's education system faces irrelevance unless we bridge the gap between how students live and how they learn" (p. 5). They live with Web 2.0 tools, but schools must help them use the tools to acquire new skills, not just play with them. Even more, today's education system faces irrelevance unless we bridge the gap between how well American students achieve and how well students in the rest of the world are doing.

The role of teachers will be to guide students in using the new tools for academically rigorous investigations and presentations. Which tools students choose to create with won't matter. Teachers will be able to let students with specific learning styles use the tools that address their particular needs. Students will be able to create a serious paper or video of robust content, great sophistication, and real depth.

Using collaboration and communication tools with educational methods that also promote these skills—such as project-based learning—will help students acquire the abilities they need for the future. They will also require access to a new generation of online educational software that can help them acquire and maintain needed skills. Providing access to the tools is essential.

Some U.S. federal policymakers agree. Alan Greenspan (2004), former chairman of the Federal Reserve System, says, "We need to be forward looking in order to adapt our educational system to the evolving needs of the economy and the realities of our changing society. Those efforts will require the collaboration of policymakers, education experts, and—importantly—our citizens. It is an effort that should not be postponed" (n.p.).

> To be literate today involves acquiring new skills, including those of using technology, understanding science, having global awareness, and most important, having the ability to keep learning.

However, action must follow rhetoric. Countries have to do more than test students on basic skills. China is revising textbooks and South Korea is developing a technology infrastructure. If education doesn't help today's students learn the skills they need, major advances will happen elsewhere.

We used to talk about reading, writing, and arithmetic as the essential skills for literacy. To be literate today involves acquiring new skills, including those of using technology, understanding science, having global awareness, and most important, having the ability to keep learning, which involves gathering, processing, analyzing, synthesizing, and presenting information as well as communicating and collaborating. Free, online tools can play a large role in helping students acquire these skills.

Businesses today focus on communicating, collaborating, and optimizing their use of data. According to David Wallen, business development director for the DataLan Corporation, "Collaboration is the key to successful innovation" (personal communication, 2006). To succeed, according to *BusinessWeek*, "Companies are finding new ways to differentiate themselves and create entirely new markets.... Many are finding that in an intensely networked age, cooperation works better than direct competition" (Zolli, 2006, pp. 80–81).

schools and change

The shift to Web 2.0 tools can have a profound effect on schools and learning, causing a transformation in thinking. This will happen because the tools promote creativity, collaboration, and communication, and they dovetail with learning methods in which these skills play a part. For example, when students collaborate on a project and present what they've learned, they've honed their thinking and organizational skills. New tools enable that possibility.

The old way of doing things is presentation-driven; information is delivered and tested. This approach prepares students for jobs that require simply following directions and rote skills. The new way is collaborative, with information shared, discussed, refined with others, and understood deeply. It prepares students to become part of a nimble workforce that makes decisions and keeps learning as the workplace changes. What makes the difference is preparing students with 21st-century skills using a flexible approach rather than teaching just what will be tested.

Indeed, the U.S. 2005 National Educational Technology Plan began, "Over the next decade, the United States will face ever increasing competition in the global economy.... It is the responsibility of this nation's educational enterprise— including policymakers—to help secure our economic future by ensuring that our young people are adequately prepared to meet these challenges." Among the action steps it suggested are encouraging broadband access and moving toward digital content (U.S. Department of Education, 2005, n.p.).

the tipping point

The Tipping Point author Malcolm Gladwell (2002) thinks of change as epidemics in which "ideas and products and messages and behaviors spread just like viruses do" (p. 7). The tipping point is "the moment within an epidemic when everything can change" (p. 191).

At what point will new tools and new methods catch on enough in schools to reach the tipping point? What forces are pushing school change? From this vantage point, it looks like the confluence of having new tools (both pedagogical and technological), the future economic need, the access to bandwidth, and tech-savvy students are driving change.

As educators, we can't sit on the sidelines watching it happen. We have to recognize that students' use of technology is stronger and work from our own strength, which is pedagogy. This means that we harness the technology and use it to help students learn thinking and analytical skills. They may know the tools better, but we have to help them use them wisely. As Jeff Utecht, a teacher in Shanghai, says, "If we want to engage students in learning, we need to first understand their world. This world is without borders, boundaries, and is limited only by the speed of one's Internet access" (personal communication, 2006).

What will make change happen? Gladwell (2002) identifies three factors necessary for change to occur: exceptional people who drive change by their own habits, stickiness or memorable qualities of the ideas that move others to act, and the power of context, which includes the skillful use of groups and the power of communities. Educators are agents of change.

They include people such as David Warlick, who speaks out on these issues and creates new tools for education; Miguel Guhlin, who creates change within a school district and generates blogs, podcasts, and articles to spread the word; Tim Lauer, who as a school principal uses and encourages new technologies for everyday practices for his staff, students, and parents; and David Jakes, who as a school district technology coordinator, presents workshops that use the tools, not as an end in themselves but so that teachers, and thus their students, will learn the power of communicating.

David Jakes (2006c), in a conference keynote presentation, described the "characteristics of school culture that are required for an innovation to become seamless and transparent" (n.p.). In other words, to become "sticky." Here are his thoughts:

MAKING IT STICK

1. There must be a high degree of organizational readiness for the innovation.

2. The innovation must have multiple entry points for a spectrum of usership; each of these entry points must support effective use by teachers and students.

3. The innovation must clearly address an instructional need, with benefits for both teacher and student.

4. The innovation must add value to an instructional process.

5. There must be visible and tangible results indicating that the innovation improves student learning.

6. The technology has been taken out of the technology or innovation.

7. The teacher has become a confident, active, and visible user; use becomes seamless and transparent. (n.p.)

new tools and learning

One exciting aspect of Web 2.0 tools is that they are free programs that could replace the traditional application suites for which schools ordinarily must pay. Some perform the familiar functions, such as word processors, spreadsheets, and presentation tools. While they may not have every single feature of Microsoft Word, Excel, or PowerPoint, there is an advantage to having software that is Web-based: people at different computers can use the software to collaborate on a single document or on sets of documents at the same time.

Web 2.0 is an ever-growing array of tools that people use to aggregate and interact with information in ways that are useful to them. Figure 1.1 shows several distinctions between the old and new ways of doing things, dubbed as Web 1.0 and Web 2.0.

Figure 1.1 | Comparison of old and new ways of working

Web 1.0		Web 2.0
Application based	▶	Web based
Isolated	▶	Collaborative
Offline	▶	Online
Licensed or purchased	▶	Free
Single creator	▶	Multiple collaborators
Proprietary code	▶	Open source
Copyrighted content	▶	Shared content

In July 2006, techLEARNING.com conducted a Question of the Week survey to find out if visitors thought that free Web tools would ever replace traditional application software. The results showed that more than 60% said yes, with people interested in the potential cost savings and believing that the free tools' features would eventually surpass those of offline tools. Nearly 20% of respondents said that getting everyone online to use the tools would pose a technical problem and 8% worried about security issues (techLEARNING.com, 2006).

One participant commented, "I think it is the wave of the future. We have to change our mindset and learn how to deal with the technical issues. When enough people are brave enough to use it, it will become the norm" (n.p.). While independent programmers write most Web 2.0 tools and make them freely accessible, some of the results are so successful that companies such as Google, Yahoo, and Microsoft are creating, acquiring, and offering them as part of their collections of free products.

taking advantage of new tools

We can take advantage of the features that new tools offer and tap into students' natural affinity for these tools in order to create learning experiences that expand their worldview and enhance what they learn. Specifically, the features are interconnectedness, immediacy, interactivity, communications, and community. These are the very features that keep global businesses competitive and workers in jobs.

Students can learn because of these features. Ideas and concepts on the Web are connected to one another through hyperlinks. Using these links, students can dig deeper to find information that stretches their ability to reason and analyze. They can interact with information online and connect instantly to relevant content that is also engaging and malleable. Students can collaborate on projects, consult experts, and share their data with the world. Most of all, they can build on others' learning by reading other students' posted work as a starting point for their own research and link back to it. The process fulfills the concept of leveraging collective intelligence in a community-building environment.

Only by learning this way and using these tools, will students be competitive for 21st-century jobs.

2

students and learning

While using the Web has changed the world and the workplace of the 21st century, nowhere has it had a greater effect than on the lives of young people. They play video games, communicate using text messaging and instant messaging, conduct Internet searches, download music and share files (legally, we hope), and use the Web for homework. These technologies have always been available to them. Their parents and teachers and the rest of us who weren't born into a technologically interactive world have to struggle to keep up.

▶ ▶ ▶ ▶ ▶

Marc Prensky is a speaker, writer, consultant, and educational software game designer whose theory about the differences between today's teens and the adults in their lives defines the generation gap. He calls students digital natives, people who live in a world where technology is omnipresent. He calls their parents and teachers (and us) digital immigrants, well-meaning adults who have to work at being comfortable with technology.

According to Prensky (2001), today's students:

- ▶ Are no longer the people our educational system was designed to teach

- ▶ Have not just changed incrementally from those of the past ... our students have changed radically

- ▶ Represent the first generations to grow up with this new technology

- ▶ Think and process information fundamentally differently from their predecessors

- ▶ Are all "native speakers" of the digital language of computers, video games, and the Internet (p. 1)

Of course, many adults (including tech coordinators and many teachers) are just as comfortable with technology as the most advanced teen. And, unfortunately, many students cannot afford 24/7 access to technology and thus cannot be facile. However, the definitions are useful for understanding that today's students are likely to be a wired generation and that today's teachers and parents are likely to need a little help from their young friends.

21st-century students

How wired are students? Of American households, 71% have Web access, and Americans age 13–24 now spend more time online than they do in front of the TV (Sloan & Kaihla, 2006). Seventy percent of YouTube's registered users are American; roughly 50% are under 20 (Gomes, 2006). They communicate with friends through instant messaging, download music to their iPods and MP3 players, hang out on MySpace, surf the Web, and meet friends online.

According to the NetDay Speak Up Survey (Project Tomorrow, 2006) of American students, 65% of students in Grades 6–12 use e-mail and/or an instant messenger every day, and personal Web site use (MySpace.com, for example) jumped at a rate of 300% from 2004 to 2005. By Grade 12, almost 50% of students reported personal Web site use on a weekly basis and 79% play video games. In Grades 6–12, 54% of students go online for news, sports, weather, and entertainment updates; 51% use graphic, design, photo, video editing, or music editing software; 47% conduct personal research; and 43% shop.

What does this tell us about students? NetDay's findings indicate that:

▶ Students are setting trends with their use of technology both in school and out of school. They are innovative users of technology, adopting new technologies to support their learning and their lifestyles.

▶ Communication is a key motivator for students and drives their use of technology for learning and for personal use. The result is an explosion of communications tool use and the desire to transcend communications obstacles.

▶ Students are strong believers in the power of technology to enrich their learning experiences. They have ideas about their futures that include using technology tools for learning and preparing themselves for a competitive job market. (Project Tomorrow, 2006, p. 6)

Technology affects how students live and communicate and when, where, and how they learn. They assume technology is there to help them. More and more students have access to technology from home. Data from the Corporation for Public Broadcasting (CPB; 2003) indicate that by 2002, 83% of family households in America reported computer ownership, a growth of 30% from 2000. By 2006, another study found that almost 70% of households in America subscribed to an online service and 60% of them had high-speed access (Leichtman Research Group, 2006).

Having digital technology at their fingertips all the time means that students think, work, and play differently from previous generations. Young people are ahead of the curve in using new Web tools and services, and social networking is causing concern. The upside is that the Internet helps people to connect with others who have similar interests whom they might not encounter in traditional ways. They can reach across vast distances to communicate and share.

MySpace, for example, is popular with teens. Youngsters post their biographies, exploits, photos, and more and link to a network of "friends." It's the place to be for teenagers to meet friends, brag, and just hang out. It has replaced the mall as the after-school haven for teens. It didn't exist three years before, but it celebrated its 100 millionth registered user on August 8, 2006. It is the most trafficked site and was acquired in 2006 by NewsCorp.

Of course there's a real downside. While social networking allows users to create an online persona, some people are eager to embellish the truth. The more hip the page, the more attention the page's author receives. Other young people accept what is written at face value. Teenagers often think that they can post outrageous information and photos about themselves without any consequences. Lately that has backfired with colleges and even prospective employers sifting through postings to determine a candidate's character. This out-of-control behavior has also raised the hackles of parents and educators. Schools block access and parents are starting to do so too.

Businesses are aware of the change in young people's habits and now spend substantial dollars in advertising online. "With children spending much of their time online, marketers are experimenting with new techniques," says Brian Steinberg (2006, n.p.), writing for *The Wall Street Journal Online*. OfficeMax, for example, produced a reality-show–type video that includes plugs for products. "Kids in middle school and high school tend to buy things differently," says Bob Thacker, OfficeMax's senior vice president of marketing. "These kids are online. They live online" (Steinberg, 2006, n.p.).

Today's students become technology-savvy early as toymakers target younger and younger children. VTech Holdings, a consumer-focused technology company, has adapted its V.Smile educational video games to reach children as young as nine months. The console was configured so that toddlers can learn vocabulary, motor skills, and even baby sign language. MGA Entertainment offers a virtual-reality gadget with animated digital characters that chat with kids on a BlackBerry-size handheld device and a Web site (Binkley, 2006; Palmeri, 2006).

According to the Corporation for Public Broadcasting (2003), "Preschool children are one of the fastest growing groups to be online. Only 6 percent of children ages 2–5 used the Internet from any location in 2000; two years later, parents reported that 35 percent of the same age group now went online from some location—the largest increase of any age or demographic group" (n.p.).

It is clear that youngsters and adults spend time in different places and use different tools. One result of the NetDay Speak Up Survey (Project Tomorrow, 2006) was an analysis of the differences in product use among different age groups and between students and educators (Table 2.1). For example, sixth grade is the tipping point when students begin to show their enthusiasm for using technology for communication. In middle schools, 50% of sixth graders say they use e-mail or instant messaging on a daily basis. It is interesting to note that only for desktop and laptop computer use do teachers employ a technology product more than students do; on all other items, students are using the technology more than teachers.

Table 2.1 │ TECHNOLOGY USE AMONG STUDENTS AND EDUCATORS				
Technology products used on a weekly basis	**K–3**	**3–6**	**6–12**	**Teacher**
Desktop computer	63%	60%	82%	93%
Laptop computer	21%	28%	35%	39%
Cell phone	39%	49%	75%	60%
Handheld device (PDA)	n/a	14%	16%	11%
Digital camera	21%	25%	43%	36%
Video camera	14%	16%	22%	9%
DVD or CD burner	24%	31%	59%	32%
MP3 player or iPod	12%	22%	46%	6%
Video game player	53%	55%	61%	3%

▶ Adapted from Project Tomorrow, 2006, p. 7.

how children get information

Students have always been social. (Watch the interaction among groups of seventh-grade girls to understand.) Older technologies such as television weren't social; individuals watched passively even if they would talk about what they had seen. Today's technologies are interactive. Students go online to meet friends, seek information, and find out what they need to know. These are social activities and involve instant messaging, e-mails, blogs, and social-networking Web sites.

Young people's personal networks of friends are always available. Youngsters are part of a group even when alone in their bedrooms. They interact, get advice, form opinions, plan events, and gather with friends. As their interests vary, their groups vary, and so they may be part of several networks at one time.

School-age youngsters use the Web to do homework and school projects—from home. According to a study commissioned by the Pew Internet & American Life Project (Levin & Arafeh, 2002), "For the most part, students' educational use of the Web occurs outside of the school day." Unfortunately, "Many schools and teachers have not yet recognized—much less responded to—the new ways students communicate and access information over the Internet" (p. iii).

> Students come to school knowledgeable about the Web and its potential, are comfortable using it, and expect learning in school to be more like learning on their own.

The Corporation for Public Broadcasting (2003) found that "In households with broadband connections, children ages 6–17 reported that high-speed access affected both their online and offline activities, including schoolwork. According to these children, since getting broadband, 66 percent spend more time online; 36 percent watch less television, and 23 percent get better grades" (n.p.). Many parents report grade increases as well.

Students do not even have to scramble to find information; now it comes to them. Using aggregators (software that checks for new content at user-determined locations and retrieves updates) and syndication (which makes part of a Web site available to other sites or to subscribers) they can receive automated updates about any information they want. Even if they don't subscribe to syndicated feeds, everything they look at has links to other things. For example, if they start a research project by looking up the topic at Wikipedia, they'll find dozens of links to other sites with more information on that topic that they can follow—and when they get there, they'll find even more links.

Today, advice is always available online. Adults make decisions about purchases by going to the Web and researching not only traditional reviewers' opinions but also by visiting sites that contain users' reviews. Online companies are themselves presenting suggestions about their own products based on what others have bought. Web sites such as Amazon.com use sophisticated software to figure out purchasing patterns and then use that information to make suggestions for additional purchases.

For example, by using word pattern analyses, Amazon can suggest additional books a reader might like, informing you that "People who bought this book also bought…" or offer a related book as a set with the one you want—at a slight discount for purchasing both. In addition, Amazon displays the opinions of other readers as reviews and as lists of related books.

This means that students come to school knowledgeable about the Web and its potential, are comfortable using it, and expect learning in school to be more like learning on their own. "Large numbers of students say they are changing because of their out-of-school use of the Internet—and their reliance on it. Internet-savvy students are coming to school with different expectations, different skills, and access to different resources" (Levin & Arafeh, 2002, p. v).

With E-Rate funding and local support, more students are going online from school as well as from home. By 2002, key findings from a U.S. Department of Education survey showed that 99% of U.S. public schools already had access to the Internet, 88–96% had classroom access, and 94% of schools had broadband connections (National Center for Education Statistics [NCES], 2003).

what students want from their schools

Today's students know that they are tech-savvy and report that their schools are not. Schools are still more text-dominated and do not integrate technology into student learning effectively. A 2005 report, "Listening to Student Voices on Technology: Today's Tech-Savvy Students Are Stuck in Text-Dominated Schools", reviews articles and papers on student attitudes, perceptions, and behaviors about using digital technology, particularly for learning. The summary also highlights what students want adults who influence education policy decisions to know about how they use technology and how schools could better meet their needs (Farris-Berg, 2005). The report's findings are:

- Computer and Internet use is growing

- Students are sophisticated users

- Technology is important to students' education

- Technology is not an "extra"

- In-school access to technology is limited

- Home use dominates

- In-school use is not integrated

- Computers and the Internet are communications tools, first

- Metaphors describe how students use the Internet for school

  - *The Internet as virtual guidance counselor*

  - *The Internet as virtual textbook and reference library*

  - *The Internet as virtual tutor, study short-cut, study group*

  - *The Internet as virtual locker, backpack, and notebook*

- Technology has caused students to approach life differently, but adults act as though nothing has changed

- Students desire increased in-school access

- Students want to use technology to learn, and in a variety of ways

- Students want challenging, technologically oriented instructional activities

- Students want adults to move beyond using the "Internet for Internet's sake"

- Students want to learn the basics, too

the customization generation

According to middle-school teacher Jeff Utecht (2006) at his Web site The Thinking Stick, "What I am starting to see is that if students cannot customize a technology device to their way, their style, then it does not interest them" (n.p.). He gives an example:

> Derek walked into technology class like he does every "A" day on his schedule. A quick "Hello Mr. U" and off to his computer. By the time I greet the other students and we begin class, Derek has done the following to his class computer:
>
> ❶ Change the desktop background to another picture in the sample picture folder. Why? Because the one that was there was not his.
>
> ❷ Change the settings of the Windows menus to reflect his colors, font, style. Why? He didn't pick those colors.
>
> ❸ Quickly go into the control panel and change the cursor to a twirling dinosaur. Why? He likes it that way.
>
> ❹ Get the height of his chair just right, move the mouse and mouse pad where it is comfortable for him. (n.p.)

Utecht (2006) is asking the right questions:

> How do we take this customization generation and apply that customization in the classroom? Allow students to choose their method of presentation, choose where they go to find their information, and choose to learn in a way that meets their needs. Can we have customized classrooms? Where each student has access and uses the tools they need to learn. Where the teacher is customizable giving each student just what he or she needs to succeed. How would our students react if we gave them the control to customize their education? (n.p.)

Outside of school, students are using the Web for homework as well as for fun, and to a great extent they do customize what and how to learn. The desire to do this is not new, however; only the tools are. With these tools, students have much more power to do as they wish. Schools may have a ways to go to match the experience students have elsewhere, but the goal is to help students use and enjoy technology in order to learn.

access to online tools and services

In any discussion of new tools, it is clear that access to them must come first. In the first national educational technology plan, issued in 1996 and titled *Getting America's Students Ready for the 21st Century,* access was defined as five students per computer (U.S. Department of Education, 1996).

If, as we saw in the previous chapter, access to online tools and services has changed the way the world operates, then students' needs have changed. If businesses have harnessed blogs and wikis, for example, then students will be expected to use these tools. For schools, this means implementing one-to-one computing programs so that each student has access where and when he or she needs it.

A 2006 American Digital Schools survey of the top 2,500 U.S. school districts found that 19.4% of all student devices today are mobile and that 52.1% will be mobile in 2011. This is not a frill. Where results were tracked, 87% of schools offering one-to-one computing reported substantial academic improvement, and the districts and states that have one-to-one programs reported higher attendance rates, fewer discipline problems, and improved student writing skills.

In 10 years of research into laptop programs, Saul Rockman, an evaluator of educational technology projects, found that one of the most important benefits of a laptop program is an increase in 21st-century skills. Students learned independently, collaborated with peers to accomplish work, and communicated the conclusions. Teachers were more likely to encourage student-led inquiry and collaborative work. Test score results improved. "These accomplishments are seen in many laptop programs, especially those that permit students to take their computer home in the evening" (Rockman, 2003, p. 27).

The kind of learning students do with these laptops will define how well they will perform the rest of their lives. Thomas Friedman points out the importance of teaching greater collaboration skills, creating a sustainable community of learning, cultivating the entrepreneurial spirit in all, and encouraging synthesis skills. "The ability to memorize is quickly fading in our information rich society where a Google search can return millions of references. Society needs more synthesizers capable of filtering divergent sources into a coherent, relevant whole" (Friedman, 2006, n.p.).

School leaders have to think differently and promote teaching methods such as those we discuss later in this chapter. According to Daniel Pink (2006), today's students will need "a new set of aptitudes. They'll need to do what workers abroad cannot do equally well for much less money: Forging relationships rather than executing transactions, tackling novel challenges instead of solving routine problems, and synthesizing the big picture rather than analyzing a single component" (p. 40).

To help students acquire these skills takes time and training as well as practice. The first step is to understand how learning works.

understanding learning

Bloom's Taxonomy (Bloom, 1956) described learning in six cognitive process dimensions: remembering, understanding, applying, analyzing, evaluating, and creating. His taxonomy, however, was one-dimensional. A team of cognitive psychologists updated the taxonomy in 2001 by developing a two-dimensional version to reflect relevance to 21st-century work (Anderson & Krathwohl, 2001).

In this adaptation, the knowledge dimension represents the kind of knowledge to be learned, and the cognitive process dimension identifies the process used to learn. The knowledge dimension is composed of the following four levels:

❶ Factual knowledge includes an elementary knowledge students must know to be acquainted with a discipline or to be able to solve problems in it; for example, knowledge of terminology and knowledge of details and elements.

❷ Conceptual (declarative) knowledge refers to an understanding of the interrelationships among the basic elements within a larger structure that enable them to function together; for example, knowledge of classifications and categories, principles and generalizations, or theories, models, and structures.

❸ Procedural knowledge is an understanding of how to do something, methods of inquiry, and criteria for using skills, algorithms, techniques, and methods.

❹ Meta-cognitive knowledge is the knowledge of cognition in general as well as awareness and knowledge of one's own cognition.

The differences between the traditional and newer versions of Bloom's Taxonomy are displayed in Figure 2.1. The distinctions indicate that new technology tools have the capacity to support higher order thinking and more engaged learning. The revised taxonomy addresses the needs of today's students (Krathwohl, 2002).

Figure 2.1 | Comparison of the revised taxonomy with Bloom's traditional version

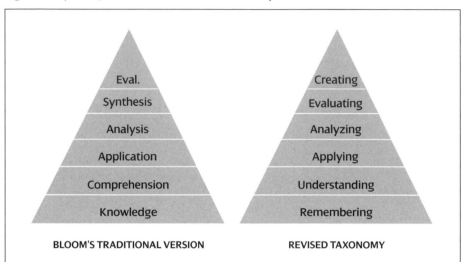

BLOOM'S TRADITIONAL VERSION (pyramid levels top to bottom): Eval., Synthesis, Analysis, Application, Comprehension, Knowledge

REVISED TAXONOMY (pyramid levels top to bottom): Creating, Evaluating, Analyzing, Applying, Understanding, Remembering

▶ Source: http://web.odu.edu/educ/llschult/blooms_taxonomy.htm

In Figure 2.1, note the change from nouns to verbs (e.g., Application to Applying) to describe the different levels of the taxonomy (Schultz, 2005). Anderson and Krathwohl (2001) explain these terms as follows:

Remembering. Retrieving, recognizing, and recalling relevant knowledge from long-term memory.

Understanding. Constructing meaning from oral, written, and graphic messages through interpreting, exemplifying, classifying, summarizing, inferring, comparing, and explaining.

Applying. Carrying out or using a procedure through executing, or implementing.

Analyzing. Breaking material into constituent parts, determining how the parts relate to one another and to an overall structure or purpose through differentiating, organizing, and attributing.

Evaluating. Making judgments based on criteria and standards through checking and critiquing.

Creating. Putting elements together to form a coherent or functional whole; reorganizing elements into a new pattern or structure through generating, planning, or producing. (pp. 67–68)

To help students acquire these skills and become synthesizers means not just providing access to technological tools but also employing the pedagogical tools that are more powerful when combined with technology. When pedagogies and technologies are grounded in how students learn, schools provide the best strategies.

To begin with, students learn in a variety of ways. They have different learning styles that are based on how they understand and process information. For example, there are visual learners, auditory learners, and tactile/kinesthetic learners. Technology makes it possible to target the right approaches for each student in order to provide individualized and differentiated instruction.

We turn to cognitive science to understand how the brain functions and how people learn. These scientific approaches have indicated that everyone learns, but schools do not always understand how best to approach each student. According to Renate and Geoffrey Caine (On Purpose Associates, 2001), the following are the core principles of brain-based learning:

1. The brain is a parallel processor, meaning it can perform several activities at once, like tasting and smelling.

2. Learning engages the whole physiology.

3. The search for meaning is innate.

4. The search for meaning comes through patterning.

5. Emotions are critical to patterning.

6. The brain processes wholes and parts simultaneously.

7. Learning involves both focused attention and peripheral perception.

8. Learning involves both conscious and unconscious processes.

9. We have two types of memory: spatial and rote.

⑩ We understand best when facts are embedded in natural, spatial memory.

⑪ Learning is enhanced by challenge and inhibited by threat.

⑫ Each brain is unique. (n.p.)

Renate and Geoffrey Caine (On Purpose Associates, 2001) also indicate that three interactive elements are essential to this process:

▸ Teachers must immerse learners in complex, interactive experiences that are both rich and real. One excellent example is immersing students in a foreign culture to teach them a second language. Educators must take advantage of the brain's ability to parallel process.

▸ Students must have a personally meaningful challenge. Such challenges stimulate a student's mind to the desired state of alertness.

▸ In order for a student to gain insight about a problem, there must be intensive analysis of the different ways to approach it, and about learning in general. This is what's known as the "active processing of experience." (n.p.)

When we understand how students learn, we can use targeted teaching methods to help them analyze, synthesize, and communicate information. Combined with appropriate uses of technology, these methods will help students prepare for the future. Examples of approaches that are customizable are constructivism, project-based learning, and a relatively new concept, connectivism.

constructivism

Constructivism views learning as a process in which the learner actively constructs or generates new ideas or concepts based upon current and past knowledge. With a constructivist approach to learning, students build on what they already know and what they learn. Rather than providing didactic instruction and expecting students to repeat facts on a test, teachers encourage students to think about what they already know about a topic, search for new information, and collaborate with others to solve realistic problems and derive new understanding.

Using Web tools helps the process along. Students are able to do more research, find information they would never encounter without Web access, and collaborate to create a product that shows how both a priori and new information are combined to become knowledge. Using Web 2.0 tools such as wikis allows students to collaborate on creating a document that displays what they have learned. They can illustrate with photos and videos, use an interesting presentation format, and engage the audience to think about what they've seen.

project-based learning

Project-based learning is a constructivist approach that encourages learning in depth by allowing students to use inquiry-based methods to engage with issues and questions that are rich, real, and relevant to their lives. It emphasizes learning activities that are long-term, interdisciplinary, and student-centered. Students form a learning community that focuses on critical thinking.

Students are expected to use technology in meaningful ways, for example, to help them investigate or present their learning. Teachers offer resources so that students can explore and develop content purposefully and creatively. Students engage in activities that are valued in the real world, manage their own tasks and time, work as part of a team, and communicate with adults and experts. They drive the accumulation of content knowledge and thus remember what they learn.

Project-based learning allows for alternative approaches that address students' individual differences, variations in learning styles, intelligences, and abilities and disabilities. Despite the current emphasis on learning and testing basic skills, many schools continue to encourage students to do higher order thinking as preparation for self-directed lifelong learning and as a way to develop workplace skills.

Web-based tools add the ability to communicate and collaborate with the world outside the classroom easily and at no cost beyond the technology. Thus, Web 2.0 tools are part of a paradigm shift in learning. Rather than delivering information from textbooks and teachers' resources, the new approach harnesses the technologies that students use outside of school to engage them in finding and analyzing resources themselves.

Because the Web has almost limitless information, students need strategies to find what they are looking for. Web 2.0 services allow them to create social networks of those with similar interests in order to interact, share information, and learn collaboratively. Achieving the goal of having students learn deeply rather than broadly can happen. They can pursue a topic thoroughly, discern the truth about it, and eventually know more than some of the experts and thus become experts themselves. They can create an authentic audience for their work by creating tags for linking, by inviting comment, or by syndicating it with RSS (Really Simple Syndication). Because they have the tools at their fingertips to publish their work online, they become resources for other students' research.

connectivism

George Siemens' (2004) theory of connectivism is an approach to learning that also considers technology as a key factor. "Including technology and connection making as learning activities begins to move learning theories into a digital age" (n.p.).

Siemens (2004) believes that:

> Learning and knowledge rests in diversity of opinions; learning is a process of connecting specialized nodes or information sources; the capacity to know more is more critical than what is currently known; nurturing and maintaining connections is needed to facilitate continual learning; the ability to see connections between fields, ideas, and concepts is a core skill; and decision-making is itself a learning process. (n.p.)

Siemens points out that using technology and making connections are linked. Combining connectivism with constructivist methods in the classroom offers students an opportunity to gain 21st-century skills. Siemens (2004) sees the trends:

- ▶ Many learners will move into a variety of different, possibly unrelated fields over the course of their lifetime.

- ▶ Informal learning is a significant aspect of our learning experience. Formal education no longer comprises the majority of our learning. Learning now occurs in a variety of ways—through communities of practice, personal networks, and through completion of work-related tasks.

▶ Learning is a continual process, lasting for a lifetime. Learning and work-related activities are no longer separate. In many situations, they are the same.

▶ Technology is altering (rewiring) our brains. The tools we use define and shape our thinking.

▶ The organization and the individual are both learning organisms. Increased attention to knowledge management highlights the need for a theory that attempts to explain the link between individual and organizational learning.

▶ Many of the processes previously handled by learning theories (especially in cognitive information processing) can now be off-loaded to, or supported by, technology.

▶ Know-how and know-what are being supplemented with know-where (the understanding of where to find knowledge needed). (n.p.)

the challenge

For a while the education pendulum had swung toward the types of learning that constructivism, project-based learning, and connectivism typify. The goals were to prepare students for the 21st century—to use higher order thinking skills, apply technology, adapt to change, acquire workplace skills, and more.

Today's educational goals are seemingly the opposite. We focus more on standards, standardized tests, and accountability, which lend themselves to traditional, teacher-directed instruction. Because "the test" is the ultimate determinant of success, many think the process is easy—teach what will be tested. However, two dangers exist: one is in not measuring what really matters even if it will matter more in the future. The other is in narrowing instruction to the exclusion of anything more than test materials.

The challenge is to find ways to support in-depth learning and increased student achievement while also employing a variety of measures, including standardized tests. If new methods engage students so they are eager to learn, allow them to acquire the ability to do serious, in-depth, "real world" activities, and support them in retaining what they've learned, can the new methods also result in their doing well not only on performance-based measures but also on high-stakes tests? If these new Web-based tools offer students the tools of production and engage them, can we harness these tools for learning? The goal is to provide an education that prepares students to have 21st-century skills and also to ace the test without breaking stride (Solomon, 2003).

When they are adults, today's students will change jobs more often than their parents did and each new job may be unrelated to the last. This means that the skills they will need will be less job-specific; rather, they will be skills that enable people to think, adapt, and continue learning. Students will acquire some of these skills informally—by communicating with a wide range of people and developing personal networks. With the kind of guidance that schools can provide, they can add the other skills they'll need. The tools students use may change where and how they get information, but only educators can make sure that students learn how to process and use that information wisely.

harnessing new technologies

How do we take advantage of students' interests and the ways they learn to create new models for learning? David Jakes (2003) had this to say in a conference presentation:

> Various types of virtual learning environments, when supported by pedagogically sound instructional models, and when combined with the content of the Web, can provide the following:
>
> ▸ A structured approach to an investigation that provides direction and guidance for students in a large, complex, and dynamic system such as the Web.
>
> ▸ An opportunity to integrate multiple types of truly unique Web resources into the learning experience, including such media as simulations and animations that can promote the development of highly interactive and multisensory learning environments.
>
> ▸ An increased level of student engagement.

- An opportunity to build information literacy and 21st-century skills in students.

- Learning experiences that are pliable and scalable, and provide opportunities for differentiation.

- Learning experiences that are inquiry-based, and focus upon the resolution of an essential question that requires the acquisition, processing and synthesis of information. (p. 1)

One of the new technologies that could be harnessed is digital storytelling. The goals are traditional; the tools are new. David Jakes explains in the Web 2.0 Wisdom sidebar, Digital Storytelling.

web 2.0 wisdom

Digital Storytelling

David Jakes

NEW TOOLS SUCH AS BLOGS, wikis, and podcasts allow everyone, including students, to contribute to a global conversation. They enable voice. The process of digital storytelling provides a voice rich in multimedia that has the potential to resonate deeply with an audience. As a result, digital storytelling has become one of the most powerful 21st-century learning processes available to teachers and students.

So what exactly is a digital story? A digital story in its truest form is a personal experience represented in narrative format. A script, or the essence of the story, is extracted from the narrative and then amplified by including video, music, still-frame imagery, and the author's voice. A digital story typically lasts between two and three minutes. The inclusion of multimedia makes the story come alive and takes the story to a place that could not be achieved by writing alone.

The process is rich in learning. Digital storytelling makes students better writers through the multiple drafts, rewrites, and script preparation that is required and helps them build essential visual literacy skills through the selection of the imagery required to construct the story. Using storytelling software such as Photo Story 3 and iMovie further advances their skill set.

The final component in the digital storytelling process is sharing the creation. The video-sharing sites now available online make this possible. The result demonstrates to students that what they have to say is important and how they say it is critical. They discover that they can be lifelong contributors to the new global conversation.

David Jakes is the instructional technology coordinator for Community High School District 99 in Downers Grove, Illinois.

One could argue that there is even yet another component beyond sharing the story. In the world of Web 2.0, the final piece involves the audience—to choose to watch or not, to choose to modify or not, to choose to re-create or collaborate or not. And then to offer it back to the original author—or not—and so on, in the ultimate peer-learning experience.

Now that we've seen what the world is like and what today's students are like, let's take a closer look at the Web tools that have such an impact.

3

new tools

On October 18, 2006, YouTube featured a music video by ClipBandits, a band with three young men that called itself "The World's First Web Band" because they formed the group, developed the music, and created the video all online. In fact, they had never met, didn't know one another's real names, and lived in New York, Los Angeles, and Austin. They were searching for a drummer by soliciting audition videos. In three days, nearly 500,000 people watched the video and almost 1,700 people posted ratings (it got four out of five stars). This is the world our students live in. How did we get here? And just what does this mean for education?

concepts

Let's begin by explaining some of the concepts we talked about earlier. Because Web 2.0 software is online and accessible to anyone with an Internet connection and a browser, we have new avenues for collaboration and communication. The tools are free and businesses, young people, and some educators are already using them.

Web 2.0 tools change the nature of the Web from distributed to participatory. People control the tools of production and publication and use them to collaborate. They can add to and change others' work online. Steven Downes (2006), a researcher with the National Research Council of Canada, believes that the emergence of Web 2.0 "is not a technological revolution; it is a social revolution. ... It's about enabling and encouraging participation through open applications and services ... with rights granted to use the content in new and exciting contexts" (n.p.).

The basis for this model is the open-source movement. Open source means that the code is available for others to use, and that they may enhance and distribute the results freely. "It enables the Web to shift from being a medium in which information is transmitted and consumed into being a platform in which content is created, shared, remixed, repurposed, and passed along" (Downes, 2006, n.p.).

the web as platform

Tim O'Reilly (2005), the CEO of O'Reilly Media and one of the best thinkers about Web 2.0 issues, says, "You can visualize Web 2.0 as a set of principles and practices that tie together a veritable solar system of sites that demonstrate some or all of those principles, at a varying distance from that core" (n.p.).

The Web 2.0 movement stems from the concept that the Web (rather than a proprietary network) is the platform on which everything is built and users control their own data. Among the advantages of having the Web as the platform is that it provides services rather than packaged software. It is also participatory, cost-effective, and scalable. The most important point is that it harnesses collective intelligence. O'Reilly's diagram (Figure 3.1) shows how ideas and tools are connected.

Figure 3.1 | Web 2.0 meme map

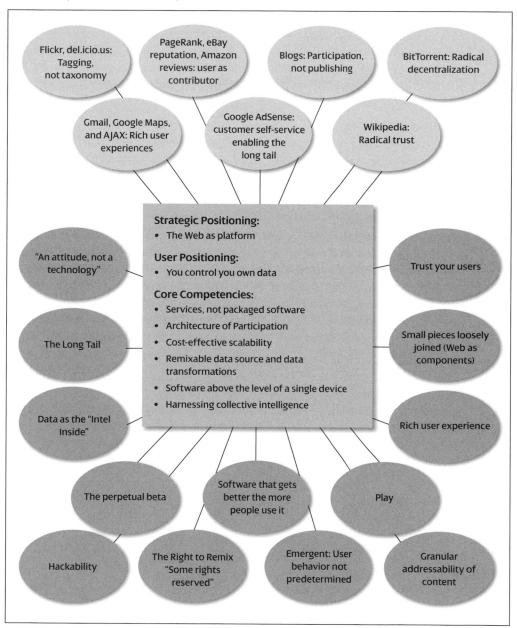

behind the web tools

Many Web 2.0 tools are based on what is commonly known as Ajax programming. Ajax, shorthand for Asynchronous JavaScript and XML, is a Web development technique used for creating interactive Web applications. The code is open source, improvements happen regularly, and users never have to wait for a new software release to get new features.

What happens is that rather than performing tasks such as word processing or crunching numbers with a spreadsheet on your desktop, you do it all online. Your browser window is the interface to Web 2.0 applications such as blogs and wikis. The greatest advantage is that these are collaborative tools that allow people to work together simultaneously from any location. All anyone needs is an Internet connection.

Ajax applications make Web pages work faster than usual to load and refresh. That's because the Ajax engine sits between the user and the server and updates pieces of data rather than reloads the entire Web page each time someone makes a change to a document. It allows work to happen asynchronously—independent of communication with the server. You can work faster because you're not waiting for the screen to reload. For example, an Ajax application such as Google Maps downloads satellite images into a browser and displays specific map segments.

There are serious tools for word, data, and business processing that companies are using to run their businesses over the Internet. These replace traditional application software installed on the computer desktop. Thomas Friedman (2005) sees this change as part of the flat world and "uploading" as one of the flatteners that he says:

> enabled more people to author more content and to collaborate on that content. It also enabled them to upload files and globalize that content—individually or a part of a self-forming community—without going through any of the traditional hierarchical organizations or institutions.

> This newfound power of individuals and communities to send up, out, and around their own products and ideas, often for free, rather than just passively downloading them from commercial enterprises or traditional hierarchies, is fundamentally reshaping the flow of creativity, innovation, political mobilization, and information

gathering and dissemination. It is making each of these things a bottom-up and globally side-to-side phenomenon, not exclusively a top-down one. (pp. 94–95)

Companies can run their businesses online, which means that workers can be anywhere and communicate, collaborate, and be as productive as if they were located in one physical location. For example, some companies are asking employees to write, change, and track changes of documents together using a wiki. Other companies record meetings that can be downloaded to iPods, use blogs so employees can reply to their bosses, and create internal blog pages where people can read their colleagues' notes and add their own. Some companies encourage employees to bookmark internal Web pages that they find useful so others can find the information by searching for keywords associated with those ideas. A public-relations manager recently tapped his social network to expand an online-marketing campaign (Vara, 2006).

If these tools are not exactly what a business is looking for, the code is available, and companies can customize applications to any of their specific needs—or hire a service to do that.

This is the world our students will work in, and the implications for school administrators, teachers, students, and parents are significant.

For administrators

Because these are free and freely shared tools that developers are using to create ever more robust and creative applications, the day may come when schools would not have to invest in new computers and software licenses because everything would be available online and at no cost.

In addition, administrators may be able to run the administrative side of school districts with these tools the way that businesses are doing. And there are implications for offering students virtual learning options as part of the bricks-and-mortar school. If this happens, districts may be able to reduce building costs and help students to benefit from learning remotely.

For teachers

Having students use these tools has implications for quality since time is no longer part of the equation. They can set high standards and require high-quality work, monitor performance at any time, and require that students keep online portfolios when excellence rather than completion is the standard.

For students

Young people are already using many of these tools for enjoyment. It's up to schools to help them apply the tools toward more serious endeavors. Because the world that today's students will work in relies on technology, they will have to use it well or risk being left behind countries with more tech-savvy workers. In addition, these tools can allow students to collaborate on projects on weekends and evenings no matter where they live; no longer is the school day limited to the time spent within brick-and-mortar walls.

For parents

It is important for parents to know what their children are doing and to monitor their progress. With these tools, parents can access student work when they have time to see what their children are doing and how well they are performing.

open source

The genesis of Web 2.0 tools is the open-source movement, whose proponents believe that the source code for programs should be available for anyone else to study, use, enhance, and distribute. The basic idea behind open source is very simple: "When programmers can read, redistribute, and modify the source code for a piece of software, the software evolves. People improve it, people adapt it, and people fix bugs. And this can happen at a speed that, if one is used to the slow pace of conventional software development, seems astonishing" (Open Source Initiative, 2006, n.p.). The epitome of open-source software is the Linux operating system (www.linux.org). There is even an open-source browser, the Mozilla Firefox Web browser (www.mozilla.org).

According to Dan Woods (2005), a seasoned CTO (chief technology officer):

> Open source usually refers to software that is released with source code under a license that ensures that derivative works will also be available as source code, protects certain rights of the original authors, and prohibits restrictions on how the software can be used or who can use it.... Open source began as, and for the most part still is, software created by a community of people who are dedicated to working together in a highly collaborative and evolutionary way. (n.p.)

What does this mean for today's youth? According to Jim Hirsch, the associate superintendent for technology in the Plano Independent School District in Plano, Texas:

> The whole open technology business is where the rest of the world is by and large now, and it's where our students are as well. ... It's a mindset. Our students are very much into a world that is collaborative, and because of that, they tend to see things a little bit differently. They are exposed to a greater number of information resources than ever before, and whether it's good or bad, they've come to expect that information to be available and free. (Villano, 2006a, n.p.)

There is confusion about open-source software, according to Robert Tinker (2005), president of the Concord Consortium. In *Freeing Educational Applications*, he identifies the following misconceptions and explains the reality:

> **Free means junk.** Not necessarily. Just like commercial software, there is a lot of open-source junk and vaporware. But there are some gems, too. Indeed, sometimes, there is such a thing as a free lunch.
>
> **Open-source software only runs on a Linux box.** Wrong. Most recent open-source software is written in Java, which will run on current Windows, Macintosh, and Linux computers, without requiring downloads. Other open-source software is available as applets that run in almost any browser.
>
> **Open-source software may be free now, but what about later?** If it's open source now, it will always be open source. The open-source copyright forbids anyone from withdrawing open-source software and making people pay for it. That said, you may want to pay someone who bundles open-source software into a convenient package, but there will always be a free option.
>
> **Open-source software will crash and burn.** Not likely. Open-source software tends to be better than commercial software when lots of people are involved in maintaining it. This hasn't happened yet for most interesting educational applications, but if enough people begin using open-source educational applications, it will.
>
> **Only geeks use open-source software.** No way. All the software described in *Freeing Educational Applications* can be downloaded

and run by most users with some (but not advanced!) technology experience, just like other educational applications.

If it's free, it must be open source. Not necessarily. Developers sometimes make early versions of their software free to get you hooked, and then begin charging later. Check the licensing to be sure it's copyrighted under one of the open-source licenses, like the GNU General Public License.

tagging and syndication

One of the ways that authors make their content available is by including information (metadata) that identifies its topics and themes. They also may add an option for readers to be alerted when new content is available, which means that information will find them. In addition, Web 2.0 sites, whether blogs, wikis, or any other, can link to one another. While any search engine will find content created with Web 2.0 services, some are specifically intended for this purpose. Technorati (www.technorati.com), for example, searches blogs by keyword and for links and provides news from general news services and blogs.

Tags

With the traditional style of Web page, search engines can find content because content managers add metadata or metatags. These are words arranged by taxonomies that people may be likely to type into a search engine. They are structured in a hierarchical form and search engines find them and list the content.

Web 2.0 is organized differently. It uses words that the authors select and attach to content. These are called folksonomies, which are keywords or "tags" that convey meaning about the content. These tags are logical, and people who tag often arrange groups of them into concept maps that they call tag clouds, which can show how the terms relate to one another. People often adopt terms that others use to describe similar content, and sites such as the bookmarking site del.icio.us suggest tags to use that are based on ones that others have identified.

For example, when attendees at *Technology & Learning's* Tech Forum conference in Chicago in April 2007 wrote in their own blogs or in the shared wiki, they tagged their entries with the topic and tag to identify the event. If someone wrote about the Web 2.0 panel that Gwen Solomon conducted at Tech Forum in Chicago in 2007, the tags might be "Web20, session, techforumChi07, solomon."

So why should tagging matter for student learning? Teachers lament that students often lack organizational skills in their writing. Adding tags to their work forces students to think about the overarching themes, the points they make, and also the value their writing could provide to a potential audience. Thinking about their writing enhances their analytical skills.

Syndication

In the traditional publishing world, articles and columns are often syndicated or distributed to publications other than the one they were written for. Other newspapers or magazines license these articles and columns for their own readers. The system is similar in television: programs are made available to other stations.

Web syndication is making information available to other Web sites or to individual subscribers. This is done by adding XML code that readers can use. When a reader wants to know when new content is added to a site, he or she can subscribe to it by grabbing the XML code and putting it into an aggregator. That software retrieves syndicated Web content. Then readers are alerted automatically when new content is added. The technique is called RSS, which stands for Really Simple Syndication.

The distinction between searching for information and using RSS is similar to the difference between going out to find something and having it come to you. When you search, you go to a search engine and plug in the terms you think will bring up the subject. Or you visit a site you've been to in the past that's likely to have the information, and search for it there. With RSS, you set up an aggregator and list the sites you've liked in the past using the RSS code provided by that site. When there's something new, you'll be alerted and can choose to read it or not. Making information available to other Web sites or to individual subscribers is syndication. In addition to students setting up RSS feeds to get new items about content they need, they can syndicate their own work so others can find it.

Hyperlinking is the basis of searching on the Web. As users add new content, pages, and sites, other users find them and link to them. Syndication is the opposite. New content on topics you decide are valuable will find you.

Aggregators

Using an aggregator means that you don't have to keep checking a particular Web site for new content. When you subscribe to a site, you determine how often you want to know when content has changed. Students can save the sites that they've researched as RSS feeds with an RSS reader such as Bloglines (www.bloglines.com). Other aggregators are My Yahoo! and Google Reader; even some browsers have the capacity to be aggregators.

from the web to web 2.0

While Web 2.0 tools rely on traditional Web pages, the Web 2.0 system is structured differently. Traditional Web pages are designed and posted in an arrangement that the designer deems important, whether it is to get a specific message across or to showcase specific content. Web 2.0 pages display their content in reverse-chronological order. The purpose of this structure is to address the immediacy of Web content so authors and collaborators can link to other 2.0 Web pages on the same topic, link to traditional Web pages, and display comments.

While most traditional Web pages simply display information, most Web 2.0 pages offer tools and services. According to Garrett (2005):

> The classic Web application model works like this: Most user actions in the interface trigger an HTTP request back to a Web server. The server does some processing—retrieving data, crunching numbers, talking to various legacy systems—and then returns an HTML page to the client. It's a model adapted from the Web's original use as a hypertext medium, but…what makes the Web good for hypertext doesn't necessarily make it good for software applications. (n.p.)

Organization on traditional Web pages, especially those run by corporations, relies on taxonomies, predetermined keywords. Web 2.0 organization uses folksonomies, which are author-assigned and fall into a more reader-centric philosophy that may change how we store and find information online. According to NCREL (2003), "It may become less important to know and remember where information was found and more important to know how to retrieve it using a framework created by and shared with peers and colleagues" (p. 2).

using the tools

The rest of this chapter will explore many of the Web 2.0 tools that educators have implemented and found useful. Chapter 4 will provide examples of how people are using the tools in classrooms and schools. There are so many ways to work with Web 2.0 tools that we can cover only a small portion of these creative ideas. Detailed lessons are beyond the scope of this book. However, in the spirit of Web 2.0, we hope you'll take these tools and ideas, put them to use, then tell the world. We have plans for a companion book that will be a practical guide to Web 2.0. This resource will showcase real-world lessons, classroom narratives, and tutorials.

basic web 2.0 tools: blogs, podcasts, and wikis

Three of the most commonly used Web 2.0 tools are blogs, podcasts, and wikis, and there are many examples of each. Bryan Alexander (2006), director for research at the National Institute for Technology and Liberal Education (NITLE), talks about the unique nature of these inventions:

> Blogs are about posts, not pages. Wikis are streams of conversation, revision, amendment, and truncation. Podcasts are shuttled among Web sites, RSS feeds, and diverse players. These content blocks can be saved, summarized, addressed, copied, quoted, and built into new projects. Browsers respond to this boom in microcontent with bookmarklets in toolbars, letting users fling something from one page into a Web service that yields up another page. (n.p.)

For examples of how to use these tools, take a look at the tutorials in chapter 10.

Blogs

A Web log, usually shortened to *blog*, is a set of personal commentaries on issues the author deems important. It contains text, images, and links to related information on other blogs, Web pages, and media. Readers can reply easily and thus participate in a discussion in which they share knowledge and reflect on the topic. Blogs promote open dialogue and encourage community building in which both the bloggers and commenters exchange opinions, ideas, and attitudes. Entries are posted in reverse chronological order. According to *Business 2.0* magazine, by the summer of 2006, there were 50 million blogs, and "two new ones are launched every second" (Sloan & Kaihla, 2006, n.p.).

Blogging has become an important method of communication within the educational technology community. With this new means of publishing, educators are free to share their ideas about issues and offer examples of what works. Classroom teachers include Jeff Utecht, who writes The Thinking Stick (http://jeff.scofer.com/thinkingstick/); Vicki Allen, who writes Cool Cat Teacher (http://coolcatteacher.blogspot.com); and Darren Kuropatwa, who writes A Difference (http://adifference.blogspot.com). Technology directors include Miguel Guhlin, who writes Around the Corner (http:/mguhlin.net), and David Jakes, who writes The Strength of Weak Ties (http://jakespeak.blogspot.com). Principals include Tim Lauer, who writes Education/Technology (http://tim.lauer.name/). This list is a small sample of the dedicated educators who are using new tools to communicate and instruct. Some of them write more than one blog, often separating instructional advice from opinions.

Blogging is the new way to express oneself and have an authentic audience. The implications for students include writing about issues and thus improving writing skills, learning from each other, thinking through topics thoroughly enough to offer an opinion or add information, peer editing, finding a community of others interested in the same topic, and becoming confident in sharing what they know. Teachers can create blog pages to communicate with students and parents about content and to have an ongoing open dialogue about coursework. Administrators can replace printed announcements and meeting agendas with blogs that allow for communication with the staff.

The danger is that blogs that students find when researching a topic may contain highly subjective or inaccurate information. However, because blogs attract an audience by having a good reputation, the audience itself may serve as a filter to protect a blog's credibility by making sure that commenters don't post inaccurate or offensive remarks.

Some blogging tools that are popular in education are Blogger (www.blogger.com), WordPress (www.wordpress.com), and Drupal (www.drupal.org). A videoblog, or vlog, is a Web log that uses video rather than text or audio.

For anyone concerned about allowing student blogs to be public, sites such as Class Blogmeister (http://classblogmeister.com) and Gaggle Blogs (www.gaggle. net) are available for schools and mandate teacher supervision. Their popularity is growing. According to David Warlick (2006a), who provides Class Blogmeister,

"We are now well over 3,500 classroom blogs on Class Blogmeister. When you throw in the student blogs as well, we are very close to 36,000 bloggers. That's pretty amazing—especially when you consider the current atmosphere around social networking—at least in the U.S."

Podcasts

Podcasting is a way to distribute multimedia files such as music or speech over the Internet for playback on mobile devices and personal computers. The term podcast, a word created by combining Apple's iPod and broadcast, can mean both the content and the method of delivery. The host or author of a podcast is often called a podcaster. Podcasters' Web sites may offer direct download or streaming audio, and a podcast is distinguished by its ability to be downloaded automatically using software capable of reading RSS feeds. Usually a podcast features one type of show, with new episodes released either sporadically or at planned intervals such as daily or weekly. In addition, there are podcast networks that feature multiple shows on the same feed (Wikipedia, 2006b).

The implications for education include students' being able to replay the audio of traditionally delivered information (even a teacher's lecture) to review or catch up. Podcasts are portable and students are used to listening on iPods and MP3 players. Podcasting is another step in having information that is portable, accessible 24/7, and user-selected.

Anyone with a simple computer, inexpensive microphone, and access to the Internet can create a podcast show and make it available online. Once the show is put on the Internet, anyone can listen to it. What makes a podcast so different from anything else on the Internet is the ability to subscribe to the show. This means that once you find something you like, you can subscribe to it, and your computer will continue to automatically update you with new shows as they are produced.

Students can create their own podcasts as a way of sharing their expertise and opinions. They can also use podcasts to keep notes, reflect on the day's lesson, or keep track of project activities as they work.

Wikis

A wiki is a Web page and as such is accessible to anyone with a Web browser and an Internet connection. This is where the similarity to a traditional Web page ends, because a wiki allows readers to collaborate with others in writing it and adding, editing, and changing the Web page's contents at any time. Its ease of use makes a wiki an effective tool for collaborative authoring.

The most well-known wiki is Wikipedia, a collaborative encyclopedia that includes more up-to-date entries than the *Encyclopedia Britannica*. The danger is that content can be modified incorrectly or to prove a point, and educators must teach students how to evaluate the accuracy and appropriateness of content. Contributors of most wikis usually monitor and edit one another's work, which serves as a way to evaluate and authenticate the content.

In addition to having students read existing wikis on topics of interest, the implications for education include group collaboration and problem solving, peer editing during the writing process, and electronic portfolios. Students can work from anywhere, which means they are able to contribute on their own schedule rather than being limited to the school day or class period. Wikis keep track of changes, so teachers can look at successive versions of documents for electronic portfolios or the contributions each student has made. When the work is complete, students can invite parents and others to read their work and comment.

Teachers can use wikis for students to collaborate on a document by writing, editing, and revising it in their own classes, across a grade, school, or district, or even outside those traditional boundaries. Districts can set up a wiki on their own servers or use commercial wiki services such as Wikispaces (www.wikispaces. com), which offers its service free to educators and removes all advertising from its pages. These wikis are secure because the teacher or someone at the district level determines who can view and edit.

MediaWiki (http://mediawiki.com) is server-based, which means that it is protected and free of advertising. Pbwiki or Peanut Butter Wiki (www.pbwiki.com) is so named because using it is supposed to be as easy as making a peanut butter sandwich. Schools can password protect their wikis but there are advertisements. Google purchased the wiki JotSpot (www.jotspot.com) in October 2006.

other popular web 2.0 tools

Social Bookmarking

Web 2.0 sites promote sharing information of various types. For example, social bookmarking is a popular Web-based service that displays shared lists of user-created Internet bookmarks. Instead of keeping long lists of "favorites" in their own browsers, people use these Web sites to organize, rank, and display their resources for others to see and use. They classify the content using tags based on folksonomies of community-acceptable keyword classifications.

Social bookmarking sites allow users to create a page of annotated URLs. You select favorite Web pages, add a sentence that describes each page, and put in keywords to use for tags. Because these tags are attached to the sites, others can initiate a search for them and get back a list of URLs for sites tagged with these words. People connect through shared tags and subscribe to one another's lists, which means that they'll receive an alert when one is updated. Some social bookmarking sites are popular for education.

On del.icio.us (http://del.icio.us/), which is owned by Yahoo!, bookmarks are public, and lists of how many other people have saved the same site are visible and accessible, which extends sharing. Backflip (www.backflip.com) stores user URLs in folders, but student teams can create folders and store URLs together. Bookmarks are private but you can choose to share them publically or with specific people, and you can even let other people add to your folders. Furl (www.furl.net) saves pages as private or public and offers a list of recommended sites that have topics or themes in common with those you've identified.

When student teams work on a project, they can divide their project's topic into subtopics, and each student can search for information on the one he or she chooses. Then they can share what they've found online, select the ones that are most relevant, and use them for the project. In addition, students can search for information by using keywords to bring up lists of Web sites related to their topic that others have compiled. This way they can find information that they might not have thought to look at. However, because the organization and tagging are not supervised, students will have to learn how to discern what is valuable.

The term "personal computer" has no meaning in K–12 unless students are assigned or buy their own computing device, be it a laptop, tablet, or handheld. So traditional bookmarking is an exercise in frustration because students use different computers each time they work. If they bookmark sites they want to remember on one computer, there's no way to access that information from another. Even if they get the same computer the next time, someone else may have erased the information. Using online bookmarking sites means that favorites are available from any computer at any time.

Photo Sharing

Flickr (www.flickr.com) is perhaps the best known of the free online photo management and sharing applications. Rather than sending photos from desktops and cell phones to friends and family using e-mail, people can post them at Flickr and invite people to view them in online albums or slideshows. They can add notes and tags to each photo, and their viewers can leave comments, notes, and tags as well. Tags are searchable so it's easier to find related photos later. Photos are secure and private.

The implication for education is that students can post digital photos and use them to illustrate their writing. One idea that teachers are using is to have students find images that have been stored on Flickr or other sites and select them as illustrations. Because many images on Flickr have Creative Commons licenses, students know what use they may make of the pictures.

Students can also upload images they have photographed themselves to illustrate narratives, document field trips, show historical sites, or display objects they want to show in school. When they do this, they learn how to copyright their own work and are better informed about intellectual property.

Photo Editing

To make their photos look good, people use photo-enhancing software. The most sophisticated are only available for purchase, but a number of good programs are free and downloadable. While the following are not open-source software, they are good alternatives:

Google's Picasa
http://picasa.google.com

Apple's iPhoto
www.apple.com/iphoto/

Microsoft's Photo Story
www.microsoftcom/photostory/

One open-source solution is GIMP (www.gimp.org), an acronym for GNU Image Manipulation Program. This freely distributed software is UNIX compatible and is useful for photo retouching, image composition, and image authoring. People find it handy both for creating graphics and editing them, as it has fairly complex tools and filters.

Video Showcasing

Several sites display videos created with a digital camcorder or cell phone with video capabilities. For example, YouTube (www.youtube.com), which was started in February 2005 and acquired by Google in 2006, is the best known of the free video-sharing services. People can post, comment on, tag, and watch videos. While it has become an entertainment hub, YouTube is also a place where people can build or join a community that produces and shows videos about shared interests. People can upload videos and make them public or private or even integrate them on other Web sites using video embeds. Viewers can create playlists of their favorites and subscribe to others' videos.

There is a free solution for downloading video, too. Video Furnace (www. videofurnace.com), a video-over-IP solution, makes video just another application on the network. It delivers high-quality, live and on-demand broadcasts to any network-connected device, such as desktop and laptop computers, without requiring any client player software.

In addition, there's a new group of sites that offer tools for merging video clips and adding soundtracks, titles, transitions, and other visual effects. The intent of sites such as Jumpcut (www.jumpcut.com), Eyespot (www.eyespot.com), Grouper (www.grouper.com), and VideoEgg (www.videoegg.com) is to make editing easier and free.

The implication for education is that students can create thoughtful and meaningful video clips that look professional and command an audience for their work. Having the simple tools available makes it easier to create and edit effective presentations. They can collaborate by uploading individual videos and editing them together into a single movie that uses the best of each clip. They can use the clips for digital storytelling and insert them into presentations and projects. If their videos are of high enough quality, other students can learn from them.

For example, a student-created video from a New Hampshire school that is on YouTube features a student who is shown speeding and a police officer who stops him. The police officer asks if the student knows why he was stopped and the student produces a card that explains he is deaf and communicates using sign language but can also read lips. The story of how and what they communicate provides a powerful lesson.

web 2.0 versions of desktop tools

The mainstays of any enterprise, whether business or education, are the applications used to write, crunch numbers, present information, send e-mail, and keep calendars. Until recently, these tools have had to reside on users' desktops, and Microsoft Office is the most commonly used suite of products.

A number of Web-based applications have recently emerged for word processing, spreadsheets, presentations, and other tasks. While they have yet to develop the robust features of Microsoft products, they are collaborative tools that several people can use at one time to work on documents together. And they are free. The use of these applications in education is the same as for the full-featured, desktop versions.

One popular source of applications is TheOpenCD project (www.theopencd.org). The software CD this organization distributes is high quality, free, and open source. The programs run in Windows and cover the most common tasks such as word processing, presentations, e-mail, Web browsing, Web design, and image manipulation. Also available is the OpenOffice productivity suite (http://openoffice.org), which is compatible with all other major office suites, yet is free to download, use, and distribute.

In today's intensely competitive business environment, both Google and Microsoft won't be left out. Google offers a number of free applications such as gmail, calendar, SketchUp, chat, telephony, Web pages, blogs, and more, and is packaging some of them for schools. Microsoft has LiveOffice available as free online tools to purchasers of Office software.

Word Processing

The potential for these early programs to become robust, feature-filled applications exists. For example, Google Docs & Spreadsheets (http://docs.google.com) started out as Writely, an online word processor that was developed by Upstartle and purchased by Google. It allows people to share ideas as they create a document. Zoho Writer (www.zohowriter.com), ajaxWrite (www.ajaxwrite.com), and Writeboard (http://writeboard.com) are similar, although each has somewhat different features. Most have simple formatting tools, and some allow users to save online or to their desktops.

Access is managed somewhat differently too. For example, with Writeboard, the person who creates the page sends e-mail to invite the others. Google Docs &

Spreadsheets also restricts access to whomever the first writer allows but will permit exporting the content into other formats such as Word for additional editing offline. Other educators use wikis for collaborative writing.

With these social writing tools, people can share documents and collaborate in real time or asynchronously, edit documents from anywhere, and store their work on their desktops or securely online. The software is easy to use and writers can limit access to documents to a selected group. Writers can assign tags and organize their documents into folders.

Some educators have begun to use blogs to teach the writing process so that their students can publish their work and invite comments from others, and Class Blogmeister (http://classblogmeister.com) is designed specifically for schools. Its creator, David Warlick (2006a), says:

> There are many freely available tools that facilitate blogging, but none seem especially suited for the classroom. Blogmeister is explicitly designed with teachers and students in mind, where the teacher can evaluate, comment on, and finally publish students' blog articles in a controlled environment. (n.p.)

Warlick explains why he created the site in the Web 2.0 Wisdom sidebar, Birth and Caring of a New Web Tool.

Spreadsheets

For anyone who relies on a spreadsheet to crunch numbers or keep track of data, a Web 2.0 version can provide new options even if it has only some of a desktop application's advanced features. For example, Google Docs & Spreadsheet (http://docs.google.com) is an emerging collaborative spreadsheet that others can update from their own computers, even at the same time. Students can import existing spreadsheets or create new ones from scratch, make changes collaboratively in real time, and store them securely online or on a hard drive. It lacks charting and graphing features but allows for sorts, various typefaces and colors, and the use of preset formulas.

Zoho Sheet (www.zohosheet.com/home.do) is another Web-based alternative to traditional spreadsheet applications that provides basic spreadsheet functionalities including charts coupled with Web-based features such as sharing, tagging, and publishing.

web 2.0 wisdom

Birth and Caring of a New Web Tool

David Warlick

IN 2004, I WAS JUST BEGINNING to learn about blogging and other Web 2.0 applications. I knew so little that I could teach it all during a one-hour presentation and have time for questions. There was a great deal of interest among teachers, especially in blogging. They recognized the power behind turning their students into authors. Not only would it be an effective platform for making them better writers, but it would also provide a voice to what they were learning and what they thought about it.

There was a problem, however. Of all of the blogging engines that were available at that time, none of them were designed for classroom use. Although some teachers were using tools such as Blogger for their high-school students, most teachers were not comfortable with student posts going public before they were screened by the teacher. We had a demand asking for a tool to quench it.

During the late weeks of 2004 and early weeks of 2005, I created Class Blogmeister, a blogging engine that was designed with features that gave teachers control over all of the content—both what the students read and what they wrote. There are varying degrees of control, but no content leaves the classroom that the teacher has not seen.

Perhaps the most important aspect of this tool is a concept called perpetual beta. This means that the tool is never finished. Teachers use it, think of a way that it can be made better, suggest it in the users' mailing list, and if enough like the idea, then I write in the feature. The software becomes buggy for a while, but it all works out, and the tool continues to get better out of the conversation between users and developer.

David Warlick, blogger, podcaster, author, programmer, and public speaker is also director of the Landmark Project, a Web development, consulting, and innovations firm in Raleigh, North Carolina.

Presentations

If you use software to create and present slides for presentations, the Web 2.0 application Zoho Show (www.zohoshow.com) serves the purpose online. You can access, import, and edit presentations from anywhere, import Microsoft PowerPoint (.ppt, .pps) or OpenOffice Presentation (.sxi) files, or build and edit presentations on-the-fly using a WYSIWYG editor. It lets you pull publicly shared images from your Flickr account into your presentation (www.zohoshow.com/login.sas).

web 2.0 management tools

Search Engines

While many Web search engines are available and everyone has his or her favorite way to find information, Technorati (www.technorati.com) is a new search tool that works best on content that is posted on blogs. Google's search engine, a favorite of many, includes blogs in its regular searches. For others such as Grokker and Squidoo, see appendix B, Web 2.0 Tools.

Electronic Portfolios (ePortfolios)

Teachers often ask students to keep portfolios to showcase ongoing work and assemble a body of evidence of intellectual growth and competence. EDUCAUSE, an organization for higher education that also speaks to K–12, established a group called IMS Global Learning Consortium, or IMS/GLC, to determine specifications for electronic portfolios. These include enhancing the learning experience and improving employee development, allowing educators and institutions to better track competencies, making exchanging portfolios from school to work transitions easier, and supporting the advancement of lifelong learning (IMS/GLC, 2006).

Some teachers are using wikis as portfolios for student projects because it is so easy to view contributions from each person and track how the work has evolved from previous pages. One example of an electronic portfolio is ELGG (www.elgg.org), which allows students to build their own "personal learning landscape" that incorporates many tools to put the students at the center of their learning environment.

Content Management

If one subscribes to a philosophy of constructivist learning and a belief that creating online communities helps students to learn, one needs the tools to support the activities. Moodle (http://moodle.org) is a free, open-source course-management system that was designed around a constructionist philosophy that says that students construct new knowledge as they interact with their environment to learn and create something.

Teachers can use it to organize learning content as a course divided into modules and lessons, complete with quizzes, tests, and discussions, and sometimes integrated into the school or district student information system. It has features that promote collaboration, activities, reflection, and other characteristics for both online classes and face-to-face learning (Moodle, 2006). Because Moodle use is confined to the school district, some districts include tools such as blogs and wikis for students to use within it.

Calendars

With a Web 2.0 calendar, the user and anyone who needs to know his or her schedule can check it online. Such calendars are good for parents to keep their own schedules, for educators to list events and due dates of assignments, and for students to keep track of homework and extracurricular activities.

With Google Calendar (www.google.com/calendar), you can see others' schedules next to your own to cross-reference and add new events quickly. You can also set up automatic event reminders and search the calendar to find events.

other web 2.0 tools for education

Mapping

Google Earth (http://earth.google.com) combines satellite imagery, maps, and the power of Google Search to put the world's geographic information at your fingertips. You start from a view of Earth from outer space and can zoom in quickly to search for places in your neighborhood. You can also do research for a trip and get directions. You can tilt and rotate the view to see 3D terrain and buildings, save and share searches and favorites, and add your own annotations.

3D Modeling

Google's SketchUp (http://sketchup.google.com) is a simple but powerful tool for quickly and easily creating, viewing, and modifying 3D designs. You can create 3D models of houses, schools, and other objects in a community for a classroom project and place them into Google Earth. You can click on a shape and push or pull it to create a desired 3D geometry, experiment with color and texture, use real-time shadow casting, and select from thousands of predrawn components to save time drawing.

Social Networking

The MySpace social-networking site (www.myspace.com) has seen a lot of controversy because many young people use it to show off, boast, and tout poor behavior. In some ways, early adopters will always test the limits of any new technology. There's always a reaction and school districts have blocked students from accessing MySpace from their school network.

Social networking itself is powerful and other sites are available that may be better equipped to monitor conduct. Certainly, if it is going to get approval from educators, it has to promote responsible behavior. A site such as imeem.com (http://imeem.com) that offers social networking and Web tools but that has community rules may be more responsible. The issue is how well community policing will work.

For younger students, Whyville (www.whyville.net) is a free but not open-source online community where 1.7 million children and young teens (ages 8–15) meet to discuss books and films in the city's Greek theater, compete at checkers, and go on art treasure hunts. More than just a social network, Whyville is an educational tool sponsored by various entities including NASA and designed to engage children in all types of activities that will support their understanding in real life.

Organizing Web Info

Google Notebook (www.google.com/notebook/) puts a little button on the frame of your browser that organizes snippets of information you find on the Web into folders that are then accessible from any computer. When you are on a Web site and you see something you want to save, you highlight it, right-click your mouse, click on "Note this" in the dropdown menu, and your search is saved.

Surveys and Polls

If you want to make a decision and need the input of others or if you want students to learn how to use surveys in class, Zoho Polls (http://zohopolls.com) offers a simple interface.

Drawing

Tux Paint (www.newbreedsoftware.com/tuxpaint/) is an open-source painting tool that is free, downloadable, and easy to use. It runs on both Macintosh and PC platforms and is a lot of fun.

Mashups

Mashup sites mix and match content from two or more sites to create something entirely new. One of the most popular is HousingMaps (www.housingmaps.com), which combines real estate information from Craigslist with Google Maps interactive data. People can enter a city and price and see a map marked with properties and a corresponding list.

Using mashups with students allows for interesting learning opportunities. For example, students could use Flash Earth (www.flashearth.com), a mashup of Google Maps and Virtual Earth satellite imagery, to zoom in on their community. They could use Bubblr (www.pimpampum.net/bubblr/) to add cartoon bubbles to photographs. They could even use TerraPass' emission calculator (www.terrapass.com/flight/flightcalc.html) to enter a starting point and destination to find out how far a trip is and how many pounds of carbon dioxide each person produces en route.

There are a lot of possibilities for student creativity with these applications. Lists of popular mashups are available on Programmable Web (www.programmableWeb.com/popular/). Maybe at some point teachers and students will design custom mashups, but for now, creating mashups is best left to programmers. For those who want to try, instructions and tools are online at Amazon Web Services (http://amazon.com/aws/) and other sites.

As you will see in the next chapter, many teachers are using these tools with students. Yet this is just the beginning of Web 2.0 tool integration, and in the future even better examples will emerge.

more new tools

eHub

Emily Chang's Web site, eHub (www.emilychang.com/go/eHub/), is a constantly updated resource of Web applications, services, and sites with a focus on next generation Web (Web 2.0), social software, blogging, Ajax, location mapping, open source, folksonomy, design, and digital media sharing.

Instant Messaging

If learning is to become a 24/7 enterprise, students will need access to real-time communication tools. Instant messaging (IM) is a form of online communication that allows real-time interaction through computers or mobile devices. Although typed text remains the primary convention for IM, the technology now allows users to send images, audio and video files, and other attachments. Hundreds of millions of people use IM to stay connected. In many ways, it epitomizes the notion of the always-connected, multitasking student, sending and receiving messages at all hours, from a wide spectrum of devices, while doing several other things at the same time. IM has become such an integral part of students' lives that some schools are working to move it beyond the social sphere into teaching and learning so that students can communicate in real time from home to create projects. Yahoo and Google offer free instant messaging tools.

Internet Telephony (VoIP)

Voice over Internet Protocol (VoIP) means routing voice conversations over the Internet or through any IP-based network. In general, phone service that uses VoIP is free or costs less than equivalent service from traditional sources. Skype (www.skype.com), which is owned by eBay, reports that it has 113 million users around the world. Google Talk is also a free Internet telephony tool.

Four educators who call themselves Women of Web 2.0 (www.womenofWeb2.com) conduct weekly SkypeChats in which they interview other educators whose experiences contribute to the body of knowledge about Web 2.0 and schools. Students can use Skype to interview experts, conduct a conversation with groups of people, and talk to one another as they work collaboratively on projects from home.

Think.com

One excellent tool that is not open source is worth mentioning because of the philosophy behind it. Think.com (www.think.com) is an online learning community run by Oracle's Education Foundation. Think.com turns students into multimedia authors who use Web sites and interactive tools to collaborate on projects, build knowledge together, and publish their ideas. The advantage that it has in being proprietary is that it is a password-protected learning community that allows entry only to member schools and commands a large but vetted audience for student work.

Projects are organized into topic categories that align with the ThinkQuest Library (www.thinkquest.org/library/). Many of the projects are submitted to the annual ThinkQuest contest, in which students collaborate to create Web pages of subject-based content that will help other students to learn. The tools they use begin with a Web page builder that allows them to include text, lists, and images. It is template-driven so it's easy to use. All of this takes place in a protected environment; accounts are free but only schools can join and teachers assign student accounts. Students exchange e-mail messages only with other members. Teachers can invite parents to participate and even create newsletters for them.

Google Tools

Earth science. Students use Google Earth to view tectonic plate-shift evidence by examining whole continents, mountain ranges, and areas of volcanic activity; they also study impact craters, dry lake beds, and other major land forms.

Social studies. Students use Google Maps and start from their home address to plan a trip to a nearby city, finding hotels, restaurants, stores, and entertainment. They can even look for additional information such as business hours of operation, types of payment accepted, and reviews.

Geometry. Students use SketchUp to visualize geometry and other mathematical concepts by constructing three-dimensional models of buildings, trees, cars, and other objects.

ADAPTED FROM GOOGLE FOR EDUCATORS (WWW.GOOGLE.COM/EDUCATORS/).

Google Education

No discussion of Web-based tools is complete without looking at Google. Some Google tools have already been discussed, but there's even more to talk about. Google has become interested in helping educators use their tools and integrate them into classrooms. Google has compiled a group of its programs into a collection of tools that are particularly appropriate for learning. Called Google for Educators (www. google.com/educators/), this part of the Google Web site is a teacher's guide to Google products such as Web Search, Earth, Book Search, Maps, Video, Docs & Spreadsheets, Blogger, SketchUp, Calendar, Picasa, and more. It includes basic information about each tool, examples of how educators are using them, and lesson ideas. Google invites users to add materials too. A few examples of the tools' potential uses are in the Google Tools sidebar.

On an enterprise level, because educators are concerned with students wandering around the Web, Google offers Google Apps for your domain, an IT solution that lets technology administrators provide e-mail, sharable online calendars, instant messaging tools, and even a dedicated Web site to faculty, students, and staff for free. Google manages the details.

Where does this leave us? So far, we have quite a collection of useful but disparate tools. Yet this is only the beginning. If we believe that innovation and ideas will come from the brightest minds no matter where they are, open source could provide robust, complex solutions that are improved continually.

educational software

One possibility is that new platforms will emerge with software designed for specific learning tasks, following the model (although not specifically the content) of traditional educational software produced with open-source tools and available free online. Writer and designer Marc Prensky (2004) proposes that:

> the educational software we use (all of it—games, non-games and anything else, at all levels, pre-school to adult), should be created by the 'world mind,' should not belong to any of us, and should be available, for free, to anybody, anywhere, who wants to use it. (n.p.)

Bob Tinker (2006), president of the Concord Consortium, envisions that "a body of educational applications that are all free, open source, and maintained by a collaborating community, could result in an exciting new generation of computer-based learning activities that are well designed, robust, and highly effective" (p. 1.). These would run on any operating system, including Windows, Apple OS, and Linux.

Tinker (2005) also says:

> Students learn from these tools and models through guided explorations of appropriate problems and challenges. To be practical, these applications need to be embedded in an educational platform that can deliver complete learning activities online and then assess student progress as they work through these activities. Teachers and educators should be able to customize the activities and assessments, so that they can tailor the learning strategies to the needs and interests of their students. (n.p.)

> Open source provides a rich and growing set of applications that can be used as learning tools and other software that is designed specifically for learning.

In the next chapter you will see how Web 2.0 tools and applications are gaining a foothold in classrooms in a variety of subject areas. As more schools adopt them, they will become commonplace. Then educators will begin to look for and use open-source educational applications that have been created specifically as curricular tools. Designers are already at work creating them. In *Freeing Educational Applications*, Robert Tinker (2005), who is in the forefront of this development, describes some of the applications already in use (see sidebar, Open-Source Educational Software).

In addition, there are groups that fund open-source solutions that focus on educational applications. For example, the Hewlett foundation is funding Open Educational Resources for teaching, learning, and research resources that reside in the public domain or have been released under an intellectual property license that permits their free use or re-purposing by others. These include full courses, course materials, modules, textbooks, streaming videos, tests, software, and any other tools, materials, or techniques used to support access to knowledge. Information is available at www.hewlett.org/Programs/Education/OER/openEdResources.htm.

Curriki (www.curriki.org), funded by Sun Microsystems, is developing an open-source repository for educational content to include tools, materials, and curriculum. Educators will be able to download, use, and enhance the content they find and post their changes to the repository, much the same as open-source programmers adapt one another's work and offer the revision to the community.

Open-Source Educational Software

THE SOFTWARE TOOLS AND MODELS showcased here were designed specifically for education in a particular discipline area or topic. Most of these are in mathematics and science, because the National Science Foundation has funded almost all this software. No comparable source of funding exists for educational software.

Mathematics

Seeing Math Interactives. The Seeing Math project has developed a series of interactive software that clarify key mathematical ideas for teachers and students of algebra. Five packages are currently available that allow students to explore various aspects of linear and quadratic functions. http://seeingmath.concord.org/resources.html

Shodor Software. This is a collection of over 60 Java applets for all levels of math, with student activities. www.shodor.org/interactivate/tools/

StarLogo is a special kind of model-building programming language like Logo. It is hard to categorize, because it can be used to create interesting models of systems in mathematics, science, and social science. These models all involve giving simple rules to an "agent," and when there are lots of these agents, the system as a whole sometimes has some unexpected "emergent" behavior. http://education.mit.edu/starlogo/

Science

BioLogica is a multilevel model of classical genetics that is often known as "Dragon Genetics," because it allows students to explore the mythical genetics of dragons as a way of discovering all the major forms of inheritance. The software is available as a series of guided explorations or as an open-ended tool called GenScope. http://molo.concord.org/database/activities/30.html

Dynamica provides guided exploration of two-dimensional kinematics and dynamics. It can trace its roots to ThinkerTools, which once ran only on a Commodore 64. Request a demonstration account at http://mac.concord.org/portal/registration/register.php?action=demo. You will then be given a username and password that will give you access to a Software button on the left-hand panel. Look for physics software.

 ▶ ▶ ▶

Molecular Workbench is a model of atoms and their interactions that can be used to explore many properties of atomic and molecular systems in biology, chemistry, and physics. A database of over 100 student activities based mostly on the Molecular Workbench can be found at http://molo.concord.org

The Molecular Workbench software provides a variety of 2D and 3D molecular dynamics engines and an authoring system to create models and activities based on these engines.

Open Source Physics is a collection of Java applets related to a text by Harvey Gold. www.opensourcephysics.org

PhET. The Physics Education Technology (PhET) project at the University of Colorado produces fun, interactive simulations of physical phenomena that make bridges to the real world. A collection of 40 Java applications for introductory physics is available. www.colorado.edu/physics/phet/

Other

PDA Participatory Simulations, developed at MIT for handhelds, use Palm computers to embed people inside simulations. Interactions between players in the game are mediated by beaming. Current systems model genetics, logic, ecology, and infection. http://education.mit.edu/pda/

Sustainable Education Software. Community Planner and Ecological Footprint help students think about environmental scenarios, communities, and their "ecological footprint." www.concord.org/resources/browse/251/

Squeak is a media authoring tool, which allows you to create your own media to share and play with others. A modern implementation of Smalltalk, it is great for kids and serious programmers alike. www.squeakland.org

Additional OS applications for educators

GIMP is an open-source photo-editing software. www.gimp.org

GRASS is a geographic information system package. http://grass.baylor.edu

ImageJ is a Java image analysis package. http://rsb.info.nih.gov/ij/

J-mol 3D visualization tool is particularly helpful for seeing large biological molecules. http://jmol.sourceforge.net

.LRN is a platform for online courses, a possible replacement for Blackboard or other proprietary course management systems. http://dotlrn.org

VideoPaper Builder makes it easy to make and share video case studies that can be used in teacher professional development. http://vpb.concord.org

WISE is a Web-based environment for easily authoring and delivering learning activities made from linked steps. http://wise.berkeley.edu

© 2005 The Concord Consortium, Inc. Reprinted with permission.

For example, contributors might develop collaborative textbooks, add provocative questions to materials, and suggest assessments to measure learning that they post so that the process can continue. The initial focus is on K–12 curricula in the areas of literacy, languages, mathematics, science, and technology.

At some point, it will be possible to find complete sets of standards-based curriculum materials and adapt them for individual classrooms and students. The tools are available for educators to work collaboratively to create and refine lessons, activities, and resources, share them with others, get enhancements, and implement the best learning materials they can imagine.

immersive environments

One other possibility might be to offer classes such as Law in the Court of Public Opinion, a course that was piloted at the Harvard law school and extension school in fall 2006 (http://blogs.law.harvard.edu/cyberone/). Students and anyone else who wanted to take this class ended up with a project-based learning experience in which they used multiple forms of media, such as blogs and wikis, to understand how digital technologies and digital forms of distribution affect the kinds of arguments people make. The setting for the course was on Second Life (www. secondlife.com), a three-dimensional environment in which users create avatars that explore, build, socialize, and participate in a virtual economy. Although created for adults, this serves as a model for how students can learn in a truly virtual world, communicating with others and creating knowledge using free, online tools within an immersive environment.

data and design

Open source provides a rich and growing set of applications that can be used as learning tools and other software that is designed specifically for learning. Beyond individual programs, however excellent they may be, a system is needed to analyze results and predict what will work best.

We've argued that it should be possible to use brain-based learning to determine how each student learns and direct learning activities to them that will address their needs. School districts use data mining software to analyze student test scores. In one Louisiana middle school, administrators have been experimenting with using this system to analyze student misbehavior and the effectiveness of disciplinary actions taken. Data mining and analysis is getting more and more sophisticated and thanks to interoperability standards, systems can share files (Whiting, 2006).

Thus, it is not a big leap to consider mining data about every student's learning style, retention of information, and interests and then harness what we know from successes in the past to predict what will be successful for each student in the future. Eventually every student may get a detailed learning plan that is adjusted automatically, based on new data.

4

new tools in schools

Thus far, this book has presented information on the changing nature of information, new ways our students understand and make sense of the world, and strategies for rethinking the ways teachers can take advantage of new methods for teaching and learning. The book also described these new tools that offer new opportunities for students to learn, explore, and present their knowledge; these models are often termed "social software," a phrase attributed to Clay Shirky (2003) to describe technologies that facilitate group communication.

▶ ▶ ▶ ▶ ▶

By now, however, you are probably asking yourselves the great "So what?" question—the "Why do I care about all of this?" or "How does this affect my school, the teachers with whom I work, or me?" Since the early 1900s technology proponents have claimed that this or that technology would fundamentally change education; so far, we haven't changed much—other than the fact that some of the tools are new.

This chapter presents concrete examples of ways the new tools are being used or could be used in various subject areas and with learners at all age or grade levels. This is not an exhaustive list by any means; rather, it is a compelling sample of creative ideas.

You may be wondering what new schools really are like; after all, schools have not really changed in the last century. We provide models of these new schools along with information from the teachers and administrators who have first-hand experience with them. We also show examples of the ways students are using the new tools to learn.

cool schools

You will notice that there are not a lot of examples as of yet in which an entire school system has reconceptualized itself to incorporate technology in order to promote an environment that supports, sustains, and even requires a pedagogical approach that includes inquiry, creativity, and full integration of technology. There may be many reasons for this, including caution, funding, leadership, or competing demands on time. Nevertheless, it is worth noting that some schools and districts are taking first steps in this process.

New Tech High

The New Technology High School model uses in-depth project- and problem-based learning that involves teamwork, critical thinking, and communication skills. Students are assessed with authentic outcomes and get real-time feedback, and technology is used to bind the collaborative learning community together. The New Tech High Learning System is a suite of tools that is currently a Lotus Notes implementation, but they are working on making the tools available in a Web Portal version. The system contains curriculum, assessment rubrics, living grade books, and communication tools.

The model was developed first at Napa New Tech High School by visionary teachers who knew that technology could help manage their unique collaborative environment, and later with funding from the Bill & Melinda Gates Foundation as part of the NTHS Replication Project, which helps reinforce best practices by shaping the way teachers think about teaching and learning. The New Technology Foundation has assisted 14 schools in replicating the New Tech High model and is working with 14 more during the 2006 and 2007 school years. Business projections show the potential to grow to 35 schools, each serving 400 students, by school year 2009, thereby reaching more than 14,000 students and preparing them for the 21st century.

> The most important aspect of the New Tech High model is that it was developed as part of an overall education reform effort and to implement a 21st-century learning environment.

The most important aspect of the New Tech High model is that it was developed as part of an overall education reform effort and to implement a 21st-century learning environment. Its use of collaborative and project-based learning was the first priority, and they looked at technology to support the pedagogy and philosophy second. For true reform to take place, according to proponents of the New Tech High model, pedagogy and technology must find a proper balance.

The results are important to note in this competitive global economy in which it is imperative to have a significant percentage of students majoring in science, technology, engineering, or math (STEM) fields. In a study of the first nine graduating classes from Napa New Tech High, 40% of the respondents either were majoring or were working in STEM professions.

The program's expansion is admirable but the weakness is the funding that is needed to make this work. For example, each school needs a Lotus Notes/Domino server, a highly functional and reliable network, one-to-one computing, and support for pedagogy and technology implementation as well as for infrastructure. When pedagogical models such as this one are available within the framework of open-source software, costs are reduced significantly. Then the expansion has the potential to be geometric rather than incremental (Computerworld Honors Program, 2006).

Lemon Grove School District

The Lemon Grove School District of California faced a large digital divide issue with respect to technology in homes, and with an innovative solution (partnerships with cable and other companies in the community) they have been able to launch a unique and inclusive project, called LemonLINK. According to the LemonLINK Web site (2007), "Project LemonLINK establishes a collaborative learning environment for students, teachers, parents, and members of the Lemon Grove community. The creation of a comprehensive technology-based educational environment stimulates students and helps them learn to challenging standards" (n.p.).

The LemonLINK program sought support to develop this collaborative learning environment by delivering high-speed intranet connectivity between the district and students' homes. Students are able to access the Internet and school resources at school and from home. Parents can easily communicate with teachers.

> The evolution of technology integration in the classroom environment has brought about changes in the structures of teaching and learning. With adequate numbers of computers in the classroom, teachers report that they are integrating its use in every curriculum area at every grade level. (LemonLINK, 2007, n.p.)

Lemon Grove accomplishes this with thin client technology. A thin client is a computer (client) that depends primarily on a central server for processing activities and contains no software, other than that necessary to connect to a network and start up a dedicated Web browser. The district also has a computer-to-student ratio of 1:2. Administrators prepare teachers for new models of learning by offering more than 120 hours of curriculum-based professional development to implement technology in their classroom; they work with 20% of the teachers each year on a five-year rotation cycle.

classroom applications: using the tools for learning

Writing Process (Blogs)

Using a Web 2.0 site for writing or a blog is similar to keeping a writer's journal, and of course, journals serve many purposes. They can be a log of daily activities and thoughts, the intellectual musings that become the foundation of a serious essay or book, or anything in between. Posting thoughts online—even on a class Web site—is communicating in a public sphere.

Blogs are natural tools for writing instruction. From brainstorming to organizing to writing, revising, and peer review, they are tools that lend themselves to the writing process. Since there's a comment box, blogs are important in peer editing and sharing thoughts on the ideas presented.

Just as students keep paper journals as a class assignment, they can maintain individual blogs on a site designed for writing. Because teachers monitor these pages, students are able to write openly and get thoughtful feedback on their ideas. When students are ready, their work can be made available to a larger audience than just classmates. Of course, because of security issues, identities have to be protected.

Because blogs and other Web 2.0 writing sites can have more of an audience than just the teacher, students are engaged in sharing, communicating, and exchanging ideas on a larger scale and see a permanency to their words that a composition paper can never equal. Because of this audience, students are motivated to learn how to write responsibly, accurately, clearly, and inoffensively. They are empowered as thinkers, communicators, and authors. One third- and fourth-grade class in Australia offers its students the opportunity to put their digital creative writing stories into a blog for all to read (http://middlepstories.learnerblogs.org). Other schools provide a forum for their students in all grades to write about current events, their experiences, and school activities. Examples include sixth graders in England (http://priestsic6.learnerblogs.org) and first graders in New Zealand (http://roomonemapua.blogspot.com).

Collaborative Writing (Wikis)

Sometimes one tool will work well for one type of project and a different tool will work well for something else. Wikis are well suited for projects in which collaborative teams write, revise, update, and contribute on a regular basis. Wikis keep track of changes and teachers can monitor progress to see if someone is taking over or if someone isn't doing his or her fair share of the work.

Illinois English teacher Jon Orech's students work on a long-term, independent literature circle project using wiki software. They begin with reading a book, answering discussion worksheets, and leading a discussion about it online. Each student must post at least twice a week as groups create book notes that include a comprehensive summary, biography of the author, passages from the book with explanations, and an analysis of important themes, symbols, or recurring motifs.

These tools are excellent resources for teaching English and literature, but collaborative writing projects can focus on almost any subject. As you will see later in this chapter, Darren Kuropatwa, a high-school math teacher in Winnipeg, Manitoba, Canada, created an Applied Math 40S Wiki Solutions Manual (http://am40s.pbwiki.com). Students help each other learn by contributing to the manual.

Student Feedback (Podcasting)

Another teacher, Cheryl Oakes, also uses Web 2.0 tools with her students. Oakes (2006) explains:

> As any teacher of technology has experienced, as soon as you learn a new tool and feel comfortable enough to begin teaching it in your classroom, that technology is old and you are moving on! Well, be brave and take a risk, our new digital learners have different strategies, different needs and totally different outcomes that WORK! (n.p.)

Oakes tries to meet them where they are, and so, for example, "Instead of teaching them about GarageBand, I jumped in and demonstrated how to use GarageBand, gave them a sentence prompt, asked them to get into groups of 2 to 3 and record their thoughts. Oh, did I mention these were third graders?" They had just taken tests online and as a response, she offered them the following prompt:

> What did you take? How many questions did you have?
> The tests shows _____
> I really _____

In 45 minutes, these students came up with thoughtful responses to the online testing questions, recorded their reflections about taking these tests, listened to their responses, and asked if they could delete and record again! Oakes stated, "There was purpose; there was a challenge; the outcome was incredible and featured on my blog. Twenty students recording all at once, not one had to wait their turn, it just happened." She then has parents listen to the podcasts or read students' thoughts on her blog. You can listen at www.cheryloakes.com. Scroll down to June 5, 2006, or type the following address into your URL bar: http://homepage.mac.com/cherylsoakes/NWEA3rds_2.mp3.

Cheryl Oakes says that students and parents around the world have listened to her students' work or read their blog. This activity addresses the Maine Guiding Principles, part of the traditional curriculum for the state, which encourage being a self-directed lifelong learner and a clear and effective communicator.

Digital Storytelling (Flickr)

Digital storytelling merges writing, photographs, music, and voice to create a personal multimedia story. It too is valuable for teaching many subjects. Students begin by composing their narrative, and from it, synthesize the story into its critical elements to develop a script. They add multimedia to the script by including photographs, music, and audio and then put it all together in a logical sequence that is compelling and engaging.

David Jakes (2005), instructional technology coordinator for Community High School in Downers Grove, Illinois, says, "Digital storytelling helps students explore the meaning of their own experience, give value to it, and communicate that experience on multiple levels to others. ... [It] not only promotes the development of life-long learners, but life-long communicators as well" (n.p.).

Teachers in his district are using digital storytelling with students. English teacher Jon Orech teaches sophomores on the college track and those who are learning disabled, and requires two projects annually. The first stems from their reading and involves their writing and illustrating personal history narratives similar in style to what they read. The second is a digital inquiry project for a combined English and history course. This focuses on learning about the events behind protest songs as they answer the question "How can you maintain a just and equitable society?" Students use Photo Story 3 to create their presentations. Orech finds that students work hard, remain engaged, and ask better questions because they know it will end up in digital media.

Ted Glazier, a physical and health education teacher in the district's North High Campus, has students use Flickr (www.flickr.com) in digital storytelling projects. He has had students create public service announcements on addiction. He also wanted students to learn to use statistics so he asked them to take two relevant statistics and make them come alive in a digital story. The images resided behind the district's firewall in a shared folder on the network with Flickr usernames built into the file name so the students would be able to include correct attribution for them.

Digital Diplomacy

In an effort to expand and improve on the popular digital storytelling projects, some teachers have moved into "digital diplomacy" using Web 2.0 tools. David Jakes reports that his project "has enlarged the voice of our students and 'broadcast' it to the larger digital world" (personal communication, 2006). The educators involved believe their students have a lot to say to the larger world and can do it through a digital story format.

They wondered what would happen if "students could tell the story of their lives as Americans or convey the realities of our culture to other students whose culture is different or even in direct conflict to theirs" (David Jakes, personal communication, 2006). They are asking their students and "those on the other side of the world" to share their experiences, lives, and perspectives with each other. They are doing this through podcasting stories, and student engagement in understanding the world has dramatically increased. The educators ask, "Will kids learn as a result? Does this project constitute enough risk, is it provocative enough, does it use the tools of their generation to publish something of value, something of meaning, and in the process, teach them about how they can be lifelong contributors and what they have to say can make a difference?" While those questions have not been answered directly, these educators are convinced that it will make a difference.

classroom applications: teaching content

English and Literature

When offered a positive and engaging activity, students may suddenly become very excited about learning literature. At Gunston Middle School in Arlington, Virginia, an assignment to study poetry was not warmly received by the students, but the teacher turned it into an incredible opportunity to create a blog on Dickinson, Frost, and Shakespeare. The students began writing to other students about what they learned and how they felt about the poems, and then published their work for others to see and comment upon. Some schools, even elementary ones, are allowing students to post their original poems, stories, and even illustrated books to represent their work.

Chris Sloan is an English, journalism, and new media teacher at Judge Memorial High School in Salt Lake City. He is also the technology liaison for the Utah Writing Project. Chris has been expanding the use of technology in his courses. His media students have been using varied tools such as video, text, photographs, and podcasts (http://judgemedia.blogspot.com) to improve their communication and writing skills.

Media Literacy

Educators have been talking about and working to teach media literacy since the first motion pictures entered the classroom. Jackie Marsh (2007), a library media specialist from the UK, asks students, "What does a news blog do that a newspaper doesn't, and vice versa?" (n.p.) She maintains that by using this simple question for each Web 2.0 tool, students can begin to see the validity and challenges for each type of information. Students really need to learn how to question the source of the information they are seeing on the Web.

Perhaps the most valuable resource in teaching our students about the advantages and pitfalls in using the information they find on the Web is the American Library Association (ALA). Its TechSource (www.techsource.ala.org/blog/2006/04/a-new-media-information-literacy-tool.html) offers a collection of information to help educators and parents assist students in understanding and assessing the variety of resources found online. The organization has also developed an e-learning tool designed to provide new media information literacy-related content. It includes a new media resource and reference guide. The organization states, "This project is intended to introduce students to the key concepts in new media and to address a host of new media issues including the collapse of distinctions between media forms and the societal effects of new technologies such as blogs, chat rooms, TiVo, and Facebook" (ALA TechSource, 2007, n.p.).

A new organization, NewMediaLiteracy.org, has evolved to promote a community that encourages "technologists, designers, educators, scholars, and businesspeople to develop new media projects for the cultivation of deep multimedia literacy among all Internet-users" (NewMediaLiteracy.org, 2006, n.p.). The organization maintains that its "definition of 'literacy' reaches beyond the technical skills one needs to perform tasks using computers and networked information and encompasses the critical faculties one needs to evaluate, criticize, and learn from those resources." The group provides interesting resources for teachers to assist in their efforts to prepare their students for Web 2.0 curricular lessons.

Social Studies

During a course of study in American history, students investigate the theme of what it means to be American in a pluralistic society. One way students can explore this question is by conducting oral histories with family members and creating a presentation of the interviews. In this way, students begin to develop a better understanding of their own family history as a means for framing a discussion as well as an understanding of who they are themselves. Web 2.0 tools are uniquely suited for this task. After a discussion on what it means to be an American, students can use an iPod and a voice recorder to interview a family member. They can then combine the interview with old photos of that relative in iMovie, and create a short video history about that person. The final movies can be presented to the class.

One history professor has dedicated his professional life to making history come alive by telling the stories of the people who experienced all the events that sound rather dry in textbooks. Professor Bob Packett loves to tell stories of the real people behind the often sterile descriptions found in history texts. He has now created podcasts filled with anecdotes, quips, and humor, presented in a conversational manner, to "bring to life the characters of history" (Packett, 2007, n.p.; see www.summahistorica.com). The Organization of American Historians has also created Talking History podcasts that focus on themes and periods of history (http://talkinghistory.oah.org). The podcasts include titles such as American Gunfight and Negro League Baseball.

Abbe Museum, in Bar Harbor, Maine, encourages the participation of students in learning about Maine's Native American tribes and then demonstrating their knowledge through the creation of movies for the museum. Their online exhibit, Wabanaki People—A Story of Cultural Continuity, will feature some of the best movies. The museum also provides support for teachers who want to use the technologies to help their students gather information and create novel approaches to learning (www.abbemuseum.org/wabanaki.html).

April Chamberlain, a former fourth-grade teacher (now district technology specialist) at Paine Intermediate School in Trussville, Alabama, created a blog to give her students a chance to communicate with soldiers who are fighting in Iraq. The interaction on this blog includes many questions from students about the daily life of the soldiers (www.paineandthesoldiers.blogspot.com). Not only are they reading and writing, but they are learning about current events and the challenges that face soldiers in the field.

The Education Podcast Network (http://epnweb.org) is devoted to bringing together a wide range of podcast programming for teachers looking for content. A variety of podcasts are available on Colonial Williamsburg at www.history.org/media/podcasts.cfm. If a teacher is looking for information related to the Middle Ages, she might try the Medieval Podcasts at http://podcasts.medievalstudies.info/.

Another organization offering resources for teachers is Teaching Matters, a nonprofit professional development group that works with educators to improve public schools (www.teachingmatters.org). Voices & Choices offers two comprehensive learning packages for teachers to use with their students on the topics of ancient Greece and the American Constitution. Along with resources for students to use for research and class assignments on these topics, the Democracy in Ancient Greece link (http://greece.teachingmatters.org) also allows students to interact with other students using class blogs and discussion boards.

Alison McBride uses a blog to teach Western Civilization and U.S. History at Arapahoe High School in Centennial, Colorado (http://arapahoe. littletonpublicschools.net). McBride poses questions about the curriculum topics on a blog (one for each type of class she teaches). A lively discussion takes place as the students respond to the prompts and to each other (see http://mcbridewc. blogspot.com or http://mcbrideus.blogspot.com).

Tom Hammond, a very experienced social studies teacher and a doctoral candidate at the University of Virginia, has used new technologies in innovative ways. Hammond reviews the latest ideas in the Web 2.0 Wisdom sidebar entitled Web 2.0 in the Social Studies.

web 2.0 wisdom

Web 2.0 in the Social Studies

Tom Hammond

WEB 2.0 TOOLS will alter students' and teachers' patterns of practice, inside the classroom and out. Each will be able to present the other with a richer array of creative expression, and each will be more connected to the other as these compositions become part of the daily library. The challenge for teachers and teacher-educators is to find compelling uses of composition tools and portable media devices to compete with the offerings on YouTube or through iTunes, or at least find a complementary niche. Otherwise, students' use of these tools and devices will become a nuisance that is as bad as or worse than cell phones. And while cell phones are a nuisance within the classroom, digital media have the potential to gain the attention of the world—for better or for worse.

Thankfully, the Internet provides access to teachers who are modeling the use of composition tools and new media in social studies. Two such models are Eric Langhorst of Liberty, Missouri, and Dan McDowell of Santee, California. Mr. Langhorst's blog (http://speakingofhistory. blogspot.com; "Teaching about George, Thomas and Abe using the latest technology") provides links to his classroom site and a library of podcasts created for his students. These podcasts demonstrate his application of this new technology to his classroom practice, such as the studycasts he posts before tests, guiding the students through a review of the material. Dan McDowell's site (http://ahistoryteacher.com) models innovative uses of wikis, including student compositions of compelling, historically-based branching narratives (http://ahistoryteacher.com/~ahistory/apwhreview/).

Not unlike Lewis and Clark mapping the Louisiana Purchase, Langhorst and McDowell and other innovative social studies teachers are charting the instructional territory that new Web-based technologies have opened up. Their examples of rich practice should serve as a source inspiration for teachers, administrators, teacher-educators, and education researchers.

Tom Hammond is an experienced social studies teacher and a doctoral candidate at the University of Virginia.

Journalism, Broadcasting, and Video Production

Many schools at all grade levels are instituting journalism or broadcast courses and experiences for their students. This type of curriculum often meets the standards for communications, creative writing, and technology. Web 2.0 tools are particularly suited for this curriculum area, because citizen journalism "is the act of citizens playing an active role in the process of collecting, reporting, analyzing and disseminating information" (Bowman & Willis, 2003, n.p.).

Communication is oral as well as written, and a traditional way to teach students to understand their own environment is to create a classroom daily newscast. These news broadcasts used to be compiled by a special group of students and used a school's sound system as the audio. We might question whether anyone listened. Today, the process can be egalitarian; every class can create a news show using podcasts or video that can be saved and heard by other students, parents, and the community at the listeners' convenience.

Some high schools are publishing their newspapers online as well as in paper, and they provide podcasts as well as open blogs for their students. The Hunterdon Central Regional High School in Flemington, New Jersey, is one school using this innovative technique. Its newspaper, Journalism2 (J2) at HCRHS, offers stories, blogs, and podcasts relevant to its audience (http://central.hcrhs.k12. nj.us/journ2/).

In fact, the My High School Journalism Web site (www.myhighschooljournalism. org) provides links to hundreds of high-school papers (481 at last count!), as well as dozens of middle- and elementary-school papers. The site's organizers also mine the papers for the "best of the best" and provide links to those as models. Individuals can search for their local paper by state or city. Another site, Cool School Newsletters, Newspapers and Magazines (http://eduscapes.com/tap/topic97.htm) also provides links and information to assist students in electronic journalism. And a third, Making the News (http://mtn.e2bn.net/rostra/news. php?r=1&t=2&id=14), provides a free online publishing system for schools hosted by the National Education Network that enables teachers and pupils to share and promote their learning experiences over the World Wide Web. This organization allows students and schools to have their news made available through broadcast using text, images, animation, audio, and video. Online publishing, in real time, is available by filling in an easy-to-use story submission form.

Journalism, broadly defined, does not have to be limited to high-school students. More specifically, there are examples of young students reporting on significant personal events. Bob Sprankle teaches third and fourth grade at Wells Elementary School in Wells, Maine. His classroom is Room 208, the name of the Web site where he and his students post news updates and links regularly. Students have their own pages but they also have areas for group projects such as poetry and journals. They also produce podcasts.

In May 2006, southern Maine experienced the worst flooding since the 1930s. How would anyone know this? Quite simply, one can listen to students in Sprankle's third- and fourth-grade classroom podcast about the disaster (www. bobsprankle.com/blog/) in Wells, Maine. Students told stories about their own personal experiences during the flood. Beyond headlines, if you wanted to hear what happened to real children and their families, this was the way. One teacher related her story of using a wet vacuum to pump water from the garage and posed a potential math problem about how many gallons of water she and her husband had pumped out over nine hours. Students questioned one another about practical concerns and doing without things that one takes for granted. How better to experience an event than by listening to the narratives of those who lived through it, especially the voices of children.

> How better to experience an event than by listening to the narratives of those who lived through it, especially the voices of children.

The potential for new journalists to learn skills that may be used throughout their careers is exciting. The Association of Electronic Journalists has recognized educators' needs concerning the technical and pedagogical strategies required to fully implement new technologies in journalism courses or projects (www.rtnda. org/hsj/). They offer workshops and even seed grants to assist in the challenge. They also have suggestions for lessons, a student handbook, and a teacher guide to establishing such programs. This organization offers a document to assist with broadcast and journalism projects, Plugged In: Using the Internet for High School (and Professional) Journalism (www.rtnda.org/hsj/pluggedin.pdf).

Taking this idea a step further, the Radio Television News Directors Association was funded to start a High School Broadcast Journalism Project. This group matches schools to broadcast stations for dissemination of video and podcasts, supports educators in learning about using the Web 2.0 tools in their journalism classes, and provides a forum for teacher interaction on the topic. It also started a

Student Television Network (STN) to foster the interaction by students about their journalism activities (http://hsbj.org).

Math

The possibilities of using Web 2.0 tools in studying mathematics are almost unlimited. In one lesson developed for young learners, students work in groups to create their own rhymes and songs for an entire family of math facts. Individual students record their math fact creations using an iPod and a voice recorder. The class then has a complete collection of math rhymes that can be used in class or saved on a CD for students to use at home.

Darren Kuropatwa, a high-school math teacher in Winnipeg, Manitoba, Canada, created an Applied Math 40S Wiki Solutions Manual (http://am40s.pbwiki.com). Students help each other learn by contributing to the manual. Participation counts in students' grades, and they have to make at least two edits or contributions to the wiki. One must be a significant contribution and the other must be a constructive modification.

He provides a table with a list of links to the various units that the class studies in his course. There are problems and also basic skills questions for students to solve in each unit. In solving these problems, students have to use all the skills they've learned in class. They also tackle test questions that the class hasn't done well with in the past. Kuropatwa tells his students, "Solving them here, in a low pressure environment, will help prepare you to ace your tests and the final exam" (2007, n.p.). Students have to solve the problems and show how they solved them by including annotated calculations and interpretations. Darren blogs at the Web site A Difference (http://adifference.blogspot.com).

Ms. Armstrong was a student teacher at Daniel McIntyre Collegiate High School in Winnipeg, Manitoba, Canada in 2006. She created a number of blogs that her students contributed to enthusiastically, including notes and homework assignments, along with general math discussions. One of these included the activity Gummy Bears—A Graduated Jellybean (http://gr10pc-gb.blogspot.com/2006/09/multiplying-and-dividing-polynomials.html).

Armstrong stated, "The blog has become an integral part of my teaching as well as my own learning" (2006, n.p.). She went on to explain that "a student that has sat dormant for the past three months, shown little more effort than simply arriving in class breathing, has not only taken the opportunity to post on the classroom blog, but has critically assessed its organization and structure. In addition to his valid concerns, he provides a well thought out solution and has taken the initiative to begin the construction of an S1 math forum (http://s13.invisionfree.com/DMCIMath/). Since I made several changes in teaching practices this year, I can in no way attribute all performance changes to the blog, but I honestly believe that student understanding, motivation, and persistence has greatly improved since the incorporation of the blog."

Students in Chris Harbeck's Grade 8 math classes at Sargent Park School in Winnipeg, Manitoba, use two blog sites (http://sp8mathextentions.blogspot.com and http://sargentparkmathzone.blogspot.com) to get updates and assignments for their math class. Students are required to complete assignments (usually math games) and then post their results on the blog. Harbeck also created a student-written wiki (Welcome to Sargent Parks Grade 8 Math Interactive Guide Book, http://sargentparkmath.pbwiki.com).

Finally, Ms. Nelson teaches several levels of math at Springfield-Clark County Joint Vocational School in Ohio. Her blog provides students with a list of homework assignments as well as class notes and solutions to previous assignments. One part of the blog is designed so that students can contribute (http://nlcommunities.com/communities/msn/archive/category/5445.aspx).

The teaching of mathematics can be exciting and challenging. In the Web 2.0 Wisdom sidebar entitled Web 2.0 in Math Education, Christopher Johnson provides insight into ways that new tools can assist students and teachers.

web 2.0 wisdom

Web 2.0 in Math Education

Christopher Johnson

During my eight years of middle-school teaching, my students had regular opportunities to write about the mathematics they were learning. These writing opportunities included daily journals where students reflected upon the day's lesson, in-class writing prompts about the day's lesson, and short answer/essay questions on assessments. The purposes of these writing assignments were generally two-fold: to allow students to reflect upon their own thinking, and to give me an insight into their thinking.

When students reflect upon not only their own writing, but also the writing of fellow classmates, the results can be even more powerful. Technology, specifically a blog, can be used to make this process more interactive for the students. For example, a class is given a "problem of the week" to consider. On Monday, the teacher posts the problem on the blog, which would most likely be related to a concept the students are currently studying. Students are given a day to think about how they would solve that problem. Then, on Tuesday, students would begin posting their responses. Their responses would include answers to the following questions: What strategies did I use to solve the problem? Was there more than one way for me to solve the problem? What did I learn as I solved the problem? (Note that this is not simply an exercise in solving a problem and then telling how it was solved.) Then, over the next two days, students would have the opportunity to read their fellow classmates' responses. Students would be encouraged to respond to their classmates' work, with the understanding that constructive criticism has already been established as part of the classroom culture. Students would also have the chance to revise their responses by posting a new response, not simply deleting an old one. On Friday, the teacher would share some of the problem-solving strategies and reflections in class.

There are many benefits to the model I propose. First, there is a permanent record of students' reflection and thought. Since no one would be able to delete a posting, all ideas would be available to both students and teacher for further reflection. Second, students, especially at the middle-school level, are more likely to be motivated to write if they are using a blog or other technology tool than if they are simply writing on paper. Third, students would have the opportunity to share their writing with other students in a nonthreatening environment, thereby allowing the "shy" students, the ones who don't speak up in class, to participate to the same degree as any other student. Finally, and perhaps most importantly, students are engaged in an ongoing metacognitive process in which they are reflecting upon their thinking and strategies.

Christopher Johnson is a doctoral candidate in mathematics education and leadership at George Mason University.

Geography

Given the nature of our world today, it is important to understand and appreciate other countries and other cultures. Web 2.0 tools provide excellent ways to help students understand cultural aspects of the world and particularly to find out something about the physical attributes of their own and other countries.

Geography Matters is a blog and set of activities designed to teach students the importance of this subject. "At the elementary level, students are naturally curious about the world around them," writes Steve Pierce (2006, p. 1) of the National Council for Geographic Education (NCGE) Curriculum and Instruction Committee, in his overview of elementary geography clubs. Do you remember playing hide-and-go-seek or going on a scavenger hunt as a kid? Well it seems this old-time favorite has taken on a new dimension in a hobby called geocaching, in which individuals and organizations set up caches (a logbook or a waterproof container) around the world and share the locations of them on the Internet. People use a GPS device and coordinates to find the caches, which might include various rewards.

One example of a Web 2.0 tool useful for geography education is World 66 (www. world66.com), which allows users to customize a map of the world for their personal travels or for an assignment to investigate a particular place. Further, individuals can contribute to the site. For instance, if your class disagrees with the description of a place, students can change it there and then. The site describes itself as "the travel guide you write." Another example of a site allowing pupils to contribute is the Royal Geographical Society's Geography in the News Web site (www.geographyinthenews.rgs.org). These are examples of geo-blogs.

National Geographic recently started a new program, My Wonderful World (www. mywonderfulworld.org), to expand geographic learning in schools, homes, and throughout the community. This site offers a variety of tools to assist educators in teaching geography at age-appropriate levels.

One evolving tool that can make geography exciting is Google Earth, basically a globe that sits inside your PC. You can point and zoom to any place on the planet that you wish to explore, as satellite images and local facts zoom into view. One Web site that helps teachers use Google Earth and other Web 2.0 tools is Juicy Geography (www.juicygeography.co.uk), which offers lesson plans and complementary ideas for encouraging and supporting student engagement in geography activities. Some of the best geography-based activities are fly-overs that can be exported to a video. This blending of technology and curriculum helps students experience events and places in deep and analytical ways. Val Vannet found this to be the case when she prepared her students for a class trip to Iceland with an exciting advanced organizer (www.hsdiceland.blogspot.com). Another tool, NASA's World Wind (http://worldwind.arc.nasa.gov), lets you zoom from satellite altitude into any place on Earth through satellite imagery and topography data. World Wind lets you experience Earth terrain in visually rich 3D, just as if you were really there.

English as a Second Language and English Language Learners

Learning a new language requires the development of listening, speaking, and memory skills. Finding new approaches and using varied methodologies is beneficial to both the teacher and learner. For middle-school students, motivation is a key factor in the learning and retention of knowledge. Using the iPod as a "language lab" is a sure way to garner interest. It allows students to record vocabulary, conduct question and answer conversations, check pronunciation, and store their language exercise for instant replay and evaluation. In this type of project, students can brainstorm topics for a conversation to be held in the language they are studying. Students generate questions and hold practice conversations. Once a practice conversation has been generated, pairs of students record questions and answers with an iPod and a voice recorder. When they are satisfied with the product, the conversation is downloaded onto a computer, renamed, and listened to by the teacher for evaluation. The recordings can be kept on the iPods for students to replay.

When families immigrate to the United States, it is sometimes challenging for them to learn a new language and become familiar with the community in which they live. In one project in Grand Island Nebraska, English language learners (ELL) use an iPod and other technology tools to help them develop language skills and learn more about their new surroundings (http://images.apple.com/education/solutions/ipod/pdf/0221205_iPod_LocalHistory.pdf).

The project incorporates multiple intelligences through the use of text, audio, and image files. English language learners are assigned a lesson that focuses on research, reading, writing, and presentation skills. The students work individually and in small groups to conduct research on their community. Students compile the results of their research, write a report, and create a presentation slideshow. They add appropriate images to illustrate each area of research. Students use an iPod and a voice recorder to create recordings of their report in both English and their native language. The audio files are added to the presentations.

Science

Science experiments can be challenging for students, especially if they are visual learners and have a difficult time with written or oral instructions. By using recordings of the teacher's instructions and student observations combined with photos of an experiment's progress, all students can review what occurred. It's a great way to reinforce student learning and to share experiments with students who weren't there. This technique can be applied to any science experiment. The teacher uses an iPod and a voice recorder to provide experiment instructions to small groups of students. Students listen to the directions first, then they observe and record their experiment steps and results using a digital camera and an iPod. The images and audio are then combined in an iMovie project or on an iPod photo (if available) to share with others.

In Norwalk, California, Margaret Munoz of Corvallis Middle School (which has a mostly economically disadvantaged student population) adopted a technology-infused, project-based learning model and her students excelled. They used iMovie to demonstrate their understanding of the concepts. She notes that their level of engagement has increased significantly and their grades clearly indicate that fact (www.apple.com/education/profiles/corvallis/). Munoz (2006) states:

> I had a student who made an iMovie for a science class that clearly demonstrated that he understood the material, and his project was just wonderful. Several other teachers wondered why he'd put in so much effort, as he isn't doing much in any of his other classes. I told everyone, "This is what students can do when they're excited about learning!" Using tools like iMovie and the Mac mini computers, our students' level of engagement is just amazing. (n.p.)

One science teacher decided to get students in his physics class involved in a project called Scribes, in which students keep a class blog. Each day a different student is given the responsibility of updating the blog. They post class notes, pictures, upcoming assignments, and useful links.

This Week in Science (www.twis.org) offers a weekly adventure through podcasting. Recent topics include What if the World Were a Giant Computer? and The String Theory Pendulum.

In a final example, students in Chris Bague's sixth-grade science class at Saugus Union School District in California created podcasts on concepts such as plate tectonics, glaciology, edaphology, and limnology. They are presented as works in progress, with requests for comments from the listeners. Their efforts show that students can use Web 2.0 tools to come to their own unique understanding of complex topics and share this understanding with others (https://Webapps. saugus.k12.ca.us/community/earthscience/Weblog/).

other tools and models

This has been a very quick look at ways that educators are using Web 2.0 tools. We hope that these resources may assist other teachers to start this adventure. The selection we have presented is by no means exhaustive and, in fact, it's hard to keep up with all the creative ideas. The educational applications seem limitless. One school, for instance, asked students to use podcasts to record thoughts, memories, and wishes as they moved from middle to high school. A dance teacher has students create their own movies to examine their form and grace, and an art teacher uses the tools for nature journaling and for artistic renderings, such as sketches and paintings, of a particular location and its surroundings. An AP psychology class produces podcasts to assist in demonstrating their knowledge and studying new topics.

> One thing is certain: we are at the very beginning of this evolution and many of you reading this book will be creating new ideas and projects that others will want to hear about.

One particular example demonstrates the brightest possibilities for incorporating the best models of teaching, learning, and student-driven content activities. ThinkQuest (www.thinkquest.org) began as a contest in 1996 and worked to encourage students and teachers across the globe to design and implement intellectually challenging, project-based learning experiences. This program has gained ongoing corporate support and now describes itself as follows:

ThinkQuest inspires students to think, connect, create, and share. Students work in teams to build innovative and educational Web sites to share with the world. Along the way, they learn research, writing, teamwork, and technology skills and compete for exciting prizes. (ThinkQuest, 2006, n.p.)

One thing is certain: we are at the very beginning of this evolution and many of you reading this book will be creating new ideas and projects that others will want to hear about.

5

professional development

In the past few decades, a transformation has occurred in American public education; now, teachers are expected and required to use educational technology in one form or another in their classrooms (Collier, Weinburgh, & Rivera, 2004). As technology improves, many school districts adopt new methods to enhance communication, teaching, and learning.

▶ ▶ ▶ ▶ ▶

Because of increased pressures to use technology placed upon teachers—by school districts, the federal government, and professional organizations—expectations to prepare teachers at the preservice and in-service levels have risen (ISTE, 2000). The No Child Left Behind Act of 2001 (U.S. Department of Education, 2001) also added pressure by increasing technology standards for teachers and by making high-stakes testing more pervasive than ever before (Amrein & Berliner, 2003).

Unfortunately, even though massive amounts of money have been spent on training educators, we have not seen a real difference in the ways technology has been integrated into the classroom (Cuban, 2001; Laffey, 2004; Norris, Sullivan, Poirot, & Solloway, 2003; Williams & Kingham, 2003). According to the U.S. Department of Education (2004), we have not done a particularly stellar job, as a recent report concluded:

> We have not realized the promise of technology in education. Essentially, providing the hardware without adequate training in its use—and in its endless possibilities for enriching the learning experience—meant that the great promise of Internet technology was frequently unrealized. Computers, instead of transforming education, were often shunted to a "computer room," where they were little used and poorly maintained. Students mastered the wonders of the Internet at home, not in school. Today's students, of almost any age, are far ahead of their teachers in computer literacy. (p. 10)

The federal government has done more than study the problem. In particular, it published the National Educational Technology Plan (U.S. Department of Education, 2004), first framed under the presidency of Bill Clinton and revised and approved by Congress in January 2005. The plan lists these seven major steps and recommendations for implementing technology in our schools:

1. Strengthen leadership
2. Consider innovative budgeting
3. Improve teacher training
4. Support e-learning and virtual schools
5. Encourage broadband access
6. Move toward digital content
7. Integrate data systems (U.S. Department of Education, 2004, n.p.)

Professional developers have tended to design programs that attempt to implement strategies to change practice; unfortunately, when the support and funding disappear, frequently so does the change in practice. Furthermore, brief classes or workshops without ongoing support seem to create few substantive changes (Cuban, 2001; Pelligrino, 2004; Sandholtz, Ringstaff, & Dwyer, 2000; Schrum, 1999).

The research firm Market Data Retrieval claims that more than 80% of public schools in the United States have broadband service, which suggests that many educators have seen some form of technology related to the Internet in their schools (Lindquist, 2004). If you are reading this book, we assume you may have resources well beyond broadband. Yet even with modern technology in so many schools, it is not being utilized in the way that has been envisioned.

Typically, teachers have been seen as one cause for this shortfall (Cuban, 2001). Many schools have attempted to provide useful professional development programs to prepare teachers to integrate technology into their curriculum. Traditional staff development has tended to be based on one model: a one-day session, often four hours right after school when everyone is tired and focused on other issues. Frequently the school hires an expert who arrives, delivers the program, and goes home. Most typically, the entire teaching staff is required to show up for the session.

Variations on the one-day program have evolved; for example, a district or individual school might choose a topic for an expanded version—an entire year of intensive staff development, often a "hot topic" found in the popular press. Regardless, they tend to be of the "chalk and talk" or "spray and pray" variety. Unfortunately, there is very little evidence that these make much difference. The research on professional development is extensive; however, most of it documents the inadequacies. Further, readers of that body of literature are often faced with contradictory statements (Guskey, 1999). Fullan and Stiegelbauer (1991) summarized this by saying, "Nothing has promised so much and has been so frustratingly wasteful as the thousands of workshops and conferences that led to no significant change in practice when the teachers returned to their classrooms" (p. 315).

creating effective programs

Most frequently, when working with adults, you will want to "meet them where they are" rather than assuming a "one size fits all" model. There are multiple ways to assess any group of faculty members, but again, using the technology will provide support in two ways. First, it states clearly that this is of utmost importance to you, and second, any additional experiences are going to prove useful and support teachers' confidence.

In his 2000 book *Evaluating Professional Development,* University of Kentucky Professor of Education Thomas Guskey outlines a comprehensive five-step evaluation program. The components are:

Participants' reactions. Evaluation at this level identifies the appropriateness of a program's content, process, and context. Was the content appropriate? Was the presenter knowledgeable? Was the coffee hot?

Participants' learning. What are participants' beliefs toward the professional development topic, and has the event changed those attitudes and beliefs?

Organizational support and change. Does the organization have the tools, services, and policies in place to support the training experience once teachers return to the classroom?

Participants' use of new knowledge. Did participants implement what they learned? Did it change classroom practice?

Student learning. Did the experience improve student learning? In most cases, that should be the most important question to ask.

preservice learning

In addition to the efforts by school districts, universities have provided classes and professional development for teacher candidates. These efforts were expanded through the Department of Education's Preparing Tomorrow's Teachers to use Technology (PT[3]) grant program from 1999 through 2003. Some PT[3] studies in particular looked at the barriers and challenges to technology integration, such as alignment with the curriculum, peer support, and faculty involvement (Brzycki & Dudt, 2005; Staples, Pugach, & Himes, 2005).

Other studies have addressed the growing challenge in modern education to remediate the fact that most teachers still feel uncomfortable using technology in their teaching (Seels, Campbell, & Talsma, 2003; Strudler & Grove, 2002). With all of the support and training seemingly provided, many teachers are still viewed as resistant to integrating technology on a more frequent basis. Now we are requesting that educators change their practice in various ways to take advantage of the opportunities of Web 2.0. How should a school or a district go about this, given the poor performance of previous professional development activities, especially as related to technology? One way might be to incorporate communities of practice into educators' daily routine and lives.

communities of practice

The investigative focus of recent theories of learning has gradually moved from the individual as learner to learning as participation in the social world, including numerous ways individuals are shaped by and shape the surrounding world (Lave & Wenger, 1991). As a result, another body of learning theories has blossomed with an emphasis on the social and cultural context of learning. Among those theories is situated cognition, which defines learning as a process of participation in communities of practice. Situated learning means that it takes place in a specific context. Lave (1988) suggests that most learning occurs naturally through activities, contexts, and cultures, but schools too often abstract learning, "unsituate" it, and teach concepts removed from natural contexts and applications.

This is particularly true of professional development activities too. We often provide "just in case" training rather than "just in time" training, which provides educators with information they need just as they need it. Just as Web 2.0 encourages the use of tools to engage and promote problem solving in authentic contexts, Web 2.0 should be used authentically to enable educators to understand and become comfortable with the tools and their potential as preparation for using them in their classrooms.

Dede (2003) notes:

> Emerging devices, tools, media, and virtual environments offer opportunities for creating new types of learning communities for students and teachers. Examples of "learning communities" include a national mix of kids working together to create an online encyclopedia

about Harry Potter's fictional world, or groups of mentor and novice teachers in Milwaukee sharing ideas about effective instruction. (n.p.)

Dede's suggestions for how students might create a learning community provide insight into how educators might use the tools to learn about the tools but, more important, to promote a learning community that fosters interaction, collaboration, and improved practice.

The participation is considered "legitimately peripheral" in the beginning, but it gradually increases in conviction and engagement with a community of practice (Lave & Wenger, 1991). The term *legitimately* implies that newcomers are not excluded from various activities of a community but involved in such activities.

Wenger (1998) suggests that a community of practice defines itself along three essential dimensions—*joint enterprise, mutual engagement,* and *shared repertoire.* The first dimension, joint enterprise, refers to what the community is about as it is understood, defined, and continuously redefined by its members. It also implies a regime of mutual accountability, meaning that members negotiate the goals and characteristics of their community, and thus, are responsible for how they are defined in a collective sense. Members of a community are engaged in common activities that often take the form of group collaboration to pursue their professional goals and interests. The second dimension describes a mutual engagement that functions to bind a community of practice together into a social entity. The last dimension, shared repertoire, refers to a wide range of artifacts that were developed by members of the community over time. The repertoire may include traditional documentary sources, routines, vocabulary, or styles that both articulate shared experience and record the history of a community.

Another view of communities of practice is explained by Bielaczyc and Collins (1999), who suggest that the defining quality of a learning community is that there is a culture of learning in which everyone is involved in a collective effort of understanding. They propose that such a culture must include four characteristics: a diversity of expertise among its members, a shared objective of continually advancing the collective knowledge and skills, an emphasis on learning how to learn, and mechanisms for sharing what is learned. If a learning community is presented with a problem, then the learning community can bring its collective knowledge to bear on the problem. The importance of the community element has been emphasized by various researchers (Rovai, 2001). They have argued that a strong feeling of community increases the willingness to share information, the passion to support each other, and the collaborative efforts to complete joint activities. Sharing interests is not enough for people to form a community of practice; rather, people form a community of practice through interaction while pursuing their interests (Wenger, 2001). Therefore, interaction and the resulting relationships are the most important catalysts in forming a community (Schwier, 2001).

Communities of practice are assisted by following some simple suggestions in organizing and planning the way these communities are structured. An article by Susan Taylor (2006) suggests the following strategies to support virtual communities:

- Establish regular times for team interaction

- Send agendas to participants beforehand

- Designate a team librarian

- Build and maintain a team archive

- Use visual forms of communication where possible

- Set formal rules for communication and/or technology use (n.p.)

In addition, continued energy to maintain participation and enthusiasm from members is required. The ideas in Encouraging Participation, from an article by Trena Noval (2006) on techLEARNING.com, are appropriate to think about when any type of professional development is being considered, and perhaps especially when dealing with Web 2.0. These ideas will help keep members energized and participatory in a professional development community.

Encouraging Participation

PROFESSIONAL LEARNING COMMUNITIES can be wonderful and exhilarating places for teachers to grow, learn, and collaborate. Communities that meet regularly face-to-face have that built-in ability to encourage participation—but this can be a little harder to maintain in online communities. Here are some tips to help keep your community actively collaborative and thriving through members' participation.

Create an environment of trust

- Involve all members in developing goals for the community.

Eliminate confusion

- ▶ Make sure they understand the purpose of your community, what they will gain through participation.

- ▶ Make sure they are clear on how the community works—this will illuminate frustration by members which can lead to lost participation.

Create productive dialogue/Make learning interactive

- ▶ If your community is local, try to have monthly or at least a few face-to-face meetings a year with the group so that they have opportunities to meet in person.

- ▶ Have a way for them to post short bios, their interests, curriculum ideas, teaching environment profiles, and maybe even a picture.

- ▶ Have a place for teachers to post questions, ideas, or things that they might want help with or to collaborate on.

- ▶ If you are a remote community, use discussion boards or live chats, or set up a listserv for your community to talk to each other on a regular basis.

- ▶ Create a space where teachers can share resources and discuss how they have used them.

Have teachers share what they are doing on a regular basis

- ▶ Give them the opportunity to ask each other questions.

- ▶ Allow for brainstorming sessions with the community participants.

- ▶ Have a show-and-tell about projects or successful learning strategies that they have had with their students or at their school.

Give constructive feedback and support as a facilitator

- ▶ Make sure that there is a way for your community members to receive feedback and encouragement—if these are done constructively it can go a long way to keep your members happy and engaged!

One of the most long-lived and well-respected educational Web sites is Tapped In (http://tappedin.org), which is credited with pioneering a multi-user virtual environment. Lectures, interactive conversations, and other resources all reside in Tapped In; however, it is important to recognize that this community, just like all communities of practice, has to work to maintain user motivation and interest. Christine Greenhow (2006) suggests social networking strategies in the following Web 2.0 Wisdom sidebar.

web 2.0 wisdom

Supporting Teachers' Development of Extended Social Networks for Teaching and Learning

Christine Greenhow

SOCIAL NETWORKS affect the way schools respond to innovation; therefore, we as teacher educators ought to cultivate an understanding of how generative networks develop and how we can help teachers and students use Web 2.0 tools to facilitate them.

Having worked with teacher educators, teachers, and students on the integration of emerging Web-based technologies into their teaching and learning practices, I offer the following recommendation to technology coordinators, administrators, and library media specialists who seek to help teachers take advantage of the social-networking capabilities of Web 2.0 technologies.

Recommendation 1
Help teachers uncover and make transparent their notions of the classroom community.

Teachers often seek to use popular new technologies found on the Internet without examining their values and assumptions about teaching and learning and considering how these fit with technology's potential. In using the social-networking capabilities of Web 2.0 to their advantage, teachers may need help identifying and making explicit their notions of time and space and where and with whom learning and teaching ought to occur in order to reconcile traditional beliefs with the technology's potential.

Consider teachers' use of Web logs, for example. I have found that often a teacher's goal for using a class blog is to get students to reflect on their beginning ideas about the subject matter and interact with other students. Blogs offer a number of advantages for student-centered and constructive teaching and learning, including giving students a vehicle for contributing to the content of the class; allowing students to comment on each other's posts and link out to other resources; enabling students to make their voice heard and to develop a sense of voice. In addition, because blogs are public, other members of the blogosphere can contribute to the evolving discussion, thereby potentially helping students and teachers to connect to other networked communities (e.g., other blogs) around their interests.

However, when teachers start out with blogs they tend to bring old assumptions and perceptions to bear on the technology that inhibit its fulfillment of this potential. Embracing traditional notions of time and space, teachers often do not conceive of building social networks beyond the classroom. Although teachers themselves may belong to online professional social networks beyond their school and see the value of such networks professionally, they need support in conceptualizing and trying out this advantage with students. Moreover, teachers are often discouraged when students' interactions within blogs seem forced or idiosyncratic. They hope that students will post ideas that substantially contribute to their own learning and to the knowledge of the class, but without modeling or linking out to other blogs, students may not recognize the potentially important and public contribution they can make. Moreover, ideally teachers' use of different media should be strategic.

What goes on in a learning blog—my term for a blog intended and designed to facilitate students' learning—should enrich face-to-face educational experiences. Again, teachers may need guidance in finding

▶▶

opportunities to improve their face-to-face teaching by building on blogged ideas and students' behaviors online. In summary, as teacher educators, we ought to develop teachers' abilities not only to operate Web 2.0 tools but to simultaneously uncover and perturb their ideas about what it means to teach with Web-enhanced social networks. We then have a better chance of promoting well-intentioned uses of technology that teachers and students perceive as successful.

Recommendation 2

Develop alternative forms of teacher professional development that embed the social-networking tools we want teachers to consider.

If we hope teaching practices will shift to benefit from Web 2.0 technologies, we ought to reexamine our own professional development models and the examples we are providing. Do our PD models benefit from Web 2.0? Do our methods mainly reinforce regular face-to-face interactions with a local group of colleagues based primarily on our own expertise? Do we draw from a broad and deep enough well of open educational resources that allow us to discover and verify information and forge creative networks?

For instance, wikis are collaborative Web sites that can be edited using a Web browser. Although this means that anyone can edit existing pages, create new pages, delete content, or rename pages, most wikis established for course-related purposes have some security features built in so only the class can view and edit them. Using wikis in education can promote genuinely collaborative environments. They can support transparent writing and editing, interdependence and teamwork among authors, public and civic engagement, and the continuous exchange of feedback on ideas. However, teaching with wikis can be difficult because they require students and teachers to reconsider their roles. For instance, students' and teachers' individual identities are subsumed by the collective. Moreover, the intellectual authority of peers is equivalent to that of the instructor or others who enter into the process of correcting, editing, revising, and even deleting work.

▶▶▶

Our professional development models should involve teachers in how we use and struggle to use such tools meaningfully and how we ourselves wrestle with and resolve such issues. To do this, we might, for example, work with teachers and wikis to collaboratively write technology integration lessons and contribute to the evolution of a relevant entry in Wikipedia. These experiences could stimulate a discussion about issues of authorship, authority, credibility, and content. Most professional development efforts are still organized around local communities often with a heavy face-to-face component. Using public wikis in distributed environments, we could emphasize a hybrid PD model, involving local and far-flung participants and balancing teachers' exploratory and disruptive experiences with opportunities to collaboratively reflect on their assumptions about the educational value and application of these tools.

Reference

Greenhow, C. (2006). From blackboard to browser: An empirical study of how teachers' beliefs and practices influence their use of the Internet in the classroom and are influenced by the Internet's affordance. Unpublished doctoral dissertation, Harvard University, Cambridge, MA.

Resources

Investigate Educational Technologies:
http://dmc.umn.edu/technologies/

University of Minnesota Wiki:
https://wiki.umn.edu/twiki/bin/view/

UThink: Blogs at the University of Minnesota:
http://blog.lib.umn.edu

Post your comments about this sidebar or your thoughts about using emerging technologies in education at http://blog.lib.umn. edu/greenhow/blog/.

Christine Greenhow is a research associate at the University of Minnesota's Digital Media Center.

technology literacy training

Many states require their new and practicing educators to demonstrate basic competencies in using and teaching with technology, and Web 2.0 tools will take those educators a bit further. Assisting educators in this task will require a concerted effort on the part of administrators. As mentioned, it is unfortunate, but most typical professional development activities have not been successful in changing behavior, for many reasons. Without significant district and building level commitment, ongoing support, and organized efforts, that reality is not likely to change. To chart a new course, administrators must agree that the use of technology is a fundamental goal, and faculty members must participate in identifying it as a shared goal.

Once the goal of enhancing teaching and learning through technology is agreed upon, there are many ways to accomplish it. One of the most successful is to use the technology to learn how to use the technology, or some might say, not just talk the talk, but truly walk the walk. Many studies of educators' lack of technology implementation have found that the lack of accountability from administrators on their actually accomplishing technological goals has been the most influential in practice (Schrum, 1999). One administrator said he had success by changing two simple things in his evaluation of the educators in his building. He required that one of the lessons he observed each year had to be in integrating technology into the curriculum and one of each educator's annual goals had to be focused on improving technology proficiency.

School districts have adopted several different approaches to preparing their educators for using and learning with technology. Some use a central model in which a wide variety of productivity and workplace skill programs are offered to interested teachers. Others have a requirement that educators attend a certain number of sessions each year. Still others poll their faculty each year and offer programs that meet specific needs. Another group of schools offers special designations to teachers who complete a specific number of training sessions and demonstrate acquired skills. A small number of districts have invested in videoconferencing technology to allow remote experts to present information and provide training without the expense and time normally required for travel.

With these possibilities for Web 2.0 tools, educators can weave in the potential for building a "learning community" as they become familiar with blogs, wikis, podcasting, and social bookmarking. Not only can educators connect with their peers, but they can have access to experts in a variety of content or process areas.

"More important, these tools enable conversation, dialogue, and reflection, which are critical to professional growth and development activities" (Jakes, 2006e, n.p.). We will examine each possible method in terms of professional development.

professional development and web 2.0 tools

Blogging

Blogs can be used to promote teachers' comfort with and understanding of Web 2.0 tools, and some teachers already use them to create their own professional and personal networks. Individuals within learning communities can determine their topics of interest, identify ways to find information, and share conversations and knowledge. Guhlin (2006a) explains:

> This idea of building your own professional development network— where you find the people from whom you can learn, ask questions of them, comment on their thoughts and links, and have them do the same for you—is one of the major benefits of blogging and podcasting. It is the art of conversation captured in digital format. (n.p.)

Conversations about teaching and perhaps every other topic are taking place in the blogosphere, and as noted in the last chapter, blogs are available on almost every issue. Guhlin (2006a) continues: "Blogs enable us to see others' thinking—or lack of thinking—as they build a Web of connected learning" (n.p.). Visiting a blog gives educators access to conference sessions or meetings that they may not be able to attend. Through interactive and public discussions, ideas can be refined, developed, or expanded.

One teacher, Karl Fisch of Centennial, Colorado, uses a staff development blog for Arapahoe High School teachers exploring constructivism and 21st-century learning skills (The Fischbowl, http://thefischbowl.blogspot.com). This blog offers information about current educational events, new technologies and their potential for schools and learners, and that's just scratching the surface.

Other schools have developed different ways to take advantage of the power of blogs for professional development. Poling (2005) described how her school,

Oakdale Elementary in Maryland, sought to raise student achievement through the use of a new model of professional development. Using the "study group" model, they created a technology study group. The group met once a month on various topics and then followed up their meetings through the use of a blog. Poling reported that:

> Blogging provided a means of ongoing communication with other group members that would not otherwise be available for an entire month until the next face-to-face session. ... Overall, the concept of blogging as ongoing support has been extremely beneficial as the staff tries to make long-term change in instruction. (p. 15)

Podcasting

Schools are starting to make professional development training sessions, lectures, and ideas available through podcasts, which leads to individualized professional development on demand. At a state level, New Hampshire offers podcasts from the New Hampshire Department of Education; one discusses the state ICT standards implementation.

King and Gura (2006) suggest that, "Developing content requires some forethought, planning and scheduling. It also requires insight into how this new technology subtly changes the dynamics of information exchange between speaker and listener and how this must be accounted for in format" (n.p.). Their Podcast for Teachers, produced and published by Fordham University's Regional Educational Technology Center (RETC), provides a large number of freely available podcasts for educators. The RETC is dedicated to serving and researching the professional development needs of educators striving to improve student and teacher performance.

Other types of podcasts for professional development are becoming available. For example, you might want to take a session on a topic, but don't have the time or it does not fit into your schedule. A variety of organizations now offer podcasts on topics you really want to hear. LearningTimes (www.learningtimes.org), for instance, is constantly updating its offerings. Recently this organization offered a podcast called Creating a CD Portfolio for Documenting Student Progress and another named Exploring the Intersection of Technology and Learning. Or you could listen to a podcast made from a live Webcast titled K–12 Professional Development: Trends and Opportunities.

A comprehensive organization, The Education Podcast Network (http://epnweb. org) offers a wide variety of podcasts for educators' professional development as well as curriculum areas, and also has links to several other content and professional podcasts. It is likely that this area will develop rapidly to support and assist educators in their learning and teaching.

Wikis

One of the most exciting opportunities for professional development is to allow all members of a community to participate in the creation of a goal, plan, or direction or to simply discuss the way a new activity is working. Wikis present the ideal manner in which to accomplish this and, at the same time, educators learn about the potential for using this tool in their classrooms. The Adult Literacy Organization models this process with a wiki focused on professional development for its members. Entitled Key Issues for Professional Development (http://wiki.literacytent. org/index.php/Key_Issues_for_ Professional_Development/),

> ### Threading a Conversation
>
> WITH WEB 1.0, many tools supported threaded discussions, and they worked well at the time. It was difficult, however, to link specific comments back to their origins or to make corrections and additions in a way that was always meaningful. With the Web 2.0 wikis, comments can be inserted precisely where they belong and the resulting "conversation" can help focus ideas. Searching for specific items is also simplified in the world of wikis, since in the past all management systems were not uniformly easy to use.

this project allows participants to collaboratively contemplate their most important topics and ways to further their mission.

Other Web sites provide a place for teachers to learn about wikis. For example, For Teachers New to Wikis (http://writingwiki.org/default.aspx/ WritingWiki/ForTeachersNewtoWikis.html) has a graphic (Figure 5.1) that shows the relationship and interaction between content and collaboration.

Other professional development sites offer lesson plans and opportunities to share ideas and ask questions of other teachers. At the Teacher's Lounge, under the link for social studies at the high-school level, one can find ideas for teaching several subjects (http://teacherslounge.editme.com/hssocialstudies/), and elementary teachers can post their lessons, talk to other teachers, or simply find ideas for teaching fractions (http://teacherslounge.editme.com/elemmath/).

Wikispaces (http://teacherconnect.wikispaces.com) is a teacher-to-teacher global network with a stated goal to "Link a profile to a network to a network" and to encourage teachers and students to provide information about the very best places to interact with others interested in education. Teachers can find information on many topics (self-directed professional development), create links to student projects throughout the world, and access links to other wikis and blogs.

Figure 5.1 | Relationship and interaction between content and collaboration

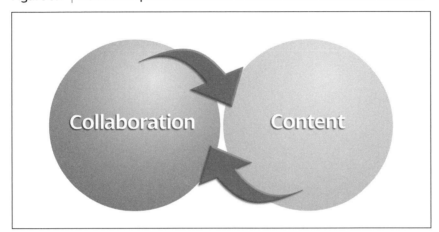

▶ Source: http://writingwiki.org/default.aspx/WritingWiki/ForTeachersNewtoWikis.html

Additionally, some organizations are working to promote the growth of interaction about particular topics for their members. One is a wiki called Library Success (www.libsuccess.org), which offers information for all types of librarians to share their successful programs and innovative projects using technology. This wiki serves as a collaborative site with information on best practices, training, and other professional topics.

Finally, even preservice educators are invited to participate in wikis to learn about their future profession and activities. Future Teachers Meet Wiki (http://en.wikibooks.org/wiki/Future_Teachers_Meet_Wiki/) is one site that encourages teacher candidates to explore new ways of teaching and learning and to promote interaction among the next generation of teachers.

Encouraging our educators and schools to use technology effectively is a complicated and challenging task. Using these new tools as models and methods to teach about them accomplishes two goals. It first provides practice and comfort with the tools, and second, offers the opportunity to experience firsthand the use of the technology for meaningful and authentic activities.

6

leadership and new tools

Being a school or district administrator has never been an easy occupation, but today they have more issues to deal with than ever before. Technology makes many tasks easier but it also adds complexities peculiar to this digital age. While much time is spent in dealing with administrative issues, a principal or district administrator is more than ever an educational leader with responsibilities for guiding classroom activities and focusing thoughtful attention on the intellectual growth of students and teachers.

Their students are part of a digital generation with new expectations and approaches to learning. They understand information from a combination of text, images, video, conversations, and more that come at them all at once. They are self-interested and self-directed; they network with peers and expect to be engaged, even entertained, at all times. This is the reality evident in classrooms around the country. The days of "Open your textbook to page 35" are over. That textbook is outdated, print is suspect, and there's only one opinion, that of the author.

With Web 2.0, however, knowledge is available from many sources and as long as teachers vet those sources for accuracy and reliability, students can get a broader range of information, perspectives, and resources.

Teachers have changed. As turnover increases and younger teachers enter classrooms, they are often well versed in using technological tools. They replace teachers who have years of experience with subject matter, student sensibilities, and the "system." Both skill sets are needed in each educator, and after years of training teachers how to use the tools, the focus is shifting to how to integrate them for new hires.

Learning has changed. "Learning is characterized not only by greater autonomy for the learner, but also a greater emphasis on active learning, with creation, communication and participation playing key roles, and on changing roles for the teacher, indeed, even a collapse of the distinction between teacher and student altogether" (Downes, 2006, n.p.).

leading in the 21st century

Leadership under these conditions is more difficult and more necessary than ever before. Leaders have to understand that things are changing, how that change is happening, and what is likely to be the result. For example, they know that the world their students will enter after graduation is very different from what it was even a few years ago. They also know that their students are using instant messaging, are blogging and downloading podcasts, and are watching YouTube outside of school. In order for schools to prepare students for the future, leaders must help teachers make the transition to using new technologies and new methods. Policies and actions at the top make it clear where a school or district is headed.

In promoting technology integration, indeed, in getting to the point of planning for new technologies, district and school leaders need to understand the issues. According to the Digital Disconnect survey:

School administrators—and not teachers—set the tone for Internet use at school. The differences among the schools attended by students [surveyed] were striking. Policy choices by those who run school systems and other factors have resulted in different schools having different levels of access to the Internet, different requirements for student technology literacy skills, and different restrictions on student Internet access. (Levin & Arafeh, 2002, p. iii)

If administrators want to make change happen, they must have a vision for the future. According to techLEARNING blogger Wesley Fryer (2006):

It is a question of leadership vision and pedagogic vision. What do the school leaders believe we need in the way of an environment to help students learn the skills they will need for life, and what does authentic teaching and learning look and sound like in the early 21st century? (n.p.)

Fryer also believes that conversations about these issues should happen at local policymaking levels as well as at classroom levels with teachers and administrators.

In addition, district and school administrators need new skills, the same ones that business leaders must have today, the personal and analytical skills required to be true leaders. Microsoft has a free tool called Education Competencies that identifies the attributes needed by those in education leadership positions (Microsoft Corporation, 2006). Their competencies are grouped into the following six qualities that individuals must have in order for a school district to achieve success in the 21st century. The six qualities are:

1. Individual excellence

2. Organizational skills

3. Courage

4. Results (goal-oriented)

5. Strategic skills

6. Operating skills

District and school leaders must have a vision for success and communicate with others to make that a shared vision. They must see the big picture—how everything fits together and what relationships exist. When new things emerge, they must be able to integrate them into the overall strategy. For example, when new tools, like Web 2.0 tools, become available, a district may have to revisit its technology plan and adapt it appropriately. The Planning for Web 2.0 sidebar offers several suggestions.

Planning for Web 2.0

1. Create a vision of how new tools will make a difference, how they will fit with existing tools, and what, if any, new policies will be needed to support it. Get a consensus on the vision so that all stakeholders buy into it.

2. Agree on goals for use. Align with other goals such as existing curricular, NCLB, career, and technology goals.

3. Evaluate how well the current infrastructure will support these goals (e.g., the network infrastructure and bandwidth).

4. Identify new instructional and technology integration strategies.

5. Identify professional development strategies that will help educators to implement new instructional and technology integration techniques.

6. Establish a realistic timetable.

7. Develop a realistic budget. While Web 2.0 tools are free, access and support are not.

8. Establish milestones. Identify ways to measure progress with tool use and growth in student learning.

9. Plan for evaluation. Find the best measures that will demonstrate whether goals were reached.

using new tools

School leaders can use Web 2.0 tools the way that business leaders do to help their organizations.

Tim Lauer, principal of Meriwether Lewis Elementary in Portland, Oregon, uses a blog (http://lewiselementary.org) to post information, announcements, class projects, and photos, and a calendar to communicate with the entire school community. He uses a separate blog to publish the staff bulletin and to encourage the staff to use the comment feature for discussions in order to build community.

Helen Nolen, principal of Buckman Arts Magnet Elementary School in Portland, Oregon, uses a blog (http://buckmanelementary.org) and wiki (www.buckmanelementary.org/wiki.html) to communicate. She posts principal and parent newsletters and school events. She installed kiosks with Internet access for those parents without their own computers. She expects teachers to use the school blog and requires that all teachers have at least one page; many have found effective uses for the technology. The librarian posts reading lists; teachers post student writing and artwork, daily journals, and science observations (Intel Education Initiative, 2006).

For teachers, blogs can replace e-mail as a way to communicate with students, parents, or other educators. Because of syndication, everyone can get updates, so teachers can post homework, long-term assignments, explanations, events, and other information. Students and parents can ask questions, react to an idea, or make suggestions in the comment box. This really matters to parents. School leaders can encourage teachers to use blogs, but the request is more accepted if the leaders themselves use the tool.

Scott McLeod (2006a), director of the UCEA Center for the Advanced Study of Technology Leadership in Education (CASTLE) at the University of Minnesota, suggests twelve reasons for an administrator to adopt blogging as a leadership strategy (see sidebar).

Twelve Reasons for an Administrator to Blog

MUCH ATTENTION HAS BEEN PAID to the value of blogging for teachers and students, but administrators can also benefit from the use of this great new tool. This discussion explores the potential value of blogging for K–12 administrators. Although the focus is primarily on principals, the same advantages hold true for superintendents, technology coordinators, and other central office administrators. This selection of reasons stems from chapter 4 of *The Corporate Blogging Book*, by Debbie Weil. So … why blog as an administrator?

Reason 1: Sharing news and events

Blogs are ideal for principals to quickly post news items for their school communities. Upcoming special events, recent awards won by students or staff, classroom highlights, reminders, lunch menus, extracurricular activities, deadlines, and other newsletter-type items are extremely well-suited for blogs and are quick and easy ways to keep a school community informed.

▶ ▶ ▶

Reason 2: Progress monitoring

Community members often are interested in the progress of a school's ongoing activities. Examples might include building a new facility, implementing new curricula, hiring new staff, trying to pass a levy or referendum, and other school initiatives. Regular posts to update stakeholders on the progress of these types of activities can go a long way toward building goodwill and keeping community members informed.

Reason 3: Status alerts

Another type of blog post might be a quick message to alert the community of a short-term problem, event cancellation, or similar news. Status alerts will be most effective when the community knows to go to the blog for the latest news.

Reason 4: Marketing

Because they're electronic, blogs are both faster and less costly than paper communication. If the savings in paper alone isn't persuasive, administrators should consider additional advantages that blogs often have over other communication channels.

Web sites and paper newsletters are static, noninteractive, and often dated. (Who wants to read about something two weeks after it occurred?) E-mails, electronic newsletters, and listservs contribute to clogged inboxes and get caught by spam filters. In contrast, blogs are timely, interactive, and avoid some of the issues that accompany e-mail communications.

If done well, blogs can "create buzz [and] loyal customers" (Weil, 2006, p. 53). One of parents' biggest criticisms of schools is that teachers and administrators don't communicate often enough about the things that parents want to hear about. Blogs can be a great way to publicize the great things that are occurring in schools.

Reason 5: Public relations

As Weil notes, a blog is a great way to bypass local media and get "your own version of the story out there and to get feedback" (p. 52). This can be either proactive or reactive. If administrators put out their spin only after some incident occurs, the message will be much less effective. School communities are going to be much more receptive and trusting if an administrator has built up goodwill beforehand through an ongoing series of posts and dialogues about less important issues.

Frequent transparent communication, with the opportunity to receive feedback through comments, is a strength of blogs that administrators can leverage to their school organization's advantage.

Reason 6: Community building

Blogs can be an excellent tool for facilitating feelings of community within a school organization. Whether a blog serves an internal or external audience, regular posts can keep stakeholders informed of important events as well as those incidents that might go unnoticed in the hectic day-to-day activity of schools. If you read the administrator blogs at Lewis Elementary School in Oregon (http://lewiselementary.org) or Mabry Middle School in Georgia (http://mabryonline.org/blogs/tyson/) you can see that the ongoing stream of news, updates, and highlights can't help but contribute to feelings of connectedness by students, staff, parents, and other community members.

Blogs are different than e-mail listservs and static Web pages because they're interactive. When a principal sends out an e-mail over a listserv or posts a notice on a Web page, there is no way for the school community to interact with that message. If someone has a question or comment, it either doesn't get made or it's merely a one-to-one communication with the principal made by e-mail, voice mail, or telephone call. In contrast, the comments feature of blogs allows anyone to post a question or comment and thus everyone else in the community can see it, see the principal's (or someone else's) response, and add his or her own two cents to the conversation. The blog thus facilitates ongoing dialogue among multiple school stakeholders rather than being a static one-way, or maybe two-way, transmission. What blogs can do that listservs and Web pages can't, is facilitate conversation.

Reason 7: Customer relations

Of course all of this is good for customer relations. Principals who are actively and publicly interacting with school stakeholders, listening to their concerns, responding to those concerns and other questions, and generally being accessible are facilitating good customer relations and building goodwill within the school community. Parents, community members, staff, and students are going to feel more positively about the school when they have the opportunity to not only get frequent updates about what is going on but also ask questions, post concerns, and give suggestions. This openness—this overt transparency—builds stakeholder confidence and satisfaction with the direction and activities of the school.

Reason 8: Branding

As real estate agents know, perhaps the first question that relocating families want answered is "Where are the good schools?" Certain school districts and certain schools within districts have reputations for providing high-quality learning experiences for children. These school organizations are the ones that attract families with high social capital and high-achieving children.

Parents are increasingly checking out school Web sites as part of their relocation decision-making. The same messages from the principal that create warm, fuzzy feelings of community, belonging, and academic excitement also are perfect for outsiders who want to see what the school is all about. It would be fairly difficult for a relocating family to acquire several months' worth of newsletters or e-mails to parents, but the public availability of a blog ensures that everyone—existing stakeholders, relocating families, realtors, potential corporate partners, and other outside community members—can see the wonderful things that are occurring in the school building.

Reason 9: Creating "customer evangelists"

Customer evangelists are those individuals who are passionate about the school and publicly advocate for the school to others. They do this of their own volition—they are not paid to do so. These are the people who talk about how great the school is to everyone they meet. They help build the reputation and the buzz of the school organization and contribute to overall feelings of satisfaction by staff, parents, students, and community members.

Evangelists are important contributors to a school's success. Indeed, as Malcolm Gladwell and others have noted, evangelists may be the only information source that others trust and believe. Nearly everyone is experiencing overload from an unlimited variety of information sources—evangelists are the folks who capture people's attention and sway opinion.

Blogs give evangelists something to talk about. Regular updates, news items, and other highlights feed the conversations that evangelists are having with others. These people can make or break a school's reputation—administrators would be wise to feed them well on a steady diet of positive information.

Reason 10: Thought leadership

A blog can be a great place to put thoughts out there for the community to chew on. Is a school considering a new initiative or an important change? Does the school want feedback on a particular topic or issue? The principal could post some information and questions on the blog and solicit community participation. This is similar to setting up a meeting with an advisory board or interested group of stakeholders, except that the potential reach is much greater because everyone in the school community can see and participate in the conversation, not just the few individuals who might attend a face-to-face meeting.

Reason 11: Advocacy

A blog also can be a good place to advocate for certain actions. For example, if state legislators were considering legislation that might negatively impact schools in some way, a principal could post a message encouraging stakeholders to become informed about the issue and let their local legislator know their opinion about the matter. Similarly, a blog can be a great place to foster community support for an upcoming levy or referendum. Regular progress updates can keep community members informed and help facilitate increased voter participation and support for the referendum.

Reason 12: Replacing the school Web site

Finally, some schools are utilizing blogs to replace key sections of their Web sites. Sometimes blogs replace the school's home page; other times they're a prominent link from the home page. Blogs would be a great tool for a FAQ page, for ongoing updates about athletic and other extracurricular programs, and for reviews of past events. Blogs also can be used to replace teachers' classroom newsletters to parents and for internal communications to staff.

That's it! Twelve reasons why an administrator's blog might be a good thing for a school organization.

Ⓒ Creative Commons attribution-share alike license, www.dangerouslyirrelevant.org.

So far, blogging is beginning to catch on as an administrative tool. Wikis are useful for creating documents collaboratively. Superintendents and district staff, for instance, can create policy documents collaboratively. Principals can post agendas for staff meetings and invite attendees to add to them in advance of the meeting as well as use the document for note-taking and end up with collaboratively written and edited minutes. Principals can ask teachers to collaborate on documents to send home to parents, including notices and newsletters.

One debate around leadership is how much administrators must use technology tools themselves. Because of new demands for accountability, most administrators are becoming facile with data management tools. The question is the extent to which they should use other applications. Scott McLeod provides his insight in the Web 2.0 Wisdom sidebar, Effective Technology Leadership.

Effective Technology Leadership

Scott McLeod

DO ADMINISTRATORS HAVE TO BE TECHNOLOGY-SAVVY to be effective technology leaders? Many folks would say yes, it is important for administrators to be able to model the use of technology if they expect teachers to integrate digital learning tools into their instruction. Otherwise it will be a situation of "Do as I say, not as I do," and some teachers will decline the invitation to use technology in their classrooms.

I am not sure I agree. Many principals and superintendents are not very fluent personally with digital technologies and yet are strong technology leaders. These folks might be able to send e-mail, surf the Web, use word processing and electronic slideshow software, and use a few administrative applications, but they are far from being the technology experts in their school or district.

Instead, what these effective technology leaders are able to do is facilitate a shared vision for technology in their school organization and mobilize staff and the local community into putting resources and effort into that vision. Although this may be harder when an administrator is not fluent with the underlying technology, it is not a big stretch, for example, to envision an administrator who knows very little about blogging and yet understands the potential power of a tool that facilitates better communication with parents and community members.

Administrators need better (and more) training in the area of technology. They need exposure to various digital tools so that they can understand the educational potential of those tools. They need help understanding what effective technology support looks like and how to find funding for appropriate staffing. They need to learn what constitutes effective technology usage in the classroom so that they can evaluate it and facilitate it schoolwide. And, of course, they need training in legal, ethical, and policy issues related to student and employee use of various digital tools.

The challenge for school leaders, then, is to surround themselves with, and listen to, technology users and visionaries. Schools have a moral obligation to prepare students for their technology-infused, globally interconnected futures. Administrators cannot simply avoid leading in the area of technology because it is an area in which they are not comfortable. We need to give principals and superintendents the knowledge and skills to be effective technology leaders despite their personal lack of digital fluency.

Scott McLeod is director of the UCEA Center for the Advanced Study of Technology Leadership in Education (CASTLE) at the University of Minnesota.

supporting new tools

As with any new tool, there's a cycle of use that begins with administrative support. If a school or district administrator is committed to implementing new technologies, the staff will get the message. Leadership starts at the top, even if the support comes without a leader actually using many of the tools him- or herself. One popular application is a course or content management system. Many districts are adopting commercial applications such as Blackboard, but there are open-source programs too. Districts, especially those without an installed base in a commercial product, are beginning to use software such as Moodle instead. Because it is open-source software, it is free; any school or district can download and customize it to address its needs.

Teachers use course management systems to manage their classes, assignments, activities, quizzes and tests, resources, student work, and other items in an online environment that's easy to access 24/7. They can create lessons, post tests, enter grades, and more, and their students can log on and do assignments anytime, anywhere.

Even districts that are not using open-source operating systems are using Moodle because it runs on most operating systems including Windows and Mac OS X without needing modification. It can be used with almost any database.

Miguel Guhlin and Greg Rodriguez (2006) in San Antonio are pleased with the results. They say:

> Imagine a content management system that enables district level staff…to share documents securely through passwored levels of access, as well as update them without knowing how to create Web pages. Imagine online help desks, frequently asked question (FAQ) repositories, and more—all management systems available to you and your district at no charge. (n.p.)

financial issues

We know that the costs of technology are far more than just the price of equipment and software. Upgrades, maintenance, and support play a large role as well. So in looking at free, Web-based tools, districts have to explore the real costs, those above and beyond the software itself, and weigh them against alternatives.

Even though there is federal, state, and other funding available for technology, especially E-Rate funds for a district's networking infrastructure, there is little support for ongoing costs. The Consortium for School Networking (CoSN) partnered with Gartner to create a tool for school districts to evaluate how well they are managing their technology infrastructure and the total cost of technology ownership (TCO). The tool measures direct and indirect costs of technology investments, such as hardware, software, direct labor costs for formal technology support, and the indirect costs for technology support. Information about the tool is available at www.classroomtco.org/gartner_intro.html.

In addition to these expenses, districts should weigh the costs of purchasing and renewing licenses to applications software such as Microsoft Windows as a platform and Microsoft Office as tools against the costs of using open-source solutions. While Linux as a platform and open-source applications are free to use, a district should look at the costs of retraining an established base of Microsoft users to use new products against the ongoing licensing and upgrade costs. In addition, districts have to consider the value of the software and the ongoing support that will be needed. Of course, if the tools that companies like Microsoft and Google provide free are robust enough, districts will benefit because educators do not commonly use advanced features.

To be sure, in order to use Web-based tools 24/7, students need Internet access. Districts must have the networking infrastructure and computer availability to take advantage of these tools. Most districts have used E-Rate funds to set up robust networks, and many districts have implemented or are considering one-to-one computing solutions. As they weigh the costs and benefits, the availability of free Web-based tools may play a role. CoSN has compiled a few case studies of districts implementing one-to-one (www.classroomtco.org/gartner_intro. html#case). In general, while they were not looking for cost savings specifically, "some financial benefits are being realized" (CoSN, 2006, p. 9).

Access 24/7 also involves the use of personal computers, best modeled in one-to-one programs. These have become popular because students can collaborate from home, and classroom use is more productive when students have their own laptops. The costs are prohibitive for some districts, however, because they require a wireless infrastructure, security, digital content, and useful applications as well as professional development and support for educators. All of which have costs.

One of CoSN's case studies focused on a small, rural Missouri school district with 450 students and 51 staff members with a total of 210 client computers. Districts this size face particular challenges when it comes to managing the costs of operating their computer networks primarily because they have limited resources. This district has three things in its favor: fast T1 communications through the Missouri Research and Education Network (MOREnet) for a nominal annual support fee, donated computers, and open-source applications such as Linux servers and Open Office. Not surprisingly, the total cost of ownership of their technology was low (CoSN, 2004).

Also, Indiana's Affordable Classroom Computer for Every Secondary Student (InACCESS) was launched in 2003 as an alternative way to put computers in the hands of every student. One effect of the new system has been cost savings. Previously, the state of Indiana was spending $100 per year per machine to license software from vendors such as Microsoft or Apple. Today, the school is paying no more than $10 per year. With 18,000 computers, this is a savings of more than $16,000 per year. And when amortized over 300,000 computers, this annual savings jumps to $27 million. The district is experiencing a similar savings with hardware, reducing total cost of ownership per machine from $1,000 to about $290 (Villano, 2006b).

Concerning a new project, Alex Inman, the technology director for the Whitfield School in St. Louis, Missouri, says (personal communication, 2006):

> Our goal was to design a new approach to laptop programs that provides the same benefits but lowers the initial and long-term costs. We implemented a program using Linux on laptops and accessed Windows programs as needed on a centralized Citrix network. We received effectively the same user satisfaction of other laptop programs in their first year and did it for about $185 less per client on an annual basis. We conservatively project that this model will extend to save the school $200,000 per year across 600 laptops.

Beyond determining the total cost of ownership, a new CoSN project explores the value of technology investments. The accompanying Web 2.0 Wisdom sidebar by Rich Kaestner, Measuring the Value of Investment, outlines this process.

web 2.0 wisdom

Measuring the Value of Investment

Rich Kaestner

OPEN-SOURCE SOFTWARE SOLUTIONS are frequently selected for reasons driven by budgets. Perhaps more important in looking at end-user applications is the value derived from product functionality and ease of use. These can be measured in terms of savings and user productivity, some of which relate to providing a better education.

Schools can do a better job of measuring the value of technology for proposed projects, which often compete for the same limited funds. Value has two major components: costs and benefits. Benefits for K–12 include qualitative benefits that are oriented to the district or school mission, goals, and mandates. A five-step process for determining the value of investment (VOI) for K–12 institutions follows:

1. Estimate costs

To implement and support technology properly, include all initial and ongoing direct costs in the budget. However, costs need to be annualized and indirect costs (e.g., user overhead time) should be considered.

2. Assess risk

Risk, for the purposes of VOI calculations, is the probability of success for the proposed project. Probability of success is generally applied to the valuation of the expected benefits of the project. (Note that probability of success could instead be applied against cost to create a risk-weighted cost.)

3. Calculate anticipated savings and revenues

Most projects, even those focused on qualitative benefits such as student achievement, have some cost savings such as lower out-of-pocket costs, better efficiencies, user productivity, or future cost avoidance. There may also be some anticipated increase of revenues based on higher attendance, grants, or state or federal aid.

4. Measure qualitative benefits

Since the business of schools is education and schools operate for the public good, many or most of the benefits of implementing technology cannot be measured in terms of dollars; we call these qualitative benefits. For these to be considered benefits they must directly or indirectly affect the school or district mission, goals, mandates, or other objectives. A suggested approach to calculating these anticipated benefits is:

- ▶ Determine the school or district mission, goals, and mandates, and assign a relative importance to each.

- ▶ Align anticipated project benefits with the appropriate school mission, goals, and mandates.

- ▶ State the anticipated project benefits in measurable terms.

▶▶

- ▶ Agree on the effect of the proposed project on the applicable mission, goals, and mandates. (On a weighting of −10 to +10, how much will the project affect each mission, goal, and mandate? Note the possibility of a negative effect.)

- ▶ Come up with a total qualitative benefits score.

- ▶ Multiply the total qualitative score by the probability of success for a risk-weighted benefits score.

5. Evaluate results

Once you have implemented your wildly successful project, you have an opportunity to review actual costs and benefits versus the projected costs and benefits. This will allow you to respond to the project skeptics. As the anticipated costs and benefits were stated in measurable terms, the actual results can be measured:

- ▶ Actual costs versus anticipated costs

- ▶ Actual savings or revenues versus anticipated savings or revenues

- ▶ Actual benefits versus anticipated benefits

For more information on TCO and VOI, including tools to help with this process, check out CoSN's TCO Web site at www.classroomtco.org and CoSN's VOI Web site at www.EdTechVOI.org.

Rich Kaestner is Total Cost of Ownership project director for the Consortium for School Networking.

infrastructure: running on open source

Setting up the infrastructure for school or district computing is a complicated and expensive effort, which requires planning for the future and selecting products that will grow as needs change. Costs are always an issue, even more so as budgets are reduced. Products must provide a good return on investment and districts now monitor the total cost of ownership of technology. One place where leaders sometimes economize is on software, and some districts are starting to rely on open-source solutions, programs for which there are no purchasing or licensing fees. While they are technically free, the overall costs of implementing and supporting open-source programs are not always less than with other choices. The San Antonio School District staff finds open-source solutions effective and cost effective. However, Miguel Guhlin cautions, "You will need to invest time" (personal communication, 2006).

Open Source

Open source is programming code that is freely available to use and to modify, upgrade, and customize. The philosophy behind it is that source code must be available to everyone to use and adapt and that any adaptations also have to be available to use and adapt. Many people contribute to open-source programming and share the programs they create.

Linux is a free UNIX-type operating system originally created by Linus Torvalds with the help of developers around the world. It is open-source software, so the source code is available to everyone. A growing number of school districts are using the Linux operating system, Apache server, and Firefox Web browser instead of commercial solutions.

There are open-source solutions for almost any task that network administrators may need, from monitoring the network and maintaining network security to fighting spam and encrypting data. These solutions run on top of any operating system, from Windows to Linux. Two Web sites for finding these programs are the OpenCD site for Windows (http://theopencd.org) and Open Source Mac for Mac OS X (www.opensourcemac.org).

According to Miguel Guhlin and Greg Rodriguez (2006), who have implemented Linux and other open-source software in the San Antonio, Texas, Independent School District, the motivation in seeking out open-source solutions is finding powerful solutions that can be readily implemented without expensive licensing and the value of using free, easily adaptable solutions on a district-wide scale.

Applications run on the servers but student and staff computers can be dumb terminals or thin clients, which mean that they have no hard drives or software. They are easy to install, reliable, require little maintenance, and are immune to viruses and other vandalism. Changes happen centrally, which saves travel time for updates and upgrades.

Information on how to set up Linux software is available on K–12 Linux Project (http://k12ltsp.org). The Web site offers downloads of software for transforming older computers into diskless clients, technical guides and tutorials for getting started with open source, and discussion forums. Because Linux is community-based, help and answers to questions are easy to find.

From the perspective of teachers and other administrators, these are useful tools. If administrators are supportive and technical staff invests the time to train and help teachers, the effect can be welcome to a district that is strapped for cash but wants to use innovative technologies. (See appendix B for an expanded list of open-source Web tools.)

If you're considering implementing Linux and open-source tools, there

> ### Full Circle?
>
> IT MAY SEEM AS THOUGH we have come full circle with computer-based learning. In the early days, students received programmed instruction through dumb terminals that were hooked up to mainframes. Companies such as PLATO created managed instruction that districts bought into to improve student scores. From the perspective of control, at least in terms of mainframe software, students had none. (The programs were often considered "drill and kill.") On today's dumb terminals, students and staff have access to Web-based applications and information, and users can control almost everything—the content they read, the ideas they espouse, and the presentations they create. Today's users control the tools of production and can reach the world with their ideas.

are support groups for education. They include The SchoolTool Project (www.schooltool.org), Schoolforge (www.schoolforge.net), K12OS (http://k12os.org), and K12 Linux Project (www.k12linux.org). Information about each of them is available in appendix B.

Miguel Guhlin (2006f) ends our chapter with a few closing thoughts on one open-source solution.

The Final Word

AFTER SEVEN MONTHS OF TRYING NEW THINGS at all hours of the night, I've learned a few things about Linux's usability. While I do not advocate a 100% switch to the Linux Operating System in all situations, I can definitely see its use in many classrooms and computer labs. Most certainly, Linux has a place in the homes of our students and teachers as an alternative to proprietary software and products. That is, instead of buying software to put on your computer, you can get Linux and use the software that comes for free on it.

A big surprise for me about Linux is that there is so much software available for download and installation. If you want a program in Windows, you buy it or you can go seek it out on the Web. While you can do the same thing in Linux, you can also run a program on your computer and do a search against the extensive software library available.

The strangest thing is that I have gone through withdrawal from Windows. I was always looking for free stuff to run on Windows … in Linux, all the free software is already there in multiple varieties. It's an amazing feeling I can't explain.

While I have left out volumes of information on using Linux, you now have more information than I did when I started down the Linux path. Has the journey been worth it? Definitely. I enjoy a freedom from proprietary software and feel part of a greater community of users.

More importantly, Linux software provides a whole new world of tools I can use to enhance my computing experience. To obtain similar tools on the Windows side would certainly have forced me to make a sizeable investment. With Linux, I can lessen my own total cost of ownership.

7

online safety and security

No conversation about students and Web-based activities would be complete without remarking on the threats that lurk online. Keeping students and data safe and secure are important—ethically and legally. School districts have to do everything in their power to prevent problems before they start.

▶ ▶ ▶ ▶ ▶

Today's new Web publishing tools such as blogs and wikis make it easy to get a message out where others can find it. However, information that's out there can be biased, inappropriate, or untruthful. And social-networking sites such as MySpace and Facebook allow youngsters to post private information, which leaves them vulnerable to harassment and other dangers. Cyberbullying may be the online equivalent of bad schoolyard behavior, but it is no less hurtful or dangerous.

College educator and lawyer Scott McLeod (2006c) says:

> Many enterprising teachers are using (or would like to use) tools provided by entities outside the school organization to enhance the classroom experience. These tools typically are not hosted by the school system, however, and there is no ability for administrators to exercise oversight effectively over teachers' and students' appropriate use of these tools. In many instances, school leaders may not even know such tools are being used. (n.p.)

Schools have to be more vigilant than ever. They want to provide access to the vast amounts of reliable, accurate information online, but they must worry about students finding incorrect data, pornography, and predators along the way. Protecting children and personal data online is a legal responsibility.

legal requirements

School districts that receive E-Rate funds are subject to the requirements put forth in the Children's Internet Protection Act (CIPA); so are districts that accept funds for Title II, Part D, the Enhancing Education through Technology (EETT) program under the No Child Left Behind Act (NCLB), or Title III monies, when used to make certain purchases related to Internet connectivity.

CIPA compliance means that districts must install filtering or blocking technology on every Internet-connected computer, whether used by students or adults. Districts also have to implement a comprehensive Internet safety policy. In addition, districts have to conduct a public meeting to discuss their Internet safety policies and the measures for protection that they have in place.

The Children's Online Privacy Protection Act (COPPA) limits the ability of Web sites to offer services to children ages 12 and younger without explicit parental consent. Its goal is to protect children's privacy and safety online.

A new law under consideration in Congress as of this writing, the Deleting Online Predators Act (DOPA), would require public schools and libraries to block student access to chat and social-networking sites. Its purpose is to thwart sexual predators.

copyright and intellectual property

Copyright law is confusing. In addition to the issues of music and video downloading, there's an even more complex area, especially for schools—students use of someone else's intellectual property to illustrate points within their own work. The fact that schools have rights for educational purposes under the Fair Use doctrine does not mean that students have the right to use someone else's work without attribution. They need guidance to understand this.

Hall Davidson outlined key facts that administrators, educators, and students should know about intellectual property. This material and related articles, charts, and information are posted at www.techlearning.com/hot_topics/copyright.jhtml. The following steps for avoiding copyright problems are from Davidson's (2005) *Copyright Primer for Administrators.*

> **Five Steps to Avoiding Copyright Problems**
>
> ❶ Create and implement a technology policy that includes a code of ethics and set of procedures.
>
> ❷ Review the entire policy with your educational community: students, teachers, and parents.
>
> ❸ Appoint a technology manager to conduct audits and maintain a log of licenses and registration materials.
>
> ❹ Teach ethical and legal behavior for technology use.
>
> ❺ Thank employees and students for supporting these steps. (n.p.)

There is a new system that can make things easier—one that enables students to use content they want and helps them to understand the conditions around that use. Creative Commons (www.creativecommons.org) is a system built within current copyright law that allows people to mark their creations with a Creative Commons license. The license allows others to use their music, movies, images, and text online for specific purposes, such as classroom use. The licenses fall between full copyright (reserving all rights, which is what traditional publishers do) and being in the public domain (where works retain no rights).

Creative Commons helps people publish work online while letting others know exactly what they can and can't do with the work. For example, you can share educational materials with students while protecting these materials from other uses. With an attribution license, people can copy, distribute, display, and perform someone else's copyrighted work—and derivative works based upon it—only if they give credit the way the holder requests. In 2005, a court in the Netherlands heard a case that involved a Creative Commons license and ruled that it is binding.

The Creative Commons Web site carries the slogan "Share, reuse, and remix—legally." The organization suggests that people include a Creative Commons "Some Rights Reserved" button on their Web sites near their work. The licenses are outlined at http://creativecommons.org/about/licenses/.

security solutions

Awareness education programs, acceptable use policies, student ethical conduct reviews, administrative restrictions, and parental involvement help, but sometimes policies that include a stronger approach such as blocking with or without alternatives are necessary—for practical and legal reasons and for peace of mind. As former principal Susan Brooks-Young (2006) says, "We can't anticipate every possible issue, but we can position ourselves so that we're being proactive rather than reactive" (n.p.).

In a survey commissioned by Thinkronize in fall 2006, four out of five school principals and administrators who were surveyed thought that danger for students on the Internet is increasing and commercial and pay sites are their greatest concern. When asked to rate the specific types of dangers facing students online, 61% said pornography and 58% said adult predators were a great or significant danger. Concern over getting useless or irrelevant results when using search engines was also high at 59%. Seventy-six percent of respondents said they were concerned about students' unauthorized redirection to commercial or pay sites when conducting online research.

Educators are seeking ways to solve these problems. According to the report, the actions they have taken to protect students include:

- Installing filters—100%
- Giving faculty instructions on safety—90%
- Giving students instructions on safety—90%
- Providing parents with tips and information—66%
- Purchased special search engines—35% (Thinkronize, 2006, n.p.)

Awareness Programs

Students do not always realize the dangers that are lurking online and having frank discussions is effective in preventing problems for students at school and at home. Deer Park Elementary School in Fairfax, Virginia, developed the Cyber Awareness Survey to initiate the conversation with students (Painter, 2004, n.p.).

Cyber Awareness Survey

Question 1. If you are using your computer and someone you don't know asks for your real name and address, what should you do?

    a. Give it to them. They probably just want to hang out.

    b. Don't give it to them. You never know who they really are.

    c. Ask them who they are first and then give it to them.

Question 2. If someone you don't know asks for your real name and address, whom should you tell?

    a. Your best friend

    b. Your parents

    c. Nobody

Question 3. With whom should you share your password?

    a. Your best friend

    b. Anybody who asks for it

    c. Nobody except your parents

▶ ▶ ▶

Question 4. If someone you meet online suggests that you should meet them in person, what should you do?

    a. Don't tell anyone, but make sure you meet in a public place for safety.

    b. Tell your best friend you are planning to meet this person in case something happens.

    c. Be sure to tell your parents if a stranger asks to meet you.

Question 5. To whom can you send an online photo of yourself?

    a. Friends and family members

    b. New people you might meet online

    c. Anyone who asks for it

Question 6. If a person is using bad language or telling people hateful things in a chat room, what should you do?

    a. Ignore them and keep chatting.

    b. Tell them to stop using such bad language.

    c. Leave the chat room and tell a parent or another adult.

Question 7. If a person sends you an e-mail or instant message with really bad language, what should you do?

    a. Reply and tell them to stop using that language.

    b. Ignore them and hope they leave you alone.

    c. Save the e-mail or instant message and give it to your parents.

Question 8. If someone you don't know e-mails you a really cool game to download, what should you do?

    a. Download and start the game. It might be really cool!

    b. Send an e-mail back and ask them who they are and why they are sending it to you.

    c. Don't download the game. It might be dangerous.

▶▶

Question 9. If somebody you don't know sends you an e-mail, should you open it?

    a. Sure. What can it hurt to open an e-mail?

    b. No, don't open it. You don't know that person.

Question 10. If a person says things online that make you feel uncomfortable, what should you do?

    a. Reply and tell them to stop using that language.

    b. Ignore them and hope they go away.

    c. Don't talk with that person and tell your parents.

Overall, these students responded correctly for most questions, with scores at least in the mid 80% range for third graders and mid 90% for fourth graders. Only question 7 had low correct responses in both grade levels. Only 68% of the third-grade students and 83% of the fourth-grade students responded correctly, which is that they would save the message and tell their parents. Most said they would reply and tell the person to stop using such bad language.

Programs that instruct students on the issues make the difference. Another successful awareness program involves students researching and creating an online safety guide. Vicki Davis, a high-school teacher at Westwood High in Camilla, Georgia, had her 10th-grade computer science class create *Online Safety and Privacy Skills* (http://westwood.wikispaces.com/Chapter+1+-+Security+and+Privacy). This guidebook was written collaboratively in a wiki. Each team selected a topic, researched the issue, and developed a team wiki. The chapters include information about viruses, intrusions, spyware, pop-up ads, e-commerce, protection, e-mail scams, and privacy. Her students learned about the issues and how to collaborate, and they created a real document that other students, parents, and educators use. Davis (personal communication, September 2006) explains:

> The method that I use to teach online safety and privacy has evolved during the last four years although the issues have always been a part of our computer science curriculum. Beginning in November 2005, my class truly became a wiki-centric classroom and this class

decided to write a "wiki book." By creating a wiki with required external sources of information, students learn to take information from their textbook and the Web and create a usable summary.

The class felt strongly that they wanted to share what they learned because they feel that there is a widespread lack of education on safety and privacy. Too many Web sites are "geek speak" and do not answer security questions in everyday language.

We will do this project again next year, and the content will focus on being current and updated and filling in the areas that need more explanation. This multi-year project will also demonstrate how things such as Wikipedia work.

Acceptable Use Policies

Most districts have acceptable use policies in place and have for years—ever since they gave students access to technology in general and to the Internet in particular. These policies outline the guidelines, procedures, and responsibilities for using school technology. They may have to be adapted or rewritten entirely to cover new online tools. It has to be clear where students may go online and what they may do when they're there.

In addition, because students are now contributors as well as consumers of information online, schools have to define their manner of participation and their rights and responsibilities concerning new technologies, the blogs, podcasts, RSS subscriptions, social networks, and more that they will encounter.

David Warlick (2006b) offers the following advice:

It's time to take those AUPs off the shelf, unfold them, and add a whole new layer—Web publishing policies. It is essential that your new technology use policy is designed not merely as a preventative tool, but as an enabling document that promotes effective uses that solve problems and accomplish goals. (n.p.)

Warlick (2006b) suggests four steps for reworking acceptable use policies:

❶ Establish goals for the use of read/write Web tools. These goals should range through administrative functions, classroom management, and instructional objectives.

❷ Itemize and describe specific uses of read/write Web applications that you will promote and support, tied to the goals established in the first section.

❸ Briefly but clearly identify those activities that will not be allowed. These might include conducting business, advertising commercial products or services, defaming the character of others, and jeopardizing in any way the safety of students.

❹ Plan your document or ancillary materials to serve as instructional resources that might be used in the classroom. Provide teachers with guidelines and procedures that not only govern student use of technology, but also help them to understand and put into practice basic foundations of information ethics. (n.p.)

Ethical Behavior

While people usually think they know what ethical behavior is, there is often a fine line between ethical and unethical actions. Nowhere is this more evident than online, where many people seem to believe that because they are physically able to copy or download files, it is OK to go ahead and do it. Teenagers too might come to the conclusion that availability equals permission. They need to learn that just because they can do something doesn't mean they should.

Suddenly, it seems that the barriers are gone and the possibilities are endless. The best example is in music downloading, where file sharing has been ubiquitous. Yet Stephen Downes (2006) and others believe that "File sharing evolves not of a sudden criminality among today's youth but rather in their pervasive belief that information is something meant to be shared" (n.p.).

Perhaps, but students can learn the finer points of ethics. The ethos of the free and open-source software movement and Creative Commons licenses for content teach a different lesson about sharing, contributing, and the value of community.

It's no wonder that teenagers are confused about copyright. Many of the adults who guide them are equally as confused. A Los Angeles Times/Bloomberg poll conducted in spring 2006 indicates that although many teens acknowledge that downloading music or DVDs for free is illegal, they feel that making a copy of music or movies they own to share with friends is OK (Duhigg, 2006). Table 7.1 shows the results of the poll, which asked teens and young adults about the perceived illegality of various activities.

Table 7.1	IS IT STEALING?				
Proportion of young people who thought the following would be committing a crime	Ages 12–14	Ages 15–17	Ages 18–20	Ages 21–24
Copying a CD from a friend who paid for it	27%	35%	33%	38%
Copying a DVD/videotape from a friend who paid for it	39%	44%	40%	41%
Downloading free music from an unauthorized file-sharing server	79%	81%	70%	79%
Downloading free movies from an unauthorized file-sharing server	83%	83%	74%	79%
Buying a bootlegged CD	84%	84%	76%	76%
Buying a bootlegged DVD/videotape	84%	84%	80%	77%
Shoplifting an item worth less than $20	97%	97%	98%	96%
Shoplifting an item worth more than $20	99%	99%	99%	97%

▶ © Los Angeles Times. Reprinted with permission.

Because there are so many new issues that confront students on the Web and new concerns for educators, adopting a code of ethics to supplement acceptable use policies may make sense. The Student and Teacher Information Code of Ethics sidebar by David Warlick (2006d) offers suggestions on creating such a document.

A Student and Teacher Information Code of Ethics

Seek Truth and Express It

Teachers and students should be honest, fair, and courageous in gathering, interpreting, and expressing information for the benefit of others. They should:

► Test the accuracy of information from all sources and exercise care to avoid inadvertent error.

► Always identify sources. The consumers of your information product must be able to make their own judgment of its value.

► Always question the sources' motives.

► Never distort or misrepresent the content of photos, videos, or other media without explanation of intent and permission from the information's owner. Image enhancement for technical clarity is permissible.

► Tell the story of the human experience boldly, even when it is unpopular to do so.

► Examine your own cultural values and avoid imposing those values on others.

► Avoid stereotyping by race, gender, age, religion, ethnicity, geography, sexual orientation, disability, physical appearance, or social status.

► Give voice to the voiceless; official and unofficial sources of information can be equally valid.

► Distinguish between opinion and fact when expressing ideas. Analysis and commentary should be labeled and not misrepresent fact or context.

Minimize Harm

Ethical teachers and students treat information sources, subjects, colleagues, and information consumers as human beings deserving of respect.

► Gathering and expressing information should never cause harm or threaten to be harmful to any one person or group of people.

► Recognize that private people in their private pursuits have a greater right to control information about themselves than do others.

▶ Consider all possible outcomes to the information you express, guarding against potential harm to others.

▶ Never use information from another person without proper citation and permission.

Be Accountable

Teachers and students are accountable to their readers, listeners, and viewers, and to each other.

▶ Clarify and explain information and invite dialogue about your conduct as a communicator.

▶ Encourage the information consumer to voice grievances about your information products.

▶ Admit mistakes and correct them promptly.

▶ Expose the unethical information practices of others.

Respect Information and Its Infrastructure

Information, in the Information Age, is property. Information is the fabric that defines much of what we do from day to day, and this rich and potent fabric is fragile.

▶ Never undertake any action that has the potential to damage any part of this information infrastructure. These actions include, but are not limited to, illegally hacking into a computer system, launching or distributing viruses or other damaging software, physically damaging or altering hardware or software, or publishing information that you know is untrue and potentially harmful.

▶ Report to proper authorities any activities that could potentially result in harm to the information infrastructure.

Posted by David Warlick in the techLEARNING blog on August 21, 2006.

Administrative Restrictions

Blogs, wikis, and other content-sharing sites can be powerful learning tools, yet many administrators have reservations about their use. In an attempt to prove a point, Miguel Guhlin (2006c) posted the following list of possible administrator concerns in the form of questions a principal might ask of a teacher who wants to use blogs with students.

1. What release form will you use for publishing student work online?

2. Has this form been approved by the District Administrative Procedures committee?

3. Are you using a District-supported Web site for hosting student and teacher content, or is a commercial site being used for this purpose? Please note that with the importance of protecting students from unauthorized access by online predators, it is important that the venues which students frequent be kept within District control.

4. Has the campus administrator approved teachers participating in potentially putting students at risk?

5. What steps have been taken to ensure all stakeholders are aware of what is going on?

6. Have parents been notified so that they understand this is an instructional activity and what the duration of such types of activities might be?

7. How does use of blogs, image galleries with RSS feeds, and other such Web sites prepare students to achieve at an "exemplary" level on our state-mandated tests?

8. Will there be sufficient access for students, or will instructional time be used for these activities? If after-hours, how will this impact existing instructional programs like Terrific Tutoring that help students achieve state mandated instructional objectives? (n.p.)

Parental Involvement

Working with parents so that they understand the issues and the policies is important. They also may need someplace to turn when the same issues confront them at home. While schools have tools to influence students' behavior, parents are often unaware of the problems and have few strategies to resolve them.

How should schools reach out to parents? Providing guides such as the ones published by MySpace, or directing them to resources such as GetNetWise (see below), help parents to cope and school personnel to work with them.

Cable in the Classroom commissioned a survey of parents in July 2006 about online safety. According to Douglas Levin, senior director of education policy for Cable in the Classroom:

> Parents want to take primary responsibility for guiding their kids' use of the Internet. Yet, as the Internet continues to change and evolve, most parents don't feel very knowledgeable about how to ensure children's Internet safety and are looking for schools to help. (n.p.)

The findings showed that 71% of parents believe that a major portion of the responsibility for ensuring children's safety on the Internet falls to schools. In addition, 49% of parents think that the government and law enforcement agencies should have a lot of responsibility in the arena of children's online safety. Of the parents surveyed, 54% reported seeking advice from other parents and from their child's school. Finally, 94% had taken steps to try to ensure their children's online safety. These steps included:

- ▶ Talking to them about how to use the Internet (88%)

- ▶ Monitoring online activities (82%)

- ▶ Confining home Internet use to the living room or other open spaces (75%)

- ▶ Setting time limits on their Internet use (74%)

- ▶ Installing software to limit or block their child's online activities (55%) (n.p.)

When parents ask for advice or help, what information should a school or district provide? *The Online Safety Guide* from GetNetWise (2003; http://kids.getnetwise. org/safetyguide/) states, "Keeping children safe on the Internet is everyone's job" (n.p.). The GetNetWise (2003) organization recommends that:

- ► Parents need to stay in close touch with their kids as they explore the Internet.

- ► Teachers need to help students use the Internet appropriately and safely.

- ► Community groups, including libraries, after-school programs, and others should help educate the public about safe surfing.

- ► Kids and teens need to learn to take responsibility for their own behavior—with guidance from their families and communities. (n.p.)

Schools often suggest that parents visit the extensive library of materials on GetNetWise (www.getnetwise.org) to help them understand the issues and protect their children. It offers many resources in one place as well as links to others.

MySpace has also published parent's and school administrator's guides to Internet safety. The parent's guide helps parents understand MySpace and answers questions about social networks and the Internet in general. The school administrator's guide, which the National School Board Association (NSBA) distributed to 55,000 public school administrators in October 2006, addresses the various challenges that students and educators face. Check out www.myspace.com/safetytips/ for more information.

Blocking

Adults and teens view the Internet very differently. For the former, the Web is a tool, a place to check e-mail, get information, and shop. For teens, it's a place to hang out with friends, especially for real-time communication, which to them is essential. But they sometimes run into problems online.

In spite of preventive measures, schools sometimes have a problem with Internet searching. The issue is primarily with the way Google and Yahoo label graphics that prevents filters from identifying cyberporn. Both search engines have internal features that block pornographic images; yet students sometimes disable them. Combinations of hardware and software filtering solutions are emerging to combat the problem. Some districts avoid the issue by licensing search engines specifically for education such as netTrekker d.i., which provides access to more than 180,000 educator-selected, standards-based online resources including an image database for safe, pornography-free images.

Almost all districts today set up firewalls or barriers to protect the network from potential hackers and inappropriate Web sites. A firewall is software or hardware or both that filters the information coming through the Internet connection into your network and blocks incoming packets of information that the filter flags. Content filtering prevents students from viewing inappropriate materials, though for filters to work properly, they depend on having all participants agree to be filtered all the time. Blocking enforces the use of the filtering server, thus preventing end users from bypassing filtering. It prevents viruses, spam, and other dangers from reaching network computers.

For technology planning teams, the challenges are urgent. In addition to keeping students from accessing inappropriate Web destinations from school and being targets of spam, viruses, and other destructive elements, some districts with one-to-one programs have to install endpoint Internet filtering systems for off-site laptops connected to their networks. Effective filtering stops spyware, malware, and other security threats as well as inappropriate content.

knotty problems

Of course, administrators worry about students circumventing even the best strategies and spending time inappropriately. Some special problems arise from instant messaging, which is possible not only from computers but also from cell phones; social networking, which is the networking activity of choice for today's Internet generation; and image sharing, whether students post digital photos on Flickr or videoclips on YouTube.

Administrators also have to determine how to handle posting photos of students online. According to Scott McLeod (2006b), an educator and lawyer:

> Schools take pictures of students all the time—for yearbooks, at athletic events, in class, at artistic performances, etc. Often they want to post those pictures to the Internet, thus making those photos potentially available to a global audience. Every school district should have a policy for dealing with student photos. That policy should comply with the federal Family Educational Rights and Privacy Act (FERPA) (www.ed.gov/policy/gen/guid/fpco/ferpa/) as well as any relevant state statutes. (n.p.)

Instant Messaging

Initially designed for conducting one-on-one personal chats, instant messaging (also referred to as IM) has made its way into schools and offices. Many people use text-based IM over phone calls and e-mail—preferring its immediacy and efficiency in getting real-time information from others. Young people in particular have adopted this technology as their own.

IM is different from other types of Internet applications in that it involves direct connections between computers—either within a school or across the Internet. While it is a popular way to send text messages, files, audio, and video for collaborative work, IM's lack of basic security features opens the door to hackers and viruses and perhaps to data capture.

IM is one of the most difficult applications to control because it attempts to hide within other network services, borrowing assigned TCP port numbers for its own communication. This stealthy approach makes traditional firewalls ineffective. Regaining control and security over this type of service is a challenge to district IT departments. Their solution is often to block access.

New Hampshire's Monadnock Community High School, for example, allows students, teachers, and parents to communicate using an internal IM. Most of the conversation revolves around students collaborating on projects, but parents can contact teachers about their students' work, and students can ask questions of their teachers with instant messages. By allowing IM in schools, implementations such as this take advantage of the benefits. Keeping it behind a firewall avoids harmful interactions, though IM use still requires careful management.

Social Networking

It is easy to understand why social-networking sites have become so compelling. Just how compelling can be seen in MySpace's astonishing growth: Estimates indicate that 5 million new members join each month. They can craft their personas and change them at will; they can be daring, popular, and attractive if they want. They can even claim accomplishments they may want to retract later.

While in real life, many teens would welcome anonymity, online they can assume an identity and be the sort of person they imagine would be fun. They can stand out and be recognized and have a shot at fame.

Social networking doesn't introduce new technologies and services. Rather, it aggregates existing standalone services in new ways, offering e-mail, instant messenging, and blogs, along with profiles and photo galleries—all from one interface. Making everything available from one screen is very conducive to building communities, but on the downside, social-networking sites make personal information public and readily available in one virtual location.

And that's only part of the problem. Despite regulations that restrict MySpace membership to users 14 and older, there's no way to prevent a 13-year-old girl from creating a profile that indicates she's 19. Similarly, there's nothing to stop a 40-year-old sexual predator from pretending to be a sympathetic 21-year-old. And making contact is merely a matter of clicking an IM or sending an e-mail.

While MySpace offers filtering tools and protection, and parents have to decide what to do about access, school districts and libraries that receive federal funds must comply with CIPA. One of the regulation's requirements states that images "harmful to minors" (children 17 or under) must be blocked. This may not be a simple process because bogus URLs evade the filters. Some filters contain a wildcard to identify all variants of a URL, no matter how it's disguised.

That's not to say that anyone objects to the use of social networking as a tool if it can be accomplished within a safe environment. One online educational community, Whyville (www.whyville.net), a blend of social networking and animated simulation, attracts almost 2 million children ages 8–15, who chat and share information. While it is not a Web 2.0 site, it is free. Students use avatars rather than personal images; they have to pass a "chat license" test, and violations of their laws are picked up in "911 reports" to adults who monitor behavior.

Occasionally we see positive change; one example is in MySpace's statistics. We don't know why—whether blocking or good sense prevailed, or there was a naturally occurring increase in interest by a different demographic group—but from August 2005 to August 2006 the percentage of visitors ages 12–17 declined by nearly half at a time when the site's traffic doubled, going from 21.8 to 55.8 million unique visitors. People ages 12–17 now represent only 11.9% of the visitors, while people ages 25–34 make up 16.7% of the visitors (Mindlin, 2006).

Image Sharing

Image-sharing sites such as Flickr that offer users the ability to upload their own photos as well as download the work of others have become controversial. Because photos at Flickr have Creative Commons copyright licenses, it's clear what uses are allowed for each picture. In addition to being a popular Web site for people to share personal photographs, Flickr also allows photos to be tagged, which makes it a good repository for bloggers' photos.

Because so many of the photos at Flickr allow use for educational purposes, they are valuable for educators in teaching digital storytelling. Because anyone can post images, students might find some that are inappropriate. For this reason, many districts block access to Flickr.

In a recent controversy over Flickr's use in K–12, techLEARNING bloggers Miguel Guhlin and David Jakes parried arguments to one another and to the community of readers.

Miguel Guhlin (2006c) states that blocking sites with inappropriate content is the responsible choice and suggests Web Gallery software such as the open-source Gallery 2 (http://gallery.menalto.com), so that "students will not be exposed to the inappropriate images found on commercial, adult sites that have been appropriated for student use" (n.p.).

David Jakes (2006a) thinks that school boards should set policy and if it's a community decision to block access to Flickr, that's the right decision for them. However, those students will miss a lot, not only because of the beautiful photography they won't see or think about but also because "there are missed opportunities to prepare students for the real world and take advantage of a teachable moment that can have lasting benefit" (n.p.).

The techLEARNING readers were asked to weigh in with their opinions in response to these two opposing viewpoints. The site stated, "School districts around the country have set district policy to block access to what some consider inappropriate social-networking sites, including sites like Flickr and YouTube. Others argue that these sites can be used to enhance teaching and learning." (Sullivan, 2006, n.p.)

Readers were asked what their districts do and how they viewed the policy. Most of them (43%) said that their districts block social-networking sites and they believe it should stay that way. Others (29%) would like to see their districts' blocking policies change. Another 24% said that they block but have alternatives in place. Only 3% said that their districts don't block.

Parents and educators are concerned about students posting private, provocative, and even untrue information on MySpace.com, and about their vulnerability there.

Schools are reaching out to parents to help them understand the issues involved with using the site. The site's owner, News Corp., is addressing security issues but many schools simply do not allow access.

other alternatives

What happens when great tools are blocked? How can students have access to them for learning? One solution is to have sites that are dedicated to education. As on Wikipedia, moderators could patrol and edit or remove inappropriate content.

One example is David Warlick's Class Blogmeister (http://classblogmeister.com), which was designed specifically for the classroom so that teachers could be the arbiter of appropriate content. The system is in a controlled environment in that teachers set up a class blog and add the names of students who should have access. Students write and do peer editing, but their teacher makes the decisions and evaluates, comments on, and eventually posts students' blogs.

Elgg (www.elgg.org), a hybrid of blogging, e-portfolios, and social networking, provides an environment for students to create their own learning space and connect to others, forming online learning communities. Students can create a profile that lists their likes and dislikes, upload their favorite files, create blogs, post podcasts, add RSS feeds, and use keywords to connect others who have the same interests. The key factor is that activities focus on learning rather than on hanging out. Access controls make it possible to keep their profiles private, available to selected users, or public. Districts can decide to allow students access or host the system on their own servers. Both are free.

Another solution is to place Web 2.0 tools on intranets so they are behind district firewalls. This limits students to collaborating only with youngsters who are already in close proximity, but it provides access to new tools and security. Miguel Guhlin (2006b) recommends a "walled garden" of safe Web 2.0 tools that can be used within a school's intranet with the ability to control or "lock" things down and eliminate social networking outside of the school environment. For example, there are wiki applications that districts can install and run from their own servers such as Socialtext (www.socialtext.com) and TWiki (www.twiki.org). Users can set up accounts, then write and revise their collaborative work.

David Jakes (2006d) provides a related example:

> We use Blackboard ... for our blogs, wikis, and discussion boards. Some might criticize that for a less-than-authentic experience, but ... it's safe and it's what our community wants. Every student post, contribution, etc. is stamped with the login information, which provides a healthy deterrent to those interested in less than appropriate contribution. So far, absolutely no issues ... no inappropriate comments, no pornographic spam, etc. Just a safe environment for learning the tools. (n.p.)

There are also free, although not open source, solutions such as Think.com, Oracle Education Foundation's philanthropic initiative, which provides online tools for education that are hosted remotely but that provide access only to teacher-designated users. Think.com allows teachers to design and coach projects for their students to work on collaboratively. Teachers can communicate with other educators around the world to share ideas and projects. Student teams create Web pages, exchange ideas, and share information on a specific topic. Projects can be self-contained within a class or school, or students can join a project from another school or open up their project for students in other schools to join. As long as schools are members, students can work together across schools, districts, and even countries. The key is that membership is limited to educators and their students.

For districts that want or need help with Web 2.0 services, there are consultants, such as Clarity Innovations (www.clarity-innovations.com) in Portland, Oregon, who can set it up (see sidebar: Implementing Web 2.0 Technologies in Schools, by Steven Burt). Companies such as CrossTec (www.crossteccorp.com) will create a school or district communication system and maintain it on their servers for security.

web 2.0 wisdom

Implementing Web 2.0 Technologies in Schools

Steven Burt

IN 2001, WE BEGAN USING WEBLOGGING TOOLS as a sort of thin content management system (CMS) to allow teachers and in some cases students to publish content on the Web. For many of these tools (syndication, podcasting, CMS selection, etc.) the willingness to adopt them now exists but the know-how of these ever-evolving tools can be a bit daunting.

One very successful school district we've been working with is the Lincolnwood School District (www.sd74.org) in Chicago, Illinois. Working with the district Web team, we developed a strategic plan for including Web 2.0 tools and built a new infrastructure (based on open-source software) to enable them to glue together the small pieces of various tools, such as a true CMS, Flickr, Google Maps (and other Google tools), RSS, and custom syndication. Their site is now based on a Web 2.0 platform that enables the best of what they find out on the Web and want to try. The platform should be stable for community interaction and communication for many years to come.

Steven Burt is content and research manager for Clarity Innovations, Inc.

8

systemic issues

Schools face challenges that are unique to their district, city, and region and must address their local constituency's concerns all the time. In addition, there are some universal or systemic issues that all schools must consider and respond to through their programs, activities, and professional development. These issues may come sharply into focus when considering technology, and in particular, the use of Web 2.0 tools. This chapter examines the implementation and possibilities for not only using these tools in the curriculum, but also using the tools in ways to create opportunities for all learners in a community.

▶ ▶ ▶ ▶ ▶

Many issues are found in educational communities and using technology often adds another layer of complexity to the questions all educators routinely address. However, Web 2.0 tools offer opportunities to address these challenges in new ways, based on what research shows us about the way learning occurs.

english language learners and english as a second language

The 5.4 million students currently classified as limited English proficient (LEP) "are our fastest-growing student population and are expected to make up one out of every four students by 2025" (U.S. Department of Education, 2006, n.p.). The number of students entering U.S. public school classrooms with a first language other than English continues to grow, according to the National Clearinghouse for Bilingual Education, as cited by Mohr (2004). Mohr continues, "The need to provide better instruction for English language learners requires an updated, invigorated approach to their schooling" (p. 18). Current literature provides many ideas on how teachers can teach learning strategies and how certain strategies, such as activating prior knowledge, making connections, visualizing, and asking questions, affect the general education student's reading comprehension. It is unfortunate that many teachers "are not well versed in how culture and language can relate positively to student learning" (Gutiérrez, 2002, p. 1049). While no one is suggesting that technology can resolve all challenges faced by second language learners, it is worth considering the possibilities for improving learning that technology may afford.

Some research has indicated promise in using technology to work with students. Daud and Husin (2004) found that the use of a computer program helped ESL (English as a second language) students develop critical analysis skills. Allowing ESOL (English for speakers of other languages) students to create electronic portfolios on personal Web sites created a nonthreatening alternate evaluation solution to traditional standardized assessments (Chang, Wu, & Ku, 2005). Similarly, Zha, Kelly, Park, and Fitzgerald (2006) found that students' use of written language for personal expression and enjoyment increased when discussion boards were introduced. Of course, teachers need to be prepared to utilize technology in their classrooms. Brown and Warschauer's (2006) study found that while new teachers were knowledgeable of the many types of technology available, they were not sufficiently prepared to integrate this technology into curricular activities.

We know that a second language is best acquired through meaningful engagement with the language (Gersten & Baker, 2000) as opposed to a set of grammatical rules to be mastered. One way to make this language usage meaningful is to create opportunities to use it in social interactions with native English speakers and with peers in general (Collier, 1997). We also know that learning a language embedded in the content areas as part of that meaningful engagement with the language helps to reduce the academic achievement gap between native and nonnative speakers (Collier, 1997; Peregoy & Boyle, 2005).

Cooperative learning activities were shown to have a positive effect on the academic achievement of English language learners, or ELL (Allen, 2006; Calderon, Hertz-Lazarowitz, & Slavin, 1998; Naughton, 2006). A study by Xu, Gelfer, and Perkins (2005) confirmed the view that informal peer interaction may have beneficial effects on the ELL student's ability to read, write, speak, and understand English. Baltova (1999) concluded that teachers should integrate traditional methods with new technologies as more computer resources become available and popular.

Pawling (1999) conducted two case studies to explore CD use for vocabulary acquisition, pronunciation, and independent learning. She reported that foreign language instruction is moving from traditional teacher-centered classrooms to student-centered resource-based classrooms with activity centers for listening, reading, playing games, working in pairs, and writing. Innovative and well-funded schools also provided video and computer stations. Pawling found positive attributes for CD use at both of the participating schools. Use of multimedia apparently provided natural differentiation, a nonthreatening environment, and cooperative work opportunities. Students stayed on task, recalled vocabulary, improved pronunciation, and demonstrated increased motivation. Jones and Plass (2002) found that for short-term retention Pauling's the hypothesis that multimedia increases multiple levels of learning, was true, but that pictorial annotations were better for long-term retention. Their study suggested that teachers should provide resources to aid comprehension while listening.

Given the evidence that technology may have a positive effect on learning, we can consider ways that Web 2.0 tools might expand students' learning of English and becoming more proficient in the educational activities required in our schools.

Blogging

Poling (2005) writes, "Blogging as a classroom application allows for enhanced comprehension and communication among students as well as the ability to build deeper understanding across the curriculum. ... Blogging is a wonderful way to enhance student understanding" (p. 12). Some second-language teachers believe that blogs can be used to give students authentic language activities (Godwin-Jones, 2003).

Campbell (2006) suggests there are three unique uses of blogs with an ESL classroom. First, one could use the blog as a tutor, with the instructor being the one who posts regularly. This would give reading practice to learners. The content could be related to students' interests and recent activities, vocabulary words could be woven into the materials, and links to English language Web sites could engage students in reading even more. Questions to be answered or "comment" buttons would encourage writing responses. Second, one of the concerns that typically is mentioned is that ESL and ELL students may learn to speak English well from classmates, but they may have more difficulty in writing and reading it. Creating a blog for the students to use may help address this through educational and recreational reading and writing. The learners might create a blog of their own, in English, to support their questions, knowledge, and ideas on class assignments or topics of common interest. Finally, a class "learning community" could create its own blog. This might encourage threaded discussions, support group activities, or identify questions or concerns. If the learners are sufficiently proficient in reading and writing English, other classrooms (in other schools or countries) could join the blog and add their own comments on a particular topic or identified problem.

Podcasting

Graham Stanley (2005) has developed several "interactive listening mazes" using podcasting (an interactive listening maze is a story that allows the reader to decide what happens and what action to take throughout the story). Stanley's interactive reading mazes allow students to use the audio as a pronunciation model to review their vocabulary, to test themselves by writing meanings from vocabulary, or simply to learn the material subliminally through short phrases and sentences.

At the same time, we are seeing efforts to expand these tools beyond podcasting. No fewer than five major universities have already begun experimenting with coursecasting, and several blogs now address the subject. Through secure sites, students may log in to download lectures from their professors. At Stanford University, professors are waiting a month before their lectures become available for download. In this case, the coursecasts are available more for review (e.g., prior to a test or for writing a paper) than for learning new material. Is this a direction that K–12 might pursue for all learners? One can imagine how students for whom English is a struggle could download lectures or interact with colleagues before an examination. If school libraries could be "stocked with compressed audio and video files for students to 'check out' onto their MP3 players (and/or if the players themselves could be borrowed from the library), this may provide a lower cost and lower space requirement than traditional media storehouses" (Kadel, 2006, p. 49).

It is possible that podcasts may be one of the most effective ways to learn a foreign language, to learn English as a second language, or to learn other subjects that may be difficult to comprehend. We are aware of the power and necessity of auditory input and repetition for a variety of topics. In learning music, for example, students have used podcasting to listen to, memorize, and critique classical music and even to share their original musical creations. Foreign language teachers have shared native music, literature, and plays through podcasting (Flanagan & Calandra, 2005).

Students have been able to create foreign language audio projects to share with their class and their teacher. In social studies or history, primary documents can include historical speeches, radio plays, interviews with experts, and audio books. The ability to hear these items as often as one wishes puts the learner in control of the learning. Audio books, newspapers, and magazines could be provided to students as podcasts. Flanagan and Calandra (2005) suggest that an audio version of Project Gutenberg would be useful so that teachers, parents, or students could download free and legal materials.

students with special needs

Hasselbring (2001) argues that in many cases, "students with disabilities have a greater need for accessing technology than do their non-disabled peers. This may be especially true for those students who need technology just to function within the school environment, such as students with sensory and physical impairments" (p. 16). Students with learning challenges are now able to have access to podcasts, learning materials, and videos, and at times that suit their individual schedules. Additionally, the multimodality of these tools allows students to learn in ways that best meet their learning styles.

Research shows that students with learning disabilities also benefit from explicit instruction of learning strategies. Swanson and Hoskyn (1999) report a positive result when a combination of strategy and direct instruction is provided to students with learning disabilities. Early intervention and reading support are critical for at-risk students and students with learning disabilities according to Short, Frye, King, and Homan (1999). They also report reading comprehension for these students increased when teachers had high expectations, provided successful reading experiences, and taught specific strategy skills. One study found that if teachers model and provide children with the language tools for talking about meaning, reading comprehension increased for students with mild disabilities (Englert, Mariage, Garmon, & Tarrant, 1998). The large majority of studies we reviewed show that explicitly teaching learning strategies positively improves the reading comprehension of general and special education students, and none reported a negative relationship. Peer-assisted learning strategies (PALS) have been shown to have a positive effect on students with learning disabilities in the general population of native English speakers (Fuchs, Fuchs, Mathes, & Simmons, 1997).

Current federal guidelines require that assistive technology must be considered for every student who has an individualized education program (IEP). Any technology that is necessary to aid a student in meeting IEP goals and objectives qualifies as an assistive technology. This might include an electronic spelling aid for a student with a spelling disability or the ability to record lectures for a student with auditory processing difficulties. Bausch (1999) created a special keyboard that consisted only of number and control keys with a computer program designed to provide math facts instruction to students with learning disabilities.

With new Web 2.0 technologies, it is possible to imagine that a wide variety of tools might be useful to the student who requires multiple input strategies or alternative methods for expressing what has been learned. Already we have seen an adaptive device for individuals with high levels of quadriplegia called a switch pod (www.tecsol.com.au/SwitchPod.htm). There are touch screens that replace the use of a mouse for students with fine motor difficulties (www.touchscreens.com). One program, Voycabulary, allows students with reading difficulties to automatically obtain definitions of unfamiliar words (www.voycabulary.com). There is even a handheld for individuals with visual difficulties (www.humanware.com/about/news/news300606.asp). All of these adaptive technologies allow Web 2.0 to become useful for every student.

In a review of research, Maccini, Gagnon, and Hughes (2002) found that auditory assistance was very helpful for secondary students with learning disabilities. This information may provide a rationale for teachers to provide podcasts of important lectures to students, but may also encourage students to get assistance through other auditory support materials. Interestingly, teachers have always known that frequently the "extra" support given to students with learning difficulties also improves the learning of all students, and perhaps Web 2.0 tools will raise the knowledge and skills of our entire K–12 population.

There are also resources to provide information, access, and a sense of community. For example, the Special Education blog (http://specialed.about.com) offers links for parents and teachers about a variety of topics, including wikis and podcasts for downloading. Another one, Family.com (http://education.families.com/blog/category/134/), has a collection of links on special accommodations for enhanced student learning, solutions that other teachers and parents have discovered, and a blog for communicating with other parents and teachers. One state site, the Connecticut Special Education Resource (www.state.ct.gov/sde/site/), has created a blog for parents and teachers to ask questions and communicate. And some institutions have created blogs for those interested in special education (www.uwstout.edu/lib/subjects/edspec.htm).

> An ongoing challenge for all schools is to provide an equal opportunity to learn and achieve to all students.

Because special needs issues are heavily connected to legal education issues, one site, Eduwonk.com (www.eduwonk.com), offers information on the legal considerations for educators and parents involved in working with schools. Additionally, a special education law blog provides information and a connection to others (http://specialedlaw.blogs.com).

Podcasts are also populating the airwaves for those interested in special education topics. Pediatrics for Parents (www.pedsforparents.com) offers podcasts for specific areas of concern, and Podcasts for Teachers (www.idiotvox.com/Education/PodCast_Review_Podcast_for_Teachers__13037.html) covers all topics including those related to teaching students with special needs. Almost every Web site devoted to this topic offers some type of podcast for those interested.

equity and the digital divide

An ongoing challenge for all schools is to provide an equal opportunity to learn and achieve to all students. This must be viewed through the reality of unequal access to technology, specifically in schools with high minority populations, high proportions of families who have cultural or linguistic diversity, or in schools located in rural areas. Female students and students who are physically challenged may also face unequal access. Equity is a complex issue and reflects the conundrum found throughout our society. There is an existing tension between families with high-speed access in their homes and those who have limited or no access, and between those who have comfort and experience with using the technologies and those who do not. Language barriers also come into play, as do educator expectations that assignments be completed using technology.

Some possible solutions to this problem have been suggested. Nicholas Negroponte, founder and chairman of One Laptop per Child, has demonstrated a working model of a proposed $100 laptop (www.laptop.org). While many of these laptops are destined for third world countries, areas of the United States are also going to be eligible to become part of this collaborative project. These machines will not require wired broadband access (with ongoing expenses that are often significant) but will work off a satellite connection.

Another option is for schools to use open-source software and tools, so that anyone with a machine is able to use the same tools from any machine. The Nonprofit Open Source Initiative (NOSI) was formed in early 2001 by a collaboration of nonprofit sector technology assistance providers who were interested in the potential of open-source software to benefit their organizations.

We have also seen the emergence of mobcasting, which is mobile audio podcasting using a mobile phone to receive the programming. Since a large percentage of students have mobile phones, this may level the playing field even further (Clyde, 2005).

Bridging the Digital Divide with Web 2.0 Tools

Although nearly all students have access to computer systems and the Internet while at school, the most recent census statistics reveal inequitable access at home. Nearly 70% of White (Non-Hispanic) and Asian-American children have both computers and Internet access at home, while fewer than 40% of American-Indian, Hispanic, and African-American children have both computers and Internet access at home (Becker, 2000). Based on these statistics, teachers should determine whether students have computers and Internet access at home before assigning blogs as instructional tools outside the school environment.

Another use of Web 2.0 tools is for those learners who routinely miss days or weeks at a time to be with their families. Several states and universities have created organizations to support migrant families through technology and distance learning initiatives (www.education-world.com/a_curr/curr347.shtml). This is an opportunity to reach out to individuals and prepare them for their return to the public schools. Through technology, students can stay in contact with their friends and teachers. Other organizations (for example, Conexiones, http://conexiones. asu.edu/mep.html) have sought to determine ways to use technology to avoid the typical disruption, lack of resources, and language difficulty that have routinely been problems for children in migrant worker families. These programs are funded by the U. S. Department of Migrant Education.

School districts are also working on strategies to level the playing field for all students. They have created a wide variety of after-school programs, clubs, technology "specials," and family technology classes.

In addition, communities have become aware of the dilemma that their members face without access to technology. The Intel Corporation has invested heavily in understanding the ways communities and individuals adopt and use technology. One example demonstrates what they are doing:

> **North Lawndale** is a low-income community on the west side of Chicago that recently had a world class wireless network installed at no cost to the community. In order to use the network, community residents must have a computer and some form of Wi-Fi capability. For residents who are using the wireless network, the main reason is to have Internet connectivity so their children can access educational resources. Other residents said convenience was a key factor in adoption. For instance, one disabled veteran uses the technology to deal with the Veterans Administration and other government agencies. In addition, a few residents use the network for their home-based businesses. Virtually everyone who spoke with the Intel researchers thought that the new wireless network would ultimately make their neighborhood a better, safer place to live, because it would bring economic development to the neighborhood and would give teens with little chance of getting jobs, access to educational materials and job skills training. That said, thus far the adoption rate has been relatively low, beyond the users cited earlier. Many non-adopters said the technology did not seem relevant to their lives. The challenge is to identify new usage models that could make a measurable impact on their lives. (Beckwith, 2006, n.p.)

assessment

It is an odd circumstance that schools find themselves in these days. All schools are driven by requirements to maintain and improve standardized test scores. And yet these efforts create a rather interesting conundrum, because frequently the "new school" model and high-stakes testing seem in conflict with each other. At the same time, we have seen an equally vigorous effort toward authentic assessment. This type of assessment involves

> engaging and worthy problems or questions of importance, in which students must use knowledge to fashion performances effectively and creatively. The tasks are either replicas of or analogous to the kinds of problems faced by adult citizens and consumers or professionals in the field. (Wiggins, 1993, p. 229)

Can assessment be authentic and simultaneously prepare students to succeed in the standardized testing that they will face? Absolutely! If we consider another definition of authentic assessment, it will become clear. Stiggins (1987) said, "Performance assessments call upon the examinee to demonstrate specific skills and competencies, that is, to apply the skills and knowledge they have mastered" (p. 34). Perhaps the most obvious use of Web 2.0 tools for assessment would be for students to be able to show what they know in a wide variety of media. If we consider the state standards for any particular subject area, it is easy for educators to plan interesting instruction around that standard, using a balanced approach that includes a variety of technological activities.

> Can assessment be authentic and simultaneously prepare students to succeed in the standardized testing that they will face? Absolutely!

Unfortunately, teachers may frequently fall back to the traditional ways of figuring out how well students have learned. However, it makes much more sense to have ongoing assessment—the way evaluators do that is known as "formative evaluation." All this means is that we don't wait until the "unit" is over to determine how well the students and we as educators are doing!

Harry Tuttle, an experienced educator, has spent considerable energy considering ways to look at using technology to authentically evaluate student progress, as he explains in the Web 2.0 Wisdom sidebar, Authentic Assessments.

web 2.0 wisdom

Authentic Assessments Made Possible by Web 2.0

Harry Tuttle

MANY TEACHERS HAVE TRIED to use the Web in the past for authentic assessment but the quality of sound, of video, and of transmission speed often made such attempts very awkward. In addition, they were limited in their concepts of how they could use the Web. As a Spanish teacher, I had a Spaniard try to assess my students' speaking, but it was hard for her to hear my students and for us to hear her; therefore, that assessment did not work. However, today with Web 2.0, a Spanish teacher can have Spanish-speakers easily assess students' progress in conducting conversations about daily life topics; the Spanish-speakers can hear and reply clearly. The following list represents a sampling of the ways teachers can do authentic assessment with the dynamically different Web 2.0.

▶ English students can listen to a podcast, answer questions about the podcast, and write about a topic using the information from the podcast just as they would on a state English exam. Furthermore, they can have students who have listened to the same podcast but who are in distant locations peer-edit their work in a shared online space. The teacher can assess that writing using the state writing rubric.

▶ Art students can prepare art projects using a certain artist's style and then, through videoconferencing, have that artist critique their work in real time. The artist can see all the subtle details because of the high quality of Web 2.0.

▶ Social studies students who work in small groups can create their own social bookmarks that not only identify critical Web sites about a topic but also demonstrate their deep understanding of the topic through their tags; teachers can use the bookmarking as authentic assessment during the process.

► ►

- Elementary math students can record the clothing that people wear in a different country with real time Web 2.0 Webcam and then analyze the country's culture through a graph of the clothing; the teacher then determines how well the students go from the lower level thinking skill of counting to the higher level thinking skill of analysis.

- Middle-school science students can add to a class wiki about stream life; the teacher can assess the students' unique contributions about the part of the stream that they analyzed and the students' ability to synthesize the information about the diverse elements of the stream ecosystem.

- Students in a school within a school can put all of their e-portfolio materials online so that distant reviewers can quickly download the e-portfolio files and assess their standards-based skills development.

- Middle- and high-school students can have regular interviews with people who have a career that they are interested in. Career people can take students on a virtual "walk-through" of their daily work life. These people can assess the students' knowledge and attitude about the careers based on the students' questions and comments.

- Students can engage in multinational conversations about school life to demonstrate their ability to communicate to diverse audiences through verbal and visual modes as their teachers assess those skills in authentic real-time situations.

If educators work together to plan their instruction and simultaneously plan ways to evaluate throughout the unit, they will develop a wide variety of interesting models. And using Web 2.0 tools the educators might also devise an interesting, authentic, and appropriate summative evaluation for the unit. After all, if you are integrating new tools, you do not want to assess these outcomes with old models— or to put it another way, you don't want to put new wine in old bottles.

This new type of assessment model is perfect for a group activity, in which teams are free to consider all possibilities. Students can blog their questions, add to a subject matter wiki, or create a phased podcast of what they are learning and what questions they are struggling with. If they see the rubric for the unit prior to the unit's start, they will understand the outcomes the school is expecting.

Helen Barrett has led educators in using electronic portfolios and has now developed the next stage of these tools. She talks about e-portfolios and Web 2.0 in the following Web 2.0 Wisdom sidebar.

web 2.0 wisdom

Authentic Assessment with Electronic Portfolios Using Common Software and Web 2.0 Tools

Helen Barrett

AN ELECTRONIC PORTFOLIO provides an environment where students can collect their work in a digital archive; select specific pieces of work (hyperlink to artifacts) to highlight specific achievements; reflect on the learning demonstrated in the portfolio, in either text or multimedia form; set goals for future learning (or direction) to improve; and celebrate achievement through sharing this work with an audience, whether online or face-to-face. When used in formative, classroom-based assessment, teachers (and peers) can review the portfolio document and provide formative feedback to students on where they could improve.

How does the Web 2.0 metaphor apply to electronic portfolios?

Web 1.0 is represented by portfolios created as traditional static Web pages that are updated rarely, if at all; Web 2.0 is represented by server-side software that is more interactive and more like desktop applications. Web 2.0 is sometimes called the "Participatory Web" based on its architecture, which is designed for interaction.

When educators think of portfolios in education, they assume the purpose is for assessment. But I always ask, "What kind of assessment?" As I have discussed in other work, there are several approaches to

▶ ▶ ▶

assessment, and thus to portfolios. Table 8.1 presents my comparison of electronic portfolios used as assessment *of* learning with those that support assessment *for* learning, based on work done in Britain by the Assessment Reform Group (see www.arg.educ.cam.ac.uk). This table has been published in previous work.

Table 8.1 Comparison of Electronic Portfolios by Type of Assessment

Portfolios used for Assessment *of* Learning	Portfolios used for Assessment *for* Learning
The purpose of the portfolio is prescribed by the institution.	The purpose of the portfolio is agreed upon with the learner.
Artifacts are mandated by the institution to determine the outcomes of instruction.	Artifacts are selected by the learner to tell the story of their learning.
The portfolio is usually developed at the end of a class, term, or program (time limited).	The portfolio is maintained on an ongoing basis—throughout the class, term, or program (time flexible).
The portfolio and/or artifacts are usually "scored" based on a rubric, and quantitative data are collected for external audiences.	The portfolio and artifacts are reviewed with learner and used to provide feedback to improve learning.
The portfolio is usually structured around a set of outcomes, goals, or standards.	The organization of the portfolio is determined by the learner or negotiated with a mentor/advisor/teacher.
Portfolios are sometimes used to make high-stakes decisions	Portfolios are rarely used for high-stakes decisions.
Portfolios are summative—what has been learned to date (past to present)?	Portfolios are formative—what are the learning needs in the future (present to future)?
The process requires extrinsic motivation.	The process fosters intrinsic motivation and engages the learner.
The audience is external; there is little choice.	The audience can be the learner, family, or friends; the learner can choose.

▶ ▶ ▶

In summary, as I review all of these comparisons, I have come up with a new look at e-portfolios from the framework of Web 2.0, which I will call ePortfolio 2.0. Other terms might be "blog-folios" or "wiki-folios" or perhaps "iPortfolios" (i=interactive). Table 8.2 offers a comparison of early electronic portfolios and Web 2.0 portfolios.

Table 8.2 Comparison of Electronic Portfolios by Type of Technology

ePortfolios 1.0		ePortfolios 2.0
Hierarchical, designed	▶	Networked, emergent
Metaphor: portfolio as checklist	▶	Metaphor: portfolio as story
Data-driven	▶	Learner-driven
Focus on standardization	▶	Focus on individuality, creativity
Feedback from authority figures	▶	Feedback from community of learners
Large, complex systems	▶	Small pieces, loosely joined—"mash-ups"
Web-based form	▶	Blog and wiki
Positivist	▶	Constructivist, connectivist
Accountability-driven	▶	Learning-focused
Proprietary	▶	Open standards
Digital paper (text and images)	▶	Digital story (multimedia)
Local storage (hard drives, CD)	▶	Network storage (lifetime personal Web space)

What are some of the advantages of an interactive portfolio? Just as the Web changed with the implementation of the architecture of interaction, we could say that portfolios have the potential to change with the pedagogy of interaction, especially as used within a paradigm of assessment for learning. With these new tools, we can post work and invite feedback, as in a blog; we can post work and invite co-authors, as in a wiki. Fortunately, wiki tools keep track of the changes, so that authorship can be tracked, if that is important for accountability. As I wrote for an article submitted to the Connected Newsletter (2006):

The use of technology can be a motivating factor for portfolios, especially if we can make the process engaging for the learners, and give them an opportunity to express their own voice and leave their own mark in their portfolios. As schools implement electronic portfolios, it will be important to do more than replicate their paper-based predecessors or adopt a database-type portfolio system that only allows students to fill in blanks on a Web-based form. Where is the individuality, creativity, and ownership? To truly engage learners, I encourage schools to incorporate emerging Web 2.0–type technologies that motivate and engage adolescent students, including digital storytelling, multimedia artifacts, podcasting and blogging (maintaining a reflective online journal).

We have seen how much students are motivated to use online social-networking sites, such as MySpace and FaceBook. The TaskStream electronic portfolio has been described by students participating in the REFLECT Initiative as an "academic MySpace." If only we could capture that level of motivation while furthering the goals of deep learning in formative electronic learning portfolios, then we may realize the real promise of using technology to both improve and showcase student achievement.

References

Assessment Reform Group. (2002). *Assessment for learning.* Retrieved June 23, 2006, from www.qca.org.uk/7659.html

Barrett, H. (2000). Create your own electronic portfolio using off-the-shelf software to showcase your own or student work. *Learning & Leading with Technology, 27*(7), 14–21. Retrieved June 23, 2006, from http://electronicportfolios.org/portfolios/iste2k.html

Barrett, H. (2000). *The "5x5" model of electronic portfolio development.* Retrieved June 23, 2006, from http://electronicportfolios.org/handouts/model5x5.pdf

Barrett, H. (2004, 2006). *My online portfolio adventure.* Retrieved June 23, 2006, from http://electronicportfolios.org/myportfolio/versions.html

Barrett, H. (2005). *White paper: Researching electronic portfolios and learner engagement.* Retrieved June 23, 2006, from www.taskstream.com/reflect/whitepaper.pdf

Barrett, H. (2006). Using electronic portfolios for formative/classroom-based assessment. Submitted to the *Connected Newsletter.*

Barrett, H. (2007, March). Researching electronic portfolios and learner engagement: The REFLECT initiative. *Journal of Adolescent & Adult Literacy, 50*(6).

Helen Barrett is a research associate with the University of Oregon's Center for Advanced Technology in Education (CATE).

Another new tool to assist in assessment goes beyond what we typically think of as an e-portfolio. Elgg is a new breed of social software that is "based around choice, flexibility and openness: a system that places individuals at the centre of their activities" according to the Elgg Web site (www.elgg.org). U.K.-based David Tosh and Ben Werdmuller developed this program in 2004 to counter what they saw as top-down e-portfolio systems in which institutions rather than students designed and drove how the systems looked.

In an interview, Tosh (2006) said that this tool was designed to promote reflective thinking, to allow users to select artifacts important to them, to promote social connections, and to focus on the process of learning rather than the end products. He explains:

> Elgg is truly a learner centric environment; it allows learners to make certain choices about their own learning landscape. It is also not designed to be an all-in-one box; it's more an ethos of choice. We have a standard tool set but the goal is to build a framework that lets learners plug in their own tools and widgets. (n.p.)

Several universities and a few K–12 schools have adopted this tool and we can expect to see more about it in the future.

into the future

The topics covered in this chapter are not in any way unique to the Web 2.0 world—in fact, they are areas of consideration throughout the educational community. However, there are some aspects of these topics that Web 2.0 tools may have the potential to improve. These tools may allow us to see these topics in new ways, or may even raise our awareness of their complexity.

9

new schools

Everything changes fast in this Web 2.0 world. Some of the applications and Web sites described in this book may already be out of fashion and new ones may have emerged as the new "new thing." However, it is certain that digital technologies and new Web applications have made a huge difference and are here to stay. The real issue is what we should do with these technologies for the future of teaching and learning. What should we expect from new schools?

▶ ▶ ▶ ▶ ▶

Marc Prensky (2001) says our digital native students "are no longer the people our educational system was designed to teach" and today's teachers "have to learn to communicate in the language and style of their students" (p. 1). "This *doesn't* mean changing the meaning of what is important, or of good thinking skills. But it *does* mean going faster, less step-by step, more in parallel, with more random access, among other things" (p. 4).

It also means using the same tools in classrooms that students use at home. The ultimate goal will be for schools to put all the pieces together and use new tools to create new models of technology-infused teaching and learning. Our vision of a new school is one in which the educators can adapt and change, model and use tools, and understand how students learn and what tools—both technological and pedagogical—will foster learning.

As the world, the students, and the technologies continue to change, what is on the horizon and beyond? This chapter presents ideas and strategies that can make a difference in the future. However, none of them is certain to happen. In a Web 2.0 world, predicting the future is risky. Some of these ideas seem possible; some merely hopeful. Some ideas are ours; many are from colleagues. Speaking of the collaborative and collegial nature of Web 2.0, we invite you to contribute to a second book we are developing on promising practice. We talk more about that at the end of this chapter.

harnessing the collective intelligence of education data

If Amazon and eBay can do it, why can't an education company create intelligent Web-based software that provides immediate feedback to students and recommends other lessons, sites, and resources that they might use, perhaps based on what has helped other students to learn? It could look at a student's learning style and suggest sites accordingly, whether simulations, games, readings, drills, or whatever has worked for that student and others.

If a student did well with project-based learning, for example, the software would provide suggestions for research (maybe an intelligent WebQuest) based on that student's preferences. These preferences would come from analyzing the data rather than asking the student or overburdened teachers what works. Teachers would become true guides, like information gurus at a help desk, to lend a hand to students along the way. These students might not be in front of them in classrooms but could be virtual learners, selected because their learning styles match the teacher's teaching style.

Years ago, Apple Computer had an advertisement that displayed the idea of a Knowledge Navigator, an electronic personal assistant that helped its user keep on track in many ways, steering him to just the right information, getting him to meetings on time, and predicting his needs.

While the technology wasn't available then, today that vision is closer to reality. In the not too distant future, an electronic personal education assistant modeled on this concept could direct students to activities that would work best for them at that moment. It would harness both cognitive science and collective intelligence. It would know what each student needs and say, "Other students who had to learn this topic found that lessons 3, 5, and 9 helped. May I suggest that you start with lesson 5 and work with Timmy?" Of course, the advice would be based on awareness of the student's learning style, interest in the subject, eagerness to collaborate, and a host of other factors.

the long tail of educational materials

Chris Anderson's 2006 book, *The Long Tail,* explains that today's opportunities for finding exactly the right book, piece of music, video, or other object are possible because of the Web's endless supply. Everything anyone could want is someplace online. This simple fact is the basis of an economic distribution model called "The Long Tail," in which companies that offer limitless products will thrive because the sum of all niche market purchases can equal the blockbusters.

Anderson says, "The story of the long tail is really about the economics of abundance, what happens when the bottlenecks that stand between supply and demand in our culture start to disappear and everything becomes available to everyone" (p. 12).

While the theory is about sales, it is also about choice and the potential to address individual interests and needs. We can apply this theory to educational materials and to student learning. If, for example, an infinite selection of products were available so that teachers could choose anything that has been published instead of just the approved textbooks, they could pinpoint precisely the right learning materials for each student. In addition, if students could choose the resources on school topics that engage them, be it simulations, games, tutorials, or some other strategy, they could learn what the standards proscribe but how they wish.

Perhaps at some point in the future, students and teachers will make the decisions and choose from among a seemingly endless supply of online content and tools that address their needs instead of having information delivered and methods mandated that someone else has decided would work.

the vision and the reality

In *A Day in the Life of Web 2.0,* David Warlick (2006c) offers his vision of a middle school. In it, teachers keep regular blogs, where they write about everything from homework assignments to reflections on course topics, with a full description posted each Monday morning of course material to be taught in the upcoming week. Many of them have a wiki site that serves as the class textbook, and students construct their own study resources using their team wikis. All significant class presentations and discussions are recorded and posted in a podcast that students, parents, community members, and other educators can subscribe to.

The school librarian subscribes to all of the teachers' Monday report blogs and uses a shared spreadsheet to maintain an ongoing curriculum map of what's being taught in the school as a way to support the teachers. The principal maintains an online school calendar with a weekly blog entry that describes happenings at the school for the next seven days. The district superintendent subscribes to the principal's blog and teachers' Monday report blogs. He uses a wiki site to develop a district improvement plan in collaboration with educators and community members. (See appendix C for Warlick's full article.)

In response, David Jakes (2006b) paints a picture of the reality in a techLEARNING blog titled Gap Analysis. He says:

> Most schools continue to educate kids in the way they always have, most teachers continue to teach in the ways they always have, and most administrators remain in their offices focusing on the things they focus on. There is a gap between what is and what should be. (n.p.)

Unless we can close that gap, "while a few will accomplish so much, many will accomplish little, and the window for imagination and boldness will be lost, perhaps forever." (n.p.)

The hope is that professional development will fill that gap for current teachers and that new teachers will enter the profession armed with the technology skills they'll need to help students learn in new ways.

polls and surveys

A series of polls conducted on techLEARNING.com attempted to capture what educators who are using technology think will happen in the future. In each case, there was a brief explanation of the issue, a series of choices, and the opportunity to comment.

The question during the week of October 3–9, 2006, asked readers what they believe about the future of the Internet. They agreed that by 2020 a low-cost global network will be thriving and creating new opportunities in a flattening world. They also agreed that people will wittingly and unwittingly disclose more about themselves, gaining some benefits in the process even as they lose some privacy.

The following week, the question asked about schooling in the future. Twenty percent of respondents agreed that schools as physical locations will become much less important as technology enables connected communities of learners located in many places. Another 20% agreed that students would be grouped by achievement level, not age, as technology allows for very granular tracking of what students know. And 43% agreed that students increasingly would work collaboratively on significant projects, with each student's individual learning goals and achievement tracked by monitoring software.

Are they right? Only time will tell.

What else should change? Some specifics include software, textbooks, and applications, to name a few. The following discussion covers these topics.

software

Mechelle DeCraene (2006) in a techLEARNING blog suggests that school districts' software selection process could use improvement. She says, "Given an ideal situation we'd all opt for open-source, but the reality is that someone has to pay" (n.p.). So she asks:

What if teachers could choose software themselves that is tailored to their students' developmental needs? What if there was a global central hub via the Web for educational software and a software smorgasbord of sorts that every teacher could pick and choose from? And what if the schools only paid for the software that teachers actually use? It would be similar to paying for the cell phone minutes that one uses. Perhaps, a subscription based on usage?

There is no one-size-fits-all software. Unfortunately, I can't tell you how many times I've walked in the ol' book closet and seen brand new software sitting sealed in its packages. Other times, it's installed but never used. When asked about it, teachers often say, "it just wasn't right for my kids." (n.p.)

textbooks

Wikis make collaborative writing possible, and David Warlick (2006e) has come up with an idea for textbooks that uses wiki technology. An advantage to students is that backpacks would shrink and students would stand a little straighter. Warlick asks:

What if teachers and preservice education students started writing little chunks of content, worthy of their textbooks?

What if a file-sharing network emerged where teachers could search, access, and download snippets of content from each other—world-wide?

What if teachers started assembling this shared content into their Moodle sites, or someone writes an open-source application specifically designed to become the next-gen digital textbook?

What if we could stop buying textbooks, and use the money to provide every teacher and learner with access to the world of digital networked content?

Our homework assignments would change just a bit from... *Ya'll read the chapter and answer the questions at the end!* to... *Ya'll read the chapter and then validate it by Friday!* (n.p.)

moving applications and data online

Terry Whitmell, a secondary school vice principal, argues that it is time to provide 24/7 access. She says:

> Investing in software that can be used only on school computers is like purchasing textbooks and then forcing students to leave them in their desks at the end of the day. Requiring that student data remain behind firewalls on school or district servers locks those same students' "notes" in their desks when they head home.

> It is time to move our classroom applications and data online. Many districts have licensed applications and utilities that are available to staff and students only when they are working in school, not at home. This restricts the flexibility of students to complete work outside of school hours and puts additional stress on school hardware resources. (Whitmell & Killingsworth, 2006, p. 8)

open-source educational applications

Bob Tinker (2006), president of the Concord Consortium, believes that we can change the paradigm used for software development to open source. He says:

> Educators and programmers worldwide could create a shared collection of educational applications based on cutting-edge open-source educational software that could help realize the potential of technology to transform education. A body of educational applications that are all free, open source, and maintained by a collaborating community, could result in an exciting new generation of computer-based learning activities that are well designed, robust, and highly effective.

> To be practical, these applications need to be embedded in an educational platform that can deliver complete learning activities online and then assess student progress as they work through these activities. Teachers and educators should be able to customize the activities and assessments, so that they can tailor the learning strategies to the needs and interests of their students. The tools, models, and platforms needed

to exploit this approach are sophisticated and probably too complex to be supported commercially. A better option is to make them open source and trust that their utility will support a broad community of users that will provide ongoing support and development. (n.p.)

---

web 2.0 wisdom

Creators in the Classroom

Jeff Utecht

IF WE THINK ABOUT HOW our current students spent their early years, we see a generation that is accustomed to information coming at them at a fast pace, multitasking as the norm, and a reliance on images to convey concepts. Their world always had cell phones, hand-held games, and the Web. They use the tools and expect to have an audience. Because of technology, these youngsters may in fact be wired differently from their predecessors.

In traditional classrooms, we restrict students to creating pieces of work only for other students in their own class, or even worse, just for the teacher. Pieces of work that could have the potential to impact many others are put out with the trash by year's end. These are the same students who go home and plug into sites like MySpace and YouTube: spaces that not only allow them to create, but to create and share with a wide audience.

If we want to engage students in our classrooms, we must start looking at the social Web as an educational tool and not something to fear. We, as teachers, fear this new Web for possible dangers and are wary of the unknown, but our students live in it. It is their home, their bowling alley, their corner hangout. These social sites turn our students into creators; creators who contribute their work not only to the twenty other students in their classroom, but potentially to the 1 billion plus Internet users on the Web. If we want to motivate students to create something, something that will last beyond the lesson and the school year, then we must find ways to use these social-networking tools in our classroom. If we continue to fight them, I'm afraid it is a battle we will lose.

Jeff Utecht is an international educator currently working in Shanghai, China.

Learning from Games

David Warlick

WE ARE FINALLY BEGINNING to pay serious attention to video games for learning. It is crucial, though, that we resist the temptation to look only at the game, and instead, study the experience, which is what students learn from, rather than the graphics and sound. I want to suggest five elements of the video game experience that makes it both compelling and instructionally potent.

Responsiveness. Video games, IM, social networks, and SMS are far more responsive to youngsters' input than anything from my childhood. These responsive information landscapes, where children play, are intensely instructional. They are learning engines.

Convert-able and convers-able rewards. We reward student work and successful learning with grades, which hold value mostly to their parents, teachers, and the government. In video games, students work to increase their level, which they value for two reasons. One is that it gives them something to talk and brag about. They share strategies and short cuts that they discovered or invented and discuss alternatives. Second, the level influences the experience. When a student moves to a new level, the game environment frequently changes dramatically.

Personal investment. One of the early lessons learned by video game developers was that players will return to a game that they have invested in. Many of today's games require players to generate currency. It might be health points, extra powers, or an inventory of tools or weapons. It may also be currency, money that can be traded for goods and services within the play of the game. Students must invest time, skill, and learning into the game to increase their level. When we have invested ourselves, we come back.

Identity building. One of the interesting aspects of many new video games is players' ability to customize their presence. One example is 1080, a snowboarding game that is fairly simple; you play against gravity. Players

▶ ▶ ▶

can choose their boards, board decorations, clothing, name, and other aspects. In car racing games, players can customize their vehicles. There is a compelling sense of personalization in the players' experience.

Dependability. There is a sense in most video games that the answer to the question or solution to the problem is always there. It is simply a matter of finding or reasoning through the answer or solution. A classroom should work the same way, with a ubiquitous sense that the answer is always close by; that it merely means turning over the right stone, and finding that stone is a matter of logic and prior knowledge.

David Warlick is director of the Landmark Project, a Web development, consulting, and innovations firm in Raleigh, North Carolina.

professional development

For two weeks in fall 2006, a group of educators convened a K–12 online conference with the theme of "Unleashing the Potential" (http://k12onlineconference. org/?p=26), for teachers, administrators, and educators around the world interested in the use of Web 2.0 tools in classrooms and professional practice. The presentations were on practical, pedagogical uses of online social tools in the classroom; advanced training for teachers who have already started using Web 2.0 tools in their classes; tips, ideas, and resources on how to orchestrate your own professional development online and on how to overcome obstacles. This conference may well be the model for professional development in the future with all events taking place online, peers helping peers, and sessions available on demand for the foreseeable future.

toward a smart future

For any of these things to happen, there has to be a commitment to education, broadband and computer access, and policies to make sure that students are able to compete in the global market.

Broadband Access in the U.S.

The U.S. Congress passed the Communications Act of 1934 to ensure that all Americans could have access to telephone service. They deemed telephone service an essential in American life and initiated the Universal Service Fund, which was supported by fees to those who paid for telephone service. Today, access to high-speed Internet is as much of an essential in all aspects of life. However, findings from a 2006 study say "America's digital divide—between rich and poor and urban and rural areas—shows no sign of closing" (Turner, 2006, n.p.). Thus the need exists to expand universal service to provide poor and rural areas with broadband. The Telecommunications Act of 1996 expanded the concept with the E-Rate program, which provided networking capabilities for schools and libraries. Homes in the U.S. remain in the digital divide.

Former FCC Chairman William Kennard (2007) says:

> Studies by the federal government conclude that our rural and low-income areas trail urban and high-income areas in the rate of broadband use. Indeed, this year the Government Accountability Office found that 42 percent of households have either no computer or a computer with no Internet connection. (n.p.)

Kennard (2007) believes that Congress should reform the Universal Service Fund and find a new source of revenue besides taxes on telephone service and "put all broadband providers on a level playing field" (n.p.).

Net Neutrality

Network Neutrality emerges as a political issue every once in a while. It is really about competition, Internet transmission speed, and freedom of speech. The large networks (cable and telecom companies) claim that Web sites should pay for content to be transmitted on the networks. Those who pay would have their content transmitted faster than those who don't. Private individuals (who are paying for cable and telecom) claim that it would create a two-tiered Internet with large companies such as Amazon and eBay able to pay for fast transmissions and mom-and-pop companies and personal sites stuck at lower speeds. Speed is everything today; no one wants to wait more than an instant for sites to refresh and content to download. Some believe that if the networks control the flow of content, democracy will suffer and so "policies must maintain Net Neutrality or 'non-discriminatory, open-access principles'" (Turner, 2006, n.p.).

Classrooms

The reality for experienced teachers is that they have too much to do and are busy with all of the regular tasks of teaching. Their comfort level with technology is low and they want to be facile before letting students use it. Then there is always the issue of time. There is never enough of it and it takes longer to figure out integration strategies than to use tried and true methods.

The reality for new teachers is that while they have used these tools themselves, they must learn how to teach plus use integration strategies. Then there is access. Most teachers have to sign up for labs and mobile carts, and the dates they get may not dovetail with their plans.

For all, the reality is that each crop of students will be more adept at using the tools for their own purposes. So teachers continue to feel that they are behind the curve. There's always something new on the horizon. How does anyone keep up?

brainstorming about schools and web 2.0

As we think about what schools might really be like in five years, it is important to keep all options on the table and our eyes firmly on the goals we set for our schools and communities. One organization, School 2.0 (www.school2-0.org), has developed a brainstorming tool to help individuals and groups do just that. The School 2.0 (2006) Web site states:

> The name *School 2.0* was chosen to encourage a discussion about the "next generation of school" that can be supported by an integrated technology infrastructure. We believe that schools must transform in order to meet the multiple challenges of the 21st century: accountability, student engagement and achievement, and economic competitiveness. By encouraging a discussion of community-based "next generation" schools, we hope communities will be inspired to think creatively about teaching, learning, and management and then explore ways that technology can help meet those goals. (n.p.)

The brainstorming tool encourages groups to talk about the next generation of schools—by considering the stakeholders, the learning ecosystem, the horizontal technology layers, and the necessary supporting elements. You can download the map and instructions and then dream up your perfect school system.

In what ways do you imagine technology supporting, encouraging, and enhancing what happens in schools?

Figure 9.1 | The school of tomorrow

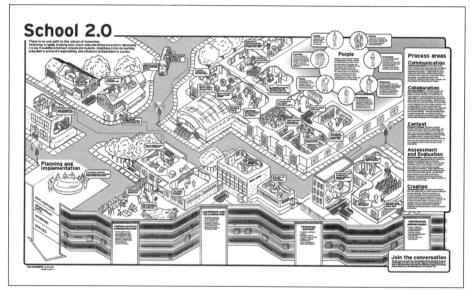

▶ © Office of Educational Technology at the US Department of Education. Reprinted with permission. Full map available at www.school2-0.org.

your turn

Our next book will focus on the many uses of Web 2.0 tools in our schools. In the spirit of Web 2.0, it is our hope that educators like you will not only actively engage in the promise of these new technologies, but will tell the world about your dreams, practical experiences, ideas, and actual plans for integrating Web 2.0 tools into classroom curriculum, professional development, school-based assessment, and administrative activities. While there are unlimited ways that these new technologies can make a difference, the real difference begins with you.

Please send your lessons, success stories, tutorials, and ideas to us at gwen_and_lynne_book2@yahoo.com.

►►

10
tutorials

In chapter 3, we discussed Web 2.0 tools such as basic applications for word processing, spreadsheets, and presentations; new communication tools including blogs and wikis; and creative tools such as those used for photo editing, audio editing, and drawing. A more extensive compendium of tools is listed in appendix B. This chapter introduces tutorials for just a few representative tools that you can use when you're ready to get started.

► ► ► ► ►

The tutorials in this chapter previously appeared elsewhere and were contributed to this book by their authors. Some tutorials came from techLEARNING.com, especially from Barbara Bray's Professional Development QuickTips (PDQ) section. Some were contributed by the people who developed the applications or Web sites, such as the Class Blogmeister tutorial by David Warlick. And some were adapted from Google, the home of so many wonderful resources for educators, and were reviewed by Google staff.

As we plan the second book in this series, we look to our readers for new tutorials, lessons, and narratives about Web 2.0 use. Maybe we'll see you online.

web-based word processor: Zoho Writer

Have you ever worked on a computer that didn't have a word processor? In the old way of doing things, a word processor was an essential tool for just about any home or classroom computer, but Web 2.0 could change all that. In fact, if your computer has Internet access, you can write with a Web-based word processor, right now. Zoho Writer's Online Word Processor (www.zohowriter.com) provides all the tools you need to write and e-mail your document to yourself or save it in your online document folder.

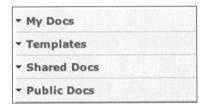

Try it as a demo user or sign up for free. Start a new document or choose from My Docs, My Templates, or Shared Documents. If you are a demo user, when you look at the left navigation panel you can see new documents created by others who are trying the program.

Zoho Writer has the same features as most word processors. Click New to bring up a blank file or select Import to load text from a different word processor. You can save your work as either a document or a template, and preview your work before you save or print.

You can format the text by choosing font type, size, style, and attributes; align or justify text; create bulleted and numbered lists; cut, copy, and paste; and undo or redo actions.

Click the Link icon to add a link to a Web site. You can also insert a table, add an image, check the spelling, find and replace words, add an emoticon, and toggle HTML source code.

Share Document

Insert /Enter the E-mail address of your friends to share

E-mail Subject | Document Shared to You o ☐ Specify Content

Give permission for shared members ○ Read Only ⊙ Read/Write

Share   Close

▶ All Zoho Writer images are © 2007 AdventNet, Inc.

Zoho Writer not only lets you create your own documents but also allows you to share your documents to collaborate with others. You give permission for your friends to read only or to read and write on your document.

web-based spreadsheet: Num Sum

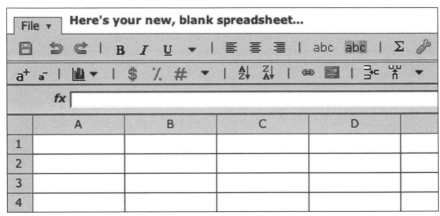

▶ © Num Sum

Have you wanted to be able to create and share a spreadsheet—online? Num Sum (www.numsum.com) is a Web-based spreadsheet application with many of the same features as Excel, as well as some pretty cool social aspects tied in. This means you can share reports, track reports, or do any number of other things you could do with a desktop spreadsheet such as Excel. Num Sum lets you input formulas, links, and other information into a spreadsheet. If you want, you can even post the spreadsheet to your blog.

Here's how it works:

❶ Name the spreadsheet.

❷ Add a description, an optional choice.

❸ Add tags—also optional—so you can share your spreadsheet.

After you create your spreadsheet you can save it so you can use it or share it with others. Search Num Sum to find other spreadsheets that you can use.

open-source painting tool: Tux Paint

Tux Paint (www.newbreedsoftware.com/tuxpaint/) is a free, downloadable, open-source painting tool that will take you back to the early Kid Pix days. It runs on both Mac and Windows systems and is a lot of fun.

To get started, download the software and go to the starter page.

Tux Paint is so easy to use with the tools and brushes on both sides of the empty canvas. The canvas is 640 x 480 and ready to go. There are even ready-to-paint coloring starter pictures like this chicken.

The Penguin tool at the bottom gives you tips on how to use the program. The drawing tools are similar to those in Kid Pix: line tools, shapes, even stamps that are very real, along with Magic tools that say what they do. When you save, you can see the pictures as thumbnails. You can also print the drawings and use them with other programs.

▶ © New Breed Software

editing sound: do you have Audacity?

Audacity (http://sourceforge.net/projects/audacity/) is a free audio editor and recorder for Windows, Mac OS X, GNU/Linux, and other operating systems. Now you can create podcasts and modify any sound. Just download to your desktop and follow the GNU General Public License (www.gnu.org/licenses/licenses.html#GPL).

You can use Audacity to:

▶ Record live audio

▶ Convert tapes and records into digital recordings or CDs

▶ Edit Ogg Vorbis, MP3, and WAV sound files

▶ Cut, copy, splice, and mix sounds together

▶ Change the speed or pitch of a recording

When you import a file, it will look like the following figure.

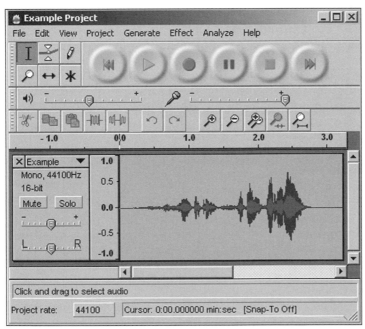

▶ © 2007 members of the Audacity development team

- ▶ You can listen to the recording by hitting the play, pause, and stop buttons.

- ▶ You can cut, copy, and paste selections.

- ▶ You can highlight the area that you would like to copy or cut.

- ▶ You can add multiple tracks.

Some tips:

❶ Audacity writes all the changed and recorded audio to a directory called Projectname_data, which is located right where you saved the project file itself. To rename your file, click Save and type in the new name.

❷ Audacity can import WAV, AIFF, AU, IRCAM, MP3, and OGG files. There are three ways to import files: drag and drop the audio file, go to Project and click on Import Audio, or select CTRL-I (PC) or Command-I (MAC).

❸ Always make a copy of the original before editing.

syndication in Firefox: RSS feeds

How do you keep up-to-date with all the information on the Internet? Because we are so busy as professional developers and technology coordinators, wouldn't it be great to have the latest news and features delivered directly to us, rather than clicking from site to site? The answer is RSS, or Really Simple Syndication.

Subscribing to an RSS feed is simple. With Firefox (www.mozilla.com/firefox/), you can create a Live Bookmark, which is easy with version 1.5 or newer. Firefox auto-detects some feeds and then provides a shortcut for subscribing by placing an orange icon either at the bottom right of the browser or in the address bar.

Here's how to add a feed from The New York Times to the Bookmarks Toolbar:

Go to www.nytimes.com/services/xml/rss/.

Click on the orange icon to bring up a list of the feeds. The following figure shows a list.

> Add 'Education' as Live Bookmark...
> Add 'Fashion & Style' as Live Bookmark...
> Add 'Health' as Live Bookmark...
> Add 'Home & Garden' as Live Bookmark...
> Add 'International' as Live Bookmark...
> Add 'Magazine' as Live Bookmark...
> Add 'Media & Advertising' as Live Bookmark...
> Add 'Most E-mailed Articles' as Live Bookmark...
> Add 'Movie News' as Live Bookmark...
> Add 'Movie Reviews' as Live Bookmark...
> Add 'Multimedia' as Live Bookmark...
> Add 'National' as Live Bookmark...

Selecting a feed brings up Add a Live Bookmark to the Bookmarks Toolbar folder.

It is OK to change the name so you know what the feed is.

Now the feed shows on your toolbar. Click on it and the latest international news feeds appear.

▶ All images on this page are © Mozilla.

del.icio.us bookmarks and favorites

Would you like to keep your favorites online and also have access to other people's bookmarks? del.icio.us (http://del.icio.us/) is a great place for you—and everyone else—to collect and share their favorite bookmarks. Use del.icio.us to:

▶ Store links to your favorite sites, articles, blogs, music, restaurant reviews, and more, and access them on the Web from any computer.

▶ Share favorites with friends, family, and colleagues.

▶ Discover new things with less work. Other del.icio.us users may have already found and posted exactly what you're looking for.

Tag your bookmarks. Tags are one-word descriptors that are assigned to a bookmark. Tags can't contain quotation marks or white space, but are otherwise unrestricted. You can assign any number of tags to a bookmark, and rename, delete, add, or merge tags together. If you want to post an article about reading and literature circles, just tag it with "reading" and "literaturecircles" or whatever other tags you'd want to use to find it again.

Bundle your tags. Bundles are a way to group together common tags. For instance, if you have the tags "stories," "literaturecircles," and "vocabulary," you may want to group these together into a bundle called "reading."

Set up your network. Your network connects you to other del.icio.us users. You can add friends, family, or anyone you find while exploring del.icio.us to your network and keep track of their latest bookmarks right here. And you can share new bookmarks with people in your network simply by clicking on their username when you save. "Your fans" is your reverse network—a list of people who have added you to their network.

Set up del.icio.us buttons. You can add two useful buttons (bookmarklets) to your browser's bookmarks toolbar. The Post to del.icio.us button posts the current page to your list and the My del.icio.us button lets you quickly view your bookmarks.

You can set up the my del.icio.us bookmark by dragging the JavaScript information to your bookmarks folder that you have available when you sign up. There is also a way to make MP3 files play on any page by dragging del.icio.us related files to your bookmark.

There are instructions available for different browsers including Internet Explorer, Firefox, Safari, and Opera.

photo editing: Photo Story 3 for Windows

Breathe life into your digital photos by adding music, narration, motion, and more, using Photo Story 3 for Windows. Go to www.microsoft.com/photostory/ to download the free program. Note, however, that it is recommended for Windows XP with 512 MB RAM.

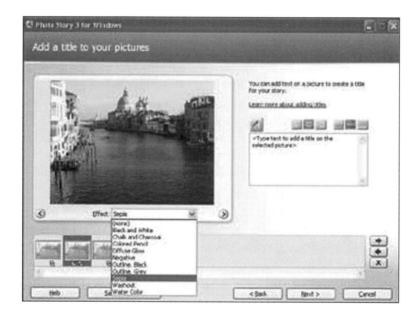

Photo Story 3 for Windows will allow you to:

- ▶ Capture your pictures from your digital camera or scanner and organize them into your own personal storybook.

- ▶ Use photo-editing tools to remove red-eye, correct lighting, and crop.

- ▶ Record your own voice to tell your story in your own words.

- ▶ Use custom panning and zooming options.

- ▶ Choose songs from the music library to add personality to your photo story.

- Add special effects and transitions to your pictures, even flips and page curls like the professionals.

- Write captions and titles for your slides.

- Share your stories on the Web, send them by e-mail, burn them to a CD, and even put them on your PDA or mobile phone.

Wikispaces for educators

Wikispaces for Educators (www.wikispaces.com/site/for/teachers) is free for K–12 education use. It offers a simple interface and a visual page editor. Community collaboration is the focus of this tool.

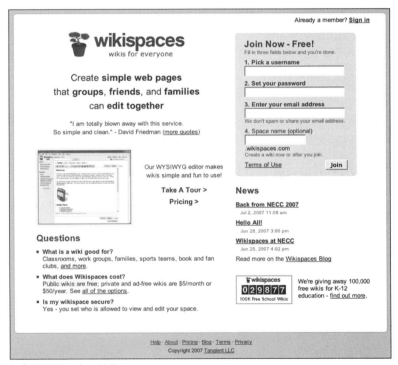

▶ © 2007 Tangient LLC

Here's how it works:

Pages

Each wikispace may contain many pages. Each page is a single Web page that can contain content and can link to other pages.

Creating Pages

To create a new page within the current space, use the Make a New Page link in the sidebar or just create a link to the new page in the editor. When you create a space, you'll start with one blank page called home. Click Edit to add content to that page.

Note that the Make a New Page link will be present only if you are a registered user and have logged in.

Editing Pages

Each editable page on Wikispaces has an Edit button at the top of the page. Click on the Edit button to bring up the page editor. The page editor allows you to add text and pictures to a page and to format that page. The editor has a visual mode and a plain text mode.

Class Blogmeister:
adding and editing blog articles

Class Blogmeister (http://classblogmeister.com) is an online blogging tool that was designed for educational use. It allows teachers to assess, comment on, and publish student blogs in a controlled environment. The program can be mastered in four simple steps.

Step 1

When you are ready to start a new blog article or edit an existing article, go to the Edit blog page (log in from the main Blogmeister page), and click the Articles tab. The article form will appear, enabling you to start a new blog or to continue work on an existing one. To begin a new blog article, simply type a title for the article in the textbox labeled Title, and begin typing the article into the larger scrolling textbox.

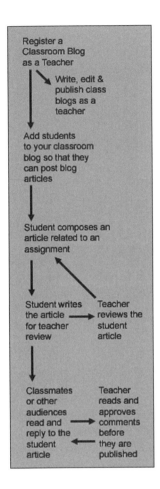

It may be a good practice to write your original blog article using a word processor so that you will have access to the spelling and grammar checkers and a thesaurus. Then when the article is finished, copy the text from the word processor and paste it into the blog textbox. To edit an existing article, click the article title in the listing below the textboxes. The title and text of the article will appear in the textboxes so that you can begin editing. Again, editing with a word processor will ensure fewer spelling and grammar errors.

Step 2

You can process blog articles in a number of ways. If you have begun editing your blog article, but must leave your work to finish later, simply click the Save button without clicking the Publish checkbox. This will save the article under your account, without its being published to the public. When you are finally ready for the article to go public, then check the Publish checkbox and click Save.

The list of articles includes three columns of indicators.

▸ The first column, Pub, will display an asterisk (*) for articles that are published and public.

▸ The Cmmt column displays the number of comments that have been posted to the article and approved for public viewing by you.

▸ The Cmmt Pndng column indicates the number of comments that have been posted to the article but have not been approved for public viewing.

Step 3

Working with comments is easy with Blogmeister. When someone comments on one of your blog articles, you will receive an e-mail message indicating that the comment has been made. The e-mail message will include the text of the reader's comment and a hyperlink to a page where you will be able to read the new addition as well as show the comment, delete the comment, or keep the comment hidden.

Step 4

To review your comments, go to the Edit blog page and click the Articles tab. In the list of existing blog articles, click the triangular twisty icon to the left of the title you wish to review. All comments posted to that article will appear. To the right of each article are links labeled Show and Delete. If the comment would not be appropriate for public viewing, click Delete. This will remove the comment from the database. If the comment is appropriate, then click Show. If you wish to continue considering the article, then leave it alone for the time being.

Select a Blog Article to Edit:

Date	Title	Pub	Cmmt	Cmmt Pndng	
▼ 12/08	Education Radio -- School Style	*	0	5	
	Socrates Crab | 12-15-04 OK. I think you are right here on this one and only this one point. (63)				Show Delete
	Appleton Snodgrasse | 12-15-04 Outstanding concept. I think that this is absolutely great great great! (61)				Show Delete
	Appleton Snodgrasse | 12-15-04 Outstanding concept. I think that this is absolutely great great great! (60)				Show Delete
	Appleton Snodgrasse | 12-15-04 Outstanding concept. I think that this is absolutely great great great! (59)				Show Delete
	Claude Claudison | 12-15-04 This is totally cool! I want one. (58)				Show Delete
▶ 12/05	What I think today...	*	2	2	
▶ 12/04	First Blog in December	*	0	0	

▶ All Class Blogmeister images are a service of David Warlick & The Landmark Project.

geography: Google Earth

Those who use Google Earth (http://earth.google.com) discover that the world is smaller than they think. The free, downloadable program combines satellite images, maps, and the power of Google Search for easy exploration of any point on our planet:

▶ Type in an address and zoom right in.

▶ Tilt and rotate the view to see 3D terrain and buildings.

▶ Search for schools, parks, restaurants, and hotels.

▶ Get driving directions.

▶ Explore rich multimedia content from sources such as National Geographic and Discovery education.

▶ Save and share your searches and favorites. Even add your own annotations.

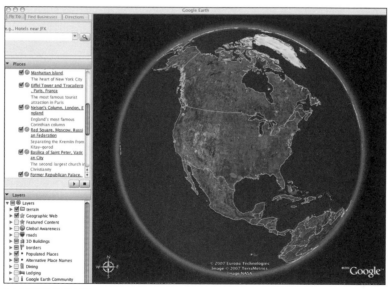

▶ View from space

▶ New York City

▶ Closer into New York City

▶ Empire State Building tilted and in 3D
All Google Earth images are © Google.

What a great way for you and your students to learn geography. You'll keep asking: Is this real? How do they do that?

creating graphics: Google SketchUp

You can show teachers how to design a do-it-yourself project that they can then show their students to build graphic skills. Google SketchUp (http://sketchup.google. com/product_suf.html) is a free, easy-to-learn modeling program that enables you to create three-dimensional models of houses, sheds, decks, home additions, woodworking projects—even spaceships. After you've built your models, you can place them in Google Earth, post them to the 3D Warehouse (http://sketchup. google.com/product_3dwh.html), or print hard copies. Google SketchUp features include the following:

- ▶ Click on a shape and push or pull it to create your 3D geometry.

- ▶ Experiment with color and texture on your model.

- ▶ Cast a shadow to see where the sun falls as you model.

- ▶ Select from thousands of predrawn components.

The Push/Pull tool lets you expand the volume of geometry in your models.

① Select the Push/Pull tool. The cursor will change to a 3D rectangle with an up arrow.

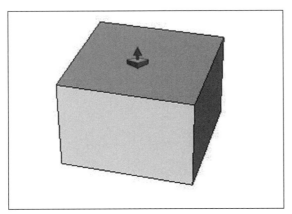

▶ © Google

❶ Click on the face that you want to expand or decrease.

❷ Move the cursor to create (or decrease) volume.

You can even create a measuring tape to measure your designs.

❶ Select the Measure tool.

❷ Click and hold on the starting point of the distance you wish to measure.

❸ Drag the mouse to the endpoint of the measurement.

❹ Release the mouse to obtain a measurement.

For more information, visit the video tutorials at http://sketchup.google.com/products.html.

Google Reader

Web sites publish lists of updates—called "feeds"—that indicate when new content has been posted. When you subscribe to a feed, Google Reader (www.google.com/reader/) starts monitoring that feed for updates. You don't have to give any personal information, it doesn't cost a dime, and it's easy to unsubscribe.

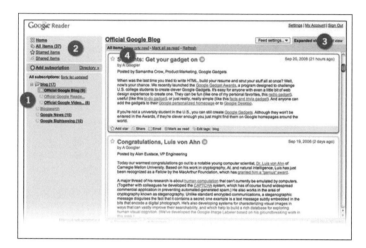

Here's how it works:

❶ The left side of the screen displays your subscriptions. Each subscription has a count of all unread posts, which indicates how many new items are available to read. Clicking on a subscription shows you items from that subscription.

❷ The "All items" link shows you items from all of your subscriptions. You can choose to auto-sort this list so that feeds with few posts (for example a friend's blog) rise above feeds that post more frequently. This allows you to catch those posts that might otherwise fall into the background because of other high-volume subscriptions.

❸ The right side of the screen displays your items. You can choose to display your items in list view or expanded view. The compact list view allows you to quickly skim the latest headlines, while the expanded view displays the full content of the items.

❹ By default Google Reader displays all items, but you may prefer to show only new items—that way, things you've already read don't keep you from finding new content.

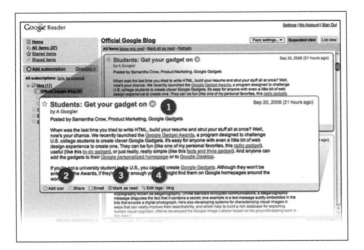

Managing your information:

❶ Click the gray arrow button to view the original source for an item. This is particularly useful if a feed only includes snippets or links.

❷ Just like in Gmail (Google e-mail), you can star your items by clicking the star. The star can be useful for many things, like indicating an item you want to read later or marking your favorite posts.

Clicking the Share button adds the item to your public page. Your public page is an easy way to share items of interest with your friends and family.

The E-mail button allows you to e-mail the item to a specific person (this requires a Gmail account).

❸ In list view, items are marked as read when you click on them. In expanded view, items are marked as read when you scroll past them. Uncheck the mark-as-read box to leave the item unread.

❹ Tags provide a way to organize items that interest you.

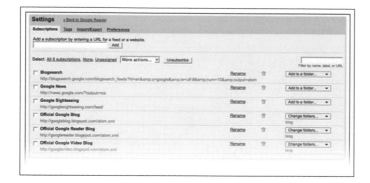

The Settings page allows you to manage your subscriptions. You can rename them, delete them, or group them by folders.

You can also manage your tags, including making some of them public so you can share them with your friends.

The Goodies section contains a number of useful tools, including instructions on how to add Google Reader to your personalized home page or access it with your mobile phone.

The Import/Export section allows you to import your subscriptions from another feed reader.

From www.google.com/help/reader/help.html. ©*Google*

web timeline

Adapted from Fifteen Years of the Web, by BBC News
http://news.bbc.co.uk/1/hi/technology/5243862.stm

AUGUST 6, 1991

Tim Berners Lee, a scientist at the world's largest particle physics laboratory, the European Organization for Nuclear Research (known as CERN), formally introduced his World Wide Web project to the world on the alt.hypertext newsgroup.

DECEMBER 12, 1991

Following a trip to CERN, where he met Tim Berners Lee, scientist Paul Kunz of the Stanford Linear Accelerator Center in the U.S. was inspired to set up North America's first Web server.

NOVEMBER 1992

26 Web servers were online.

APRIL 22, 1993

Mosaic, the first Web browser to run on the Windows operating system, was released. Developed at the National Center for Supercomputing Applications in Illinois, it provided a user-friendly way to navigate Internet information.

APRIL 30, 1993

CERN announced that the World Wide Web could be used for free by anyone. Tim Berners Lee and Robert Cailliau persuaded CERN to provide the Web technology and program code for free so that anyone could use and improve it. The decision is credited as one of the key reasons the Web grew so quickly.

MAY 1993

The Tech, published by students at the Massachusetts Institute of Technology, became the first online newspaper.

JUNE 1993

Hypertext markup language (HTML), used to create Web pages, was released.

NOVEMBER 1993

The Webcam went online. It was set up by a group of computer scientists at Cambridge University to watch a coffee pot.

FEBRUARY 1994

The precursor to Yahoo, started by two Stanford University students, went online. Called Jerry's Guide to the World Wide Web, it was originally described as a site featuring a hierarchical directory of other sites.

OCTOBER 13, 1994

President Bill Clinton put whitehouse.gov on the Web.

OCTOBER 25, 1994

Banner advertisements for AT&T and a drink called Zima appeared on Web sites.

JULY 1, 1995

The online book store Amazon.com was launched. Originally founded as Cadabra.com by Jeff Bezos in 1994, it was one of the first major companies to sell goods on the Web.

AUGUST 1995

18,957 Web sites were online.

AUGUST 9, 1995

The dotcom boom began on the stock markets, and a number of Web companies went public. The Web browser company Netscape received the third largest ever NASDAQ IPO share value.

AUGUST 24, 1995

Microsoft's Internet Explorer was released as part of Windows 95.

SEPTEMBER 4, 1995

The online auction site eBay was founded by computer programmer Pierre Omidyar as AuctionWeb. The first item ever sold was a broken laser pointer.

DECEMBER 15, 1995

The first multilingual search engine Alta Vista was launched.

JULY 4, 1996

Hotmail was launched on Independence Day in the U.S.

AUGUST 1996

342,081 Web sites were online.

DECEMBER 17, 1997

Web commentator Jorn Barger coined the term Weblog, later shortened to blog.

MARCH 1, 1998

Kozmo.com was founded by investment bankers and promised free one-hour delivery of anything from DVDs to coffee. The company raised about $280 million including $60 million from Amazon.com. Many analysts pointed out that the business model would not work. The company collapsed in April 2001, one of the casualties of the bursting dotcom bubble.

SEPTEMBER 1998

Google opened its first office in a garage in California. Larry Page and Sergey Brin, two postgraduate students at Stanford University, began the search engine as a research project that analyzed the relationships between Web sites to rank their importance.

OCTOBER 19, 1998

Open Diary, the first blog community, launched.

JUNE 1, 1999

Shawn Fanning, a student in Boston who founded Napster, released the first widely used peer-to-peer file-sharing service. Fanning wrote the original program at college to allow himself and his friends to find and share MP3 files. It immediately caught the attention of the recording industry, which accused it of massive copyright theft. After a protracted legal battle, the service was shut down in July 2001.

AUGUST 19, 1999

MySpace was originally an online storage and file-sharing firm that launched in 1999 but was shut down in 2001. The social-networking site in its present form launched in July 2003. It now has more than 100 million users. The site lets users build a personalized home page and allows for blogs, photos, music, and messaging. In 2005, media tycoon Rupert Murdoch paid $580 million for the site.

JANUARY 10, 2000

AOL bought Time Warner; it was the largest corporate merger ever.

JANUARY 14, 2000

The dotcom bubble had been growing since 1997. The excitement surrounding the Web caused share prices to soar. In January 2000 it reached its peak when the Dow Jones Industrial Average closed at a record level. On March 10 the NASDAQ Composite Index also reached an all-time high. Soon after, the markets began to crash and with it went many of the start-up companies bankrolled during the dotcom boom.

AUGUST 2000

Nearly 20 million Web sites were online.

JANUARY 11, 2001

A Grateful Dead track demonstrated podcasting for the first time.

JANUARY 15, 2001

Jimmy Wales founded the online encyclopedia Wikipedia.

SEPTEMBER 4, 2001

Google was awarded a patent for its PageRank algorithm used in its search engine.

APRIL 28, 2003

Apple launched its iTunes music download service.

JANUARY 27, 2004

Amazon.com made its first ever full year profit since its launch.

AUGUST 19, 2004

Google went public. Shares were offered at $85. Fifteen months later they were worth more than $400 each.

NOVEMBER 9, 2004

The Mozilla Firefox Web browser was launched.

FEBRUARY 2005

The video-sharing site YouTube.com went online.

OCTOBER 2005

The Web grew more in 2005 than during the whole dotcom boom. 17 million new sites went online.

APRIL 12, 2006

Google launched a restricted service in China called Gu Ge.

OCTOBER 9, 2006

Google acquired YouTube for $1.65 billion.

OCTOBER 31, 2006

Google acquired the Web 2.0 wiki tool JotSpot.

NOVEMBER 2006

By November 5, 2006, the number of Web sites had surpassed the 100 million mark.

B

web 2.0 tools

Blogging

Blogger (www.blogger.com). A really easy-to-use site that allows even non-technical types to start a blog in just three basic steps using a range of templates. The site was started in the dotcom boom of 1999 and is now part of Google.

Class Blogmeister (http://classblogmeister.com). David Warlick created this site specifically for classroom educators who want full control over the blogs created by, read by, and used by students. Teachers can evaluate, comment on, and publish students' blogs entries in a controlled environment.

Drupal (http://drupal.org). Drupal is software that allows an individual or a community of users to publish, manage, and organize content on a Web site. It can enable blogs, collaborative authoring environments, content management systems, forums, newsletters, and picture galleries.

Edublogs (http://edublogs.org). An easy-to-use blog-creation site with customizable templates (themes) for educators, K–12 and college students. Blogs created with it will include links to Chalkface, an assessment tool; to IncSub, dedicated to online projects; and to BlogSavvy, which helps bloggers become better bloggers.

Gaggle Blogs (www.gaggle.net). Part of Gaggle.net, dedicated to providing a safe e-mail experience for students, this site also provides a great deal of control over content. Blogs are filtered for inappropriate words and phrases and scanned for pornographic content, and all links are checked for pornographic content. Offending entries are blocked and sent to the administrator.

Wikis

Jotspot (www.jotspot.com/learn/). Recently purchased by Google, Jotspot has more features than other wiki sites, and is intended for businesses as well as education. Jotspot allows users to create Web-based spreadsheets, calendars, documents, and photo galleries, all without having to know HTML. It also offers varied levels of access from read-only to full editing.

Pbwiki (www.pbwiki.com). The site's slogan is "Make a free wiki as easily as a peanut butter sandwich." Educators can use the wiki to create a multi-user Web page or to have students write online collaborative essays or develop PowerPoint presentations. Basic wikis are free, and wikis with extra features are available for a fee.

Wikispaces (www.wikispaces.com/site/for/teachers/). Another site dedicated to educators, it offers sites with three levels of security: public (viewable by all), protected (viewable by all but editable by members only), and private (viewable and editable by members only). It is free to educators.

Aggregators

Bloglines (www.bloglines.com). Students can learn how quickly information changes if they allow Bloglines to deliver the RSS feeds for whichever sites they register. This is especially appropriate if they are researching current events, science, and other swiftly changing topics. The site allows users to share their feeds with others.

Google Reader (www.google.com/reader/). This aggregator from Google allows users to keep up with the latest on Web sites without laboriously searching for new information each day.

Social Bookmarking

Backflip (www.backflip.com). Students can collaborate to create folders of bookmarked URLs, which can be made public or have limited access. The site offers "My Daily Routine," allowing users to easily visit the sites they mark as daily necessities.

Blinklist (www.blinklist.com). Educators can create individual lists of recommended sites by tagging bookmarked sites. They can also create and serve as a moderator for a collective Blinklist Space, to which students can contribute recommended sites.

del.icio.us (http://del.icio.us/). Bookmarking a site is an excellent idea, and using del.icio.us allows people to store and find bookmarks from any computer with Internet access. Using tags helps users organize bookmarks into virtual folders, which is helpful for group research projects.

Furl (www.furl.net). Calling itself "Your Personal Web File," this site allows users to save a Web page and to easily find it again by using either the site's "canned" tags or unique tags, as many as desired. To find a site, users search for their tag, and to see what others have been saving, they search the Tagstream.

Simpy (www.simpy.com). This site emphasizes the social aspect of bookmarking, allowing users to locate like-minded people by virtue of their tags and even create a Watchlist to see what interesting sites they have bookmarked. It also constantly checks for broken links and compiles a list.

Spurl (www.spurl.net). Spurl-ing a Web page does more than save its URL. It also saves a copy of that page. Thus, should the URL change or the link be broken, the information on that page will still be available. Spurl files are Web based, but may also be downloaded and saved on a hard drive. The site offers a full-text search of all your Spurled pages.

File Sharing

Allmydata (http://allmydata.com). This is more file backup than file sharing. The site creates either a fixed permanent version of files or dynamic backups, which are updated as users make changes to the files on their hard drives. It also employs "grid-storage," asking users to share storage space on their hard drives.

Glide Personal (http://glidedigital.com). Permits the sharing of pictures, music, and even document files. According to the site, when such files are uploaded they are available both in Glide Personal and in the appropriate environment for that medium, such as Glide Music or Glide Docs.

Google Docs and Spreadsheets (http://docs.google.com). This is a Web-based word processing and spreadsheet program that keeps documents current and lets the people you choose update files from their own computers. Users may either import existing files or create new files from scratch, and multiple users may edit the same file simultaneously.

Openomy (http://openomy.com). Rather than e-mailing files to members of a group, people can store them on the Web and provide degrees of access to various users. Adding tags maintains the relationships among files by assigning them to virtual folders.

Xdrive (http://xdrive.com). This site performs automatic backups and file sharing with levels of access controlled by the user. Users decide who is invited and who can view, edit, and upload designated folders stored in the Xdrive. You can even use your shared folder as a virtual space to work together on the same project.

Photo and Drawing

GIMP (www.gimp.org). GIMP stands for GNU Image Manipulation Program, an open-source, UNIX-based, free piece of software from the GNU program. It offers a range of powerful photo-editing tools at no cost.

Google SketchUp (http://sketchup.google.com). This sophisticated drawing tool is ideal for creating three-dimensional models of houses, schools, and other objects in a community for a classroom project and placing them into Google Earth. It offers "real-time" shadow-casting and thousands of predrawn components.

iPhoto (www.apple.com/iphoto/). One of the many reasons Mac devotees are so loyal is this powerful photo-manipulation software that does so much, including organize photos, edit and add special effects, create slideshows, and publish to the Web.

Microsoft Photo Story 3 for Windows (www.microsoft.com/photostory/). This powerful and free download allows users to create super slideshows (with motion, music, and narrative) from just a set of digital photographs. It is an excellent tool for student presentations.

Picasa (http://picasa.google.com). A very powerful—and free—download for organizing photos, for performing minor enhancements (lighting, contrast), as well as for creating photo collages, e-mailing, burning CDs, and publishing to the Web. Using labels (tags), users may create all sorts of virtual folders.

Tux Paint (www.tuxpaint.org). Geared to a younger clientele, Tux Paint provides a colorful, easy-to-use, and fun online drawing application with some relatively sophisticated features such as Magic tools (they create realistic bricks, grass, and mirror images), plus Rubber Stamp, Shape Tool, and lots more.

Photo Sharing

Flickr (www.flickr.com). Although commonly thought of as a place to show off one's prowess as a photographer, Flickr can be very useful for group work. The Organizr feature, for instance, allows individuals to add photos to a group pool. Photos can also be organized by tags, which would make for some collaborative decision-making.

WebShots (www.Webshots.com). Permits uploading of photos as well as downloading, which could be useful for students compiling presentations. Also useful are the photos in the News/Current Events section.

Zoto (http://zoto.com). The site claims that it "supports more blogging sites than any other service" and that it publishes to Blogger, TypePad, and WordPress. It also permits Geo-tags, which plot the location of a photo on a map, a useful tool for social studies projects.

Video

EyeSpot (www.eyespot.com). The site's slogan is "Movie Making For All Of Us," and it adheres to that slogan by providing easy-to-use editing tools for producing sophisticated finished products. The site advocates sharing by posting finished films to blogs, and allows users to view such posted films.

Grouper (www.grouper.com). Setting this site apart from the others is its acceptance of video from Webcams, which are much less expensive than digital cameras. However, it is more focused on letting users view videos and offers fewer slick editing features.

JumpCut (www.jumpcut.com). More than just a place to upload videos, JumpCut actually helps users to create video and even to "borrow" parts of public videos for their finished product, which may then be shared with the world or made private with restricted access. The site encourages budding directors to write stories explaining their digital creations.

VideoEgg (www.videoegg.com). This site focuses on ease of uploading, and offers an instructional clip (a nice touch) demonstrating that a video may be uploaded from a camcorder, Webcam, or mobile phone in less than two minutes.

Video Furnace (www.videofurnace.com). This program brings live video to any Internet-connected networked computer and does not require any software to be stored on the hard drive, as the viewing software is part of the video stream. This makes it platform-independent, accommodating PCs, Macs, and Linux-based computers.

YouTube (www.youtube.com). Purchased by Google in 2006, this video-display and sharing site has become the most popular of the group. It is the place to be seen. Unlike some others, it is used for storing and displaying videos only and offers no editing capabilities.

Web-based Word Processing

ajaxWrite (www.ajaxwrite.com). The two big advantages are that the program can read and create MS Word files, and it has the look and feel of MS Word, making it more intuitive and eliminating the need to learn a new program. In addition, it allows files to be saved to one's own computer as well as to the server. Note that it requires the Mozilla Firefox browser, version 1.5 or higher, but that browser is available as a free download from Mozilla (www.mozilla.com/firefox/).

Google Docs and Spreadsheets (http://docs.google.com). The word-processing part of this program was once known as Writely. It enables users to import and edit existing documents and spreadsheets or to create new ones from scratch. Users can share changes in real time or invite others to make changes together at the same time.

Writeboard (http://writeboard.com). This site makes it easy to compare several users' versions of a document, as saved edits never overwrite an earlier version. A link to each edit is visible in the sidebar. Select two (or more) and click Compare. It is excellent for peer editing.

Zoho Writer (http://zohowriter.com). As the site says, "Access, edit, share documents from anywhere." The program accepts a wide range of file formats, including PDF, RTF, and even HTML. It also offers support for multiple languages, a significant advantage for ELL classes.

Language Arts—Creative Writing

FanFiction.Net (www.fanfiction.net). Users submit a work of fiction in any of a huge range of categories. Others then read and review the submitted content.

glypho (www.glypho.com). Think of it as a collaborative, peer-edited fiction-writing site. Users may submit an original idea for a plot or add to one of the stories already submitted. Possibilities include creating new characters, plot twists, or entire chapters. Users also rate the postings.

Web-based Spreadsheets

Google Docs and Spreadsheets (http://docs.google.com). Although it lacks charting and graphing capability, it does offer the ability to sort data, the ability to work in various typefaces and colors, and the ability to insert pre-set formulas or functions.

Numbler (http://numbler.com). A big advantage of Numbler is its similarity to the look and feel of MS Excel. Multiple users can work with a spreadsheet, view changes in real time, discuss changes, and edit the master. Users can import data from and export data to desktop spreadsheet applications.

Num Sum (http://numsum.com). Num Sum allows people to create and then share a spreadsheet. One person starts it and e-mails the specific URL to others. It also permits spreadsheets to be added to a blog.

Zoho Sheet (www.zohosheet.com). This tool has charting and graphing capabilities plus Web 2.0 features such as tagging and publishing.

Presentation Tools

Microsoft Photo Story 3 for Windows (www.microsoft.com/photostory/). This powerful and free download allows users to create super slideshows with motion, music, and narrative from a set of digital photographs. It is an excellent tool for student presentations.

SlideShare (www.slideshare.net). Teachers may create a mini-lesson slideshow to explain or enhance a concept, and student teams may create their presentations and post them. Presentations are accessible from any computer, and users are able to post comments.

Thumbstacks.com (www.thumbstacks.com). Allows users to create presentations in their Web browser and then share them simply by publishing the URL. Early versions may lack some of the bells and whistles to which MS PowerPoint users are accustomed.

Zoho Show (www.zohoshow.com). Three major features: (1) import existing presentations, done either in MS PowerPoint or in OpenOffice Presentation, (2) edit collaboratively from any computer, and (3) embed the finished presentation into a user's blog or Web site. It also allows users to access their photos stored on the Flickr photo-sharing site.

Desktop Tools

TheOpenCD (www.theopencd.org). These free and open-source programs cover the most common tasks such as word processing, presentations, e-mail, Web browsing, Web design, and image manipulation. The organization claims they are tested for stability and are appropriate for a wide audience.

OpenOffice.org (www.openoffice.org). Sounding almost too good to be true, OpenOffice.org is a multiplatform and multilingual office suite and an open-source project. Compatible with all other major office suites, it is free to download, use, and distribute. The components include word-processing, presentation, mathematical function creating, vector drawing, spreadsheet, and database software.

Surveys and Polls

Zoho Polls (www.zohopolls.com). An excellent tool for social studies and language arts classes. Users create a poll, publish it to the Web, and wait for respondents to vote. Classes may create their own pools or search for polls using tags.

Search Tools

Google Notebook (www.google.com/notebook/). No more laborious and frustrating copying and pasting from Web pages to a Word or Excel file! This new tool allows users to clip and save text, images, and other Web data to one or more Notebooks without leaving the site. The Notebooks are accessible from any computer with access to the Web, they can be organized and edited, and they can be made either public or private.

Grokker (http://live.grokker.com/grokker.html). Enter a search term and Grokker searches Yahoo, Wikipedia, and even Amazon.com to return an impressive set of results in outline format, with major categories expandable. Clicking on any item in the outline produces an annotated list of clickable links in a frame to the right.

Rollyo (http://rollyo.com). Not only does it allow customizable searches from a variety of sources (top news sites, tech news, reference, health, etc.) but it incorporates aspects of the "social" Web by allowing users to share search "rolls" (its term for a completed search) as well as view and even edit others' search rolls.

Squidoo (www.squidoo.com). This tool allows users to find or create personal searches called Lenses. A Lens on the 1962 Cuban Missile Crisis included complete details by the Lens Master plus links to various news sources, film clips of President Kennedy, books on Amazon.com, and even items for sale on eBay.

Technorati (www.technorati.com). This tool specializes in searching through the 57+ million blogs out there, and also highlights the videos to which many blogs are currently pointing at any one moment.

Task Management

Ta-da Lists (www.tadalist.com). Offers the option of sharing lists with the world or just with a few people. Educators can maintain a list of lists to determine the status of various projects in a particular class. One unusual feature—a dot before each list indicates progress or lack of same. The larger the dot the more is left to do on that particular list.

Voo2do (www.voo2do.com). Useful for managing collaborative projects involving a large number of participants. The Collaborative Contexts feature includes a person column that reveals who is responsible for a particular task.

Online Calendars

CalanderHub (http://calendarhub.com). This site's self-promotion implies that it is designed for today's really time-stressed families (you can create reminders for all your children's scheduled activities), but students and teachers can make use of its features, especially the capability to publish a calendar to the Web and make it either public or private.

Google Calendar (http://calendar.google.com). This site allows users to set up separate calendars for each class and share them with designated groups of students, parents, or the entire community. It can include information about class topics and descriptions for each session, assignment deadlines, test and quiz dates, field trips, and other activities. Administrators can keep students and families updated on events. It can also be useful for managing group projects.

WebCalendar (www.k5n.us/webcalendar.php). This is a PHP-based calendar configurable for use by individuals or groups. It can even be used as an event calendar for visitors to a site. It requires MySQL, PostgreSQL, Oracle, DB2, Interbase, MS SQL Server, or ODBC.

Content Management

Moodle (http://moodle.org). A free, open-source course-management system based upon the constructionist philosophy. A powerful tool for online learning communities, it claims 130,000 registered users in 160 countries speaking 75 languages. There is also a print MoodleZine newsletter and now a book on e-learning communities.

Mapping

Google Earth (http://earth.google.com). This mapping product combines satellite imagery from around the globe with Google search capabilities. Its navigational features allow users to explore the world and gather geographical information by zooming in from space to street level views. It offers tools for measuring, drawing, saving, printing, and GPS device support. Teachers can use Google Earth to get students excited about geography, economics, and demographics.

Web Start Pages

No more boring home pages! That could be the motto of the five sites below, each of which allows users to customize a home (start) page with a range of easily-added items that perform a wide range of tasks, including showing the current time, the weather, breaking news, tagged pictures, tech news, RSS feeds, search tools, and even a link to eBay.com. With such a wide range of add-ons available, teachers will have to be sure their students understand the concept of appropriate use.

Google Personalized Homepage (www.google.com/ig/). Google's familiar start page may be customized to include calendars, to-do lists, maps, blogs, weather, Gmail, Wikipedia, and news.

Netvibes (www.netvibes.com). As the site says, "This is your personalized page, you can now modify everything: move modules, add new RSS/ATOM feeds, change the parameters for each module, etc. Modifications are saved in real-time and you'll find your page when you get back on Netvibes.com. If you want to be able to access your page from any computer, you can sign in (at the top right) with your e-mail and a password."

Pageflakes (www.pageflakes.com). A "Flake" is a tool such as a weather display or a calculator. Users may choose from more than 100 such tools and may also add RSS feeds (including those in foreign languages) to create customizable pages.

Protopage (http://protopage.com). Allows user to create a totally customized start page featuring four different search bars (Google, Yahoo, a dictionary, and an encyclopedia) plus news feeds, sticky notes, and more. Even better, all are easily modified at any time.

C

a day in the life of web 2.0

David Warlick

**The latest powerful online tools can be harnessed to transform
and expand the learning experience.**

An eighth-grade science teacher, Ms. S, retrieves her MP3 player from the
computer-connected cradle where it's spent the night scanning the 17 podcasts she
subscribes to. Having detected three new programs, the computer downloaded the
files and copied them to the handheld. En route to work, Ms. S inserts the device
into her dash-mounted cradle and reviews the podcasts. She selects a colleague's
classroom presentation on global warming and a NASA conference lecture about
interstellar space travel.

As with all the teachers at her middle school, Ms. S keeps a regular blog, where
she writes about everything from homework assignments to reflections on course
topics, with a full description posted each Monday morning on the how, what, and
why of course material to be taught in the upcoming week.

The teachers' blogs are all syndicated using RSS—Rich Site Summary, or the
more informal and descriptive Really Simple Syndication. With aggregation
software, students, parents, administrators, and other teachers can subscribe and
have the freshly written blog entries immediately and automatically delivered
to their desktops. Professional development, communication, cross-curricular
lesson planning, and articulation among grade levels are all served as educators

regularly read each other's blogs and learn about topics and activities taking place in the various classrooms.

The Monday reports in particular enable them to benefit by sharing strategies and materials with colleagues who teach the same subject or those in other departments. For instance, Mr. K, a health and P.E. teacher, frequently finds ways of integrating science issues covered in Ms. S's classroom with his health topics. He knows that Ms. S will focus on genetics this week, and he will be teaching about disease next week, so he arranges for them to meet and discuss a combination assignment. In preparation for the meeting, Mr. K conducts a Web search to find the most informative sites and adds the Center for Disease Control (CDC) to his social bookmarks.

Meanwhile, social studies teacher Ms. L scans through sites tagged *genetics* in the school's social bookmark service. Her students may need quick access to them as they discuss genetic engineering current events during class. Mr. K's CDC site appears along with other genetics sites that have been saved and tagged. All assignments in Ms. L's class are turned in as blog entries, because she finds that their conversational nature encourages students to think and write in more depth than traditional formal essays or short answer assignments. Another advantage of receiving assignments in blog format is that both she and her students can subscribe, which means all of the kids' blogs appear in her aggregator, and students can reap the benefits of seeing each other's work.

Ms. L crafts the blog assignments with an eye toward training students to think critically and to post informed, well-considered opinions. A common classroom activity, for instance, is to have students read the blogged entries of others and write persuasive reactions—one in agreement, another in disagreement—and post these writings as comments to their classmates' blogs. Initially, the students struggled with the task, but they eventually learned the goal was not necessarily to find an idea with which they personally disagreed but to find another side to an idea and write persuasively from that perspective. For the genetics assignment, students assume a range of positions—some that discourage work in genetic manipulation based on security, cost, and ethics, and others that support it based on the potential cure for disease, life extension, and increased food production. In response to these blogged assignments, Ms. L posts assessments in the form of comments.

A few doors down the hall, veteran English teacher Mr. P is reviewing a new batch of student wikis. In an effort to help the students become better communicators, he never provides study guides for tests, instead relying on students to construct their own study resources using their team wikis. He rewards teams that create the most useful study guides.

Mr. P uses a wiki tool installed on the school's network. He devotes one part of the wiki site to general information and resources that he and the most accomplished students can edit. This part of the site serves as the class textbook. He also maintains other parts of the site for class teams, usually four students per team. These sections have their own passwords, and team members can log in to their wikis and enter text, images, and links to audio and video files. Teams can also format their content in a variety of ways. Mr. P is able to track the number of unique views for each page so that he can measure and reward teams for producing the most useful communications.

Earlier in the day, Student A had left Mr. P's room in a jubilant mood, because she'd just learned that her team produced the most useful study guide for the previous day's test, which earned them 10 points toward level three in the class. Level three will give the team much more editing access to the class wiki and more opportunities to contribute to the class literary Web site and the literary book the students will publish at the end of the school year.

Mr. P begins adjusting the volume on the microphone that hangs from his classroom ceiling. Today's discussion about *The Grapes of Wrath* will be recorded and posted in an audio file as a class podcast, as are all significant class presentations and discussions. Students, parents, community members, and other educators subscribe to his podcast programs. In fact, on the other side of town, Mrs. B, the parent of one of Mr. P's students, is listening to a podcast classroom conversation about a science fiction short story the students recently read. She and other parents subscribe to the podcasts so they can more easily engage their children in conversations about school.

At about the same time Mrs. B is listening to the lively classroom discussion, her son, Student B, is keying a text message from his school desk to his social studies class team. He briefly describes an idea for putting together a video as part of their current class project on rural cultures. The video idea had occurred to him a few days earlier while he and his mother were talking about one of the lesson recordings she'd listened to. Student C happens to be in study hall when she receives Student B's message and is excited about using a video in their presentation. She immediately accesses the school's social bookmarks, looking for sites that have been submitted by their science teacher, Ms. S, tagged with *soil* and *plantgrowth*. She identifies two sites, one from the Discovery Channel and the other from the USDA, called Ask a Worm. The idea is to create a video animation illustrating how soil quality affects cultures.

As Student C tags the sites for her team, school librarian Ms. J is conducting research on behalf of a new math teacher. She and the school tech facilitator both subscribe to all of the teachers' Monday report blogs. They use a shared spreadsheet to maintain an ongoing curriculum map of what's being taught in the school, based on the weekly updates. The librarian and tech facilitator use the map to support teachers by finding and identifying resources and strategies related to what they are teaching. Ms. J is using a blogging search engine to find some serious Web logs about mathematics so that the new teacher can include more practical applications in her current unit on real-world math. She finds several blogs: Galileo's Dilemma (math, physics, and chemistry), Dr. Katte's Blog (engineering), and BizImpresario (entrepreneurship). The librarian then adds the three blogs to the school's social bookmarks and tags them for the meeting that she has just noted on the school's collaborative social calendar.

Meanwhile, the principal is also looking at the school calendar. She is finishing up a weekly blog entry that describes happenings at the school for the next seven days, including two class podcasts, a band concert (also to be podcasted), a guest speaker, an interesting lesson about ancient civilizations, and the PTO meeting. The administrator subscribes to and scans all of the teachers' Monday report blogs for material to include in her weekly report. She always posts the blog entry by the end of the day on Monday, which is read not only by parents but also by educators at other schools, district leaders, and people from other parts of the community and country.

Early that evening the district superintendent reads the principal's recently posted blog. He also subscribes to the teachers' Monday report blogs, because he finds that their writing gives him a bank of ideas for promoting the district and its efforts toward continued improvement. After he finishes the reading, he briefly accesses the wiki site where he and a committee of educators and community members are collaborating to develop a district improvement plan. He jots down a couple of ideas that occurred to him while reading the digital conversations that have come to define the middle school. He moves on to publish the wiki version of the improvement plan, which invites interested community members to edit the improvement plan within the wiki and insert their reflections and ideas through attached comments. This superintendent truly believes that "It takes a village... "

David Warlick is a blogger, podcaster, author, programmer, and public speaker.

Reprinted with permission from *Technology & Learning*, Volume 27, Issue 3, October 2006.

D

references

A

ALA TechSource. (2007). *A "new media" information-literacy tool*. Available:
www.techsource.ala.org/blog/2006/04/a-new-media-information-literacy-tool.html

Alexander, B. (2006). Web 2.0: A new wave of innovation for teaching and learning?
[Electronic version]. *EDUCAUSE Review, 41*(2), 32–44. Retrieved December 8, 2006,
from www.educause.edu/apps/er/erm06/erm0621.asp

Allen, L. Q. (2006). Investigating culture through cooperative learning. *Foreign Language
Annals, 39*(1), 11–21.

American Digital Schools. (2006). *The America's Digital Schools 2006 national survey*.
Retrieved November 3, 2006, from www.ADS2006.org

Amrein, A. L., & Berliner, D. C. (2003). The effects of high-stakes testing on student
motivation and learning. *Educational Leadership, 60*(5), 32–38.

Anderson, C. (2006). *The long tail: Why the future of business is selling less of more*.
New York: Hyperion.

Anderson, L. W., & Krathwohl, D. R. (Eds.). (2001). *A taxonomy for learning, teaching
and assessing: A revision of Bloom's Taxonomy of educational objectives: Complete edition*.
New York: Longman.

Armstrong, E. (2006). *Gummy Bears: A graduated jellybean*. Available:
http://gr10pc-gb.blogspot.com/2006/09/multiplying-and-dividing-polynomials.html

B

Baltova, I. (1999). Multisensory language teaching in a multidimensional curriculum: The use of authentic bimodal video in core French. *Canadian Modern Language Review, 56*(1), 31–48.

Bausch, M. E. & Hasselbring, T. S. (2004). Assistive technology: Are the necessary skills and knowledge being developed at the preservice and inservice levels? *Teacher Education and Special Education, 27*(2), 97–104.

BBC News. (2006). *Fifteen years of the Web*. Retrieved October 10, 2006, from http://news.bbc.co.uk/1/hi/technology/5243862.stm

Becker, H. J. (2000). Who's wired and who's not: Children's access to and use of computer technology. *Children and Computer Technology, 10*(2), 44–75.

Becker, H. J., & Riel, M. M. (2000). *Teacher professional engagement and constructivist-compatible computer use* (Report No. 7 from the Center for Research on Information Technology and Organizations, University of California, Irvine, and University of Minnesota). Retrieved December 15, 2006, from www.crito.uci.edu/tlc/findings/report_7/report7.pdf

Beckwith, R. (2006). Meet our researchers. Intel Technology & Research. Retrieved from www.intel.com/research/researchers/r_beckwith.htm

Bedigian, B. (2006). *Rethinking education in a flat world*. Retrieved December 14, 2006, from www.hezel.com/strategies/Summer2006/education.html

Bielaczyc, K., & Collins, A. (1999). Learning communities in classrooms: a reconceptualization of educational practice. In: C. Reigeluth (Ed.), *Instructional-design theories and models. A new paradigm of instructional theory*, (vol. 2, pp. 269–292). Mahwah, NJ: Lawrence Erlbaum Associates.

Binkley, C. (2006, August 7). News from toyland: Gadgets that chat. *The Wall Street Journal Online*. Retrieved October 10, 2006, from http://online.wsj.com/article/SB115490389274028228.html

Bloom, B. S. (1956). *Taxonomy of educational objectives, Handbook I: The cognitive domain*. New York: David McKay.

Bowman, S., & Willis, C. (2003). *We Media: How audiences are shaping the future of news and information*. Available: www.hypergene.net/wemedia/download/we_media.pdf

Bradsher, K. (2006, September 1). A younger India is flexing its industrial brawn. *The New York Times*. Retrieved September 1, 2006, from www.nytimes.com/2006/09/01/business/worldbusiness/01rupee.html?hp&ex=1157169600&en=8767b2f151ae460a&ei=5094&partner=homepage

Bransford, J., Brown, A., & Cocking, R. (Eds). (1999). *How people learn: Brain, mind, experience, and school*. Washington, DC: National Academy Press.

Brooks-Young, S. (2006, September 20). *Reply to Scott McLeod's blog: Should schools allow teachers to use outside technology tools?* Retrieved September 20, 2006, from www.techlearning. com/blog/main/archives/2006/09/should_schools.php#comments

Brown, D., & Warschauer, M. (2006). From the university to the elementary classroom: Students' experiences in learning to integrate technology in instruction. *Journal of Technology and Teacher Education, 14*(3), 599–621.

Brown, J. S., Collins, A., & Duguid, P. (1989). Situated cognition and the culture of learning. *Educational Researcher, 18*(1), 32–42.

Bryant, T., & Bitikofer, J. (2006, August 1). *Open source network monitoring.* Retrieved August 1, 2006, from www.techlearning.com/showArticle.php?articleID=190301954

Brzycki, D., & Dudt, K. (2005). Overcoming barriers to technology use in teacher preparation programs. *Journal of Technology and Teacher Education, 13*(4), 619–641.

BusinessWeek. (2006, August 21). *How to hit a moving target.* Retrieved August 21, 2006, from www.businessweek.com/magazine/content/06_34/b3998423.htm

BusinessWeek. (n.d.). *Tip sheet: How to harness the power of Web 2.0.* Retrieved November 10, 2006, from www.businessweek.com/technology/ceo_tipsheet/2006_1.htm

C

Cable in the Classroom. (2006). *Parenting the MySpace generation.* Retrieved December 10, 2006, from www.ciconline.org/parenting

Caine, R. N., & Caine, G. (1994). *Making connections: Teaching and the human brain.* Boston: Addison Wesley.

Calderon, M., Hertz-Lazarowitz, R., & Slavin, R. (1998). Effects of bilingual cooperative integrated reading and composition on students making the transition from Spanish to English reading. *The Elementary School Journal, 99*(2), 153–166.

Campbell, A. (2006). Blogs and ESL. Retrieved from http://iteslj.org/Techniques/Campbell-Weblogs.html

Chang, Y., Wu, C., & Ku, H. (2005). The introduction of electronic portfolios to teach and assess English as a foreign language in Taiwan. *TechTrends, 49*(1), 30–35.

Clyde, L. A. (2005). Some new Internet applications coming now to a computer near you. *Teacher Librarian, 33*(1), 54–55.

Collier, S., Weinburgh, M., & Rivera, M. (2004). Infusing technology skills into a teacher education program: Change in students' knowledge about and use of technology. *Journal of Technology and Teacher Education, 12*(3), 447–468.

Collier, V. (1997). *Promoting academic success for ESL students: Understanding second language acquisition for school.* Jersey City, NJ: NJTESOL-BE.

Computerworld Honors Program. (2006). *New technology foundation: New Tech High Learning System.* Retrieved November 10, 2006, from www.cwhonors.org/case_studies/NewTechnologyFoundation.pdf

Consortium for School Networking (CoSN). (2004). *A report and estimating tool for K–12 school districts. Consortium for School Networking: Missouri District Case Study.* Retrieved November 10, 2006, from www.classroomtco.org/2004_case_studies/missouri.pdf

Consortium for School Networking (CoSN). (2006). *A report and estimating tool for K–12 school districts, One-to-one student computing, total cost of ownership, value of investment: District 1 TCO/VOI Case Study.* Retrieved November 10, 2006, from www.classroomtco.org/one_to_one_case_studies/District1CaseStudy.pdf

Corporation for Public Broadcasting. (2003). *Connected to the future: A report on children's Internet use.* Retrieved October 20, 2006, from www.cpb.org/stations/reports/connected/connected_report.pdf

Coy, P. (2006, September 27). Is the U.S. losing its competitive edge? *BusinessWeek.* Retrieved September 27, 2006, from www.businessweek.com/bwdaily/dnflash/content/sep2006/db20060927_387654.htm?chan=rss_topStories_ssi_5

Cuban, L. (2001). *Oversold and underused: Reforming schools through technology 1980–2000.* Cambridge, MA: Harvard University Press.

D

Daud, N. M., & Husin, Z. (2004). Developing critical thinking skills in computer-aided extended reading classes. *British Journal of Educational Technology, 35*(4), 477–487.

Davidson, H. (2005). *Copyright primer for administrators.* Available: www.techlearning.com/copyrightguide/

Davis, J. (2006, September 20). *Intel unveils Amazon River WiMax network.* Retrieved September 20, 2006, from www.edn.com/index.asp?layout=articlePrint&articleID=CA6373875

Davis, V., & Her 10th Grade Computer Science Class. (2006). *Online safety and privacy skills.* Retrieved November 10, 2006, from http://westwood.wikispaces.com/Chapter+1+-+Security+and+Privacy

DeCraene, M. (2006, September 19). *Let's flatten the schoolhouse!* Available: www.techlearning.com/blog/2006/09/lets_flatten_the_schoolhouse.php

Dede, C. (2003). No cliché left behind: Why education policy is not like the movies. *Educational Technology* (43) 2: 5–10. Retrieved from www.ncrel.org/tech/netc/2002/present.htm

Downes, S. (2006). E-learning 2.0. *National Research Council of Canada Elearn Magazine.* Retrieved November 10, 2006, from www.elearnmag.org/subpage.cfm?section=articles&article=29–1

Duhigg, C. (2006, August 9). Is copying a crime? Well ... *The Los Angeles Times.* Retrieved August 9, 2006, from www.latimes.com/news/printedition/la-fi-pollmusic9aug09,1,2427529.story

E

EDUCAUSE Learning Initiative. (2005). *7 things you should know about blogs.* Retrieved December 10, 2006, from www.educause.edu/ir/library/pdf/ELI7006.pdf

8e6 Technologies. (2005). *White paper: Instant message blocking and filtering.* Retrieved October 30, 2006, from www.8e6.com/products/R3000/pdf/R3000 White Paper_IMBlocking.pdf

8e6 Technologies. (2006). *White paper: MySpace: Safeguard your students, protect your network.* Retrieved October 30, 2006, from www.8e6.com/docs/white_papers/Myspace1.pdf

Englert, C. S., Mariage, T. V., Garmon, M. A., & Tarrant, K. L. (1998). Accelerating reading progress in early literacy project classrooms: Three exploratory studies. *Remedial and Special Education, 19*(3), 142–159.

F

Fadel, C., & Lemke, C. (2006). *Technology in schools: What the research says.* Cisco Systems: Metiri Group.

Farris-Berg, K. (2005). *Listening to student voices on technology: Today's tech-savvy students are stuck in text-dominated schools.* Retrieved October 20, 2006, from www.educationevolving.org/studentvoices/pdf/tech_savy_students.pdf

Flanagan, B., & Calandra, B. (2005). Podcasting in the classroom. *Learning & Leading with Technology, 33*(3), 20–25.

Friedman, T. L. (2005). *The world is flat: A brief history of the twenty-first century.* New York: Farrar, Straus & Girous.

Friedman, T. L. (2006, September 22). Anyone, anything, anywhere. *The New York Times.* Retrieved September 22, 2006, from http://select.nytimes.com/2006/09/22/opinion/22friedman.html

Fryer, W. (2006, August 19). *Thoughts on school district filtering.* Retrieved August 19, 2006, from www.techlearning.com/blog/main/archives/2006/08/thoughts_on_sch.php

Fuchs, D., Fuchs, L. S., Mathes, P. G., & Simmons, D. C. (1997). Peer-assisted learning strategies: Making classrooms more responsive to diversity. *American Educational Research Journal, 34,* 174–206.

Fullan, M. G., & Stiegelbauer, S. (1991). *The new meaning of educational change* (2nd ed.). New York: Teachers College Press.

G

Garrett, J. J. (2005, February 18). *Ajax: A new approach to Web applications.* Retrieved October 20, 2006, from www.adaptivepath.com/publications/essays/archives/000385.php

Gee, J.P. (2003). *What video games have to teach us about learning and literacy.* New York: Palgrave Macmillian.

Gersten, R., & Baker, S. (2000). What we know about effective instructional practices for English-language learners. *Exceptional Children, 66*(4), 454–470.

GetNetWise. (2003). *Online safety guide.* Available: http://kids.getnetwise.org/safetyguide/

Gewirtz, S. (1998). Conceptualizing social justice in education: Mapping the territory. *Journal of Education Policy, 13*(4), 469–484.

Gladwell, M. (2002). *The tipping point: How little things can make a big difference.* New York: Little, Brown and Company.

Godin, S. (2006). *Seth Godin's Web 2.0 traffic watch list.* Retrieved December 4, 2006, from www.alexaholic.com/sethgodin/

Godwin-Jones, R. (2003). Blogs and wikis: Environments for online collaboration. *Language Learning and Technology, 7,* 12–16.

Gomes, L. (2006, August 30). Will all of us get our 15 minutes on a YouTube video? *The Wall Street Journal Online,* p. B1. Retrieved August 30, 2006, from http://online.wsj.com/article_print/SB115689298168048904.html

Greenhouse, S. (2006, September 14). From author, help for white-collar workers. *The New York Times.* Retrieved September 14, 2006, from www.nytimes.com/2006/09/14/us/14labor.html?_r=1&oref=slogin

Greenhow, C. (2006). *From blackboard to browser: An empirical study of how teachers' beliefs and practices influence their use of the Internet in the classroom and are influenced by the Internet's affordances.* Unpublished doctoral dissertation, Harvard University, Cambridge, MA.

Greenspan, A. (2004, February 20). *The critical role of education in the nation's economy.* Address presented at the Greater Omaha Chamber of Commerce Annual Meeting, Omaha, NE [Transcript]. Retrieved December 15, 2006, from www.federalreserve.gov/boardDocs/Speeches/2004/200402202/

Greenstein, H. (2006). *Web 2.0 meets the Enterprise.* Retrieved December 5, 2006, from www.techlearning.com/showArticle.php?articleID=187202695

Guhlin, M. (2006a). *Blogs: Webs of connected learning.* Retrieved November 20, 2006, from www.techlearning.com/showArticle.php?articleID=189500884

Guhlin, M. (2006b). *Creating the walled garden: Setting up Web 2.0 apps on school district servers.* Available: http://mguhlin.wikispaces.com/walledgarden/

Guhlin, M. (2006c, August 15). *Flickr-ing—OUT.* Retrieved August 15, 2006, from www.techlearning.com/blog/2006/08/flickring_out.php

Guhlin, M. (2006d, June 1). *Forklifts for your mind.* Retrieved June 1, 2006, from www.techlearning.com/showArticle.php?articleID=188100264

Guhlin, M. (2006e, July 5). *Learning imprisoned.* Retrieved July 5, 2006, from www.techlearning.com/blog/main/archives/Web20/

Guhlin, M. (2006f, May 1). *Making the leap to Linux.* Retrieved May 1, 2006, from www.techlearning.com/story/showArticle.php?articleID=185303819

Guhlin, M., & Rodriguez, G. (2006, February 1). *Solving problems with open source solutions.* Retrieved February 1, 2006, from www.techlearning.com/showArticle. php?articleID=177100339

Guskey, T. R. (1994). Results-oriented professional development: In search of an optimal mix of effective practices [Electronic version]. *Journal of Staff Development, 15*(3), 42–50.

Guskey, T. R. (1999). Results-oriented professional development: In search of an optimal mix of effective practices. NCREL. [Online] Retrieved from www.ncrel.org/ncrel/sdrs/areas/ rpl_esys/pdlitrev.htm

Guskey, T. R. (2000). *Evaluating professional development.* Thousand Oaks, CA: Corwin Press.

Gutiérrez, R. (2002). Beyond essentialism: The complexity of language in teaching mathematics to Latina/o students. *American Educational Research Journal, 39*(4), 1047–1088.

H

Hasselbring, T. A. (2001). A possible future of special education technology. *Journal of Special Education Technology, 16*(4), 15–21.

Hof, R. (2006, June 5). Web 2.0 has corporate America spinning. *BusinessWeek.* Retrieved June 5, 2006, from www.businessweek.com/print/technology/content/jun2006/tc20060605_ 424102.htm

Honawar, V. (2006, July 12). NEA opens campaign to rewrite federal education law. *Education Week, 25*(42), 8.

Horrigan, J. B. (2006). *Home broadband adoption 2006.* Washington, DC: Pew Internet & American life project. Available: www.pewinternet.org/pdfs/PIP_Broadband_trends2006.pdf

I

IMS Global Learning Consortium. (2006). *IMS Global Learning Consortium, Inc.* Retrieved December 10, 2006, from www.imsglobal.org/background.html

Intel Education Initiative. (2006). *Going paperless.* Retrieved December 10, 2006, from www97.intel.com/odyssey/Story.aspx?storyid=355

International Society for Technology in Education (ISTE). (2000). *National educational technology standards for teachers.* Eugene, OR: Author.

J

Jakes, D. (2003, April 29). From creating virtual workspaces: New models for developing online curriculum. Presentation at TechForum: Breakthrough Technologies for 21st Century Schools, Chicago, IL. Retrieved December 10, 2006, from www.techlearning.com/ techlearning/pdf/events/techforum/chi03/vault/Jakes_Presentation.pdf

Jakes, D. (2005, December 1). *Making a case for digital storytelling.* Retrieved December 1, 2005, from www.techlearning.com/story/showArticle.php?articleID=174401140

Jakes, D. (2006a, August 17). *Flickr-ing IN*. Retrieved August 17, 2006, from www.techlearning.com/blog/2006/08/flickring_in.php

Jakes, D. (2006b, October 18). *Gap analysis*. Available: www.techlearning.com/blog/2006/10/gap_analysis.php

Jakes, D. (2006c, October 27). *Making IT stick*. Keynote address presented at the Technology Forum, Austin, TX. Available: www.techlearning.com/techlearning/events/techforum06/DavidJakes_MakingITStick.pdf

Jakes, D. (2006d, September 20). *Reply to Scott McLeod's blog: Should schools allow teachers to use outside technology tools?* Retrieved September 20, 2006, from www.techlearning.com/blog/main/archives/2006/09/should_schools.php#comments

Jakes, D. (2006e, May 15). *Staff development 2.0*. Retrieved May 15, 2006, from www.techlearning.com/showArticle.php?articleID=187002843

Jana, R. (2006, September 25). InShort. *BusinessWeek*, p. 4. Available: www.businessweek.com/magazine/content/06_39/b4002405.htm

Jana, R. (2006, September 25). Learning from informal urban economies. *BusinessWeek*. Retrieved September 25, 2006, from www.businessweek.com/innovate/content/sep2006/id20060925_363389.htm?chan=search

Jones, L. C., & Plass, J. L. (2002). Supporting listening comprehension and vocabulary in French with multimedia annotations. *The Modern Language Journal, 86*(4), 546–561.

K

Kadel, R. (2006). Coursecasting: The wave of the future? *Learning & Leading with Technology, 33*(5), 48–49.

Kahn, J. (2006, September 1). Where's Mao? Chinese revise history books. *The New York Times*. Retrieved September 1, 2006, from www.nytimes.com/2006/09/01/world/asia/01china.html?hp&ex=1157169600&en=6ad0b40aa76be4c4&ei=5094&partner=homepage

Kelly, K. (2005). We are the Web. *Wired Magazine, 13*(8). Retrieved December 10, 2006, from www.wired.com/wired/archive/13.08/tech.html

Kennard, W. E. (2007, January 1). Beyond taxes and regulation: Ways to unleash the broadband revolution. *Info Tech & Telecom News*. Available: www.heartland.org/Article.cfm?artId=20337

King, K. P., & Gura, M. (2006, May 1). *Professional development as podcast*. Retrieved May 1, 2006, from www.techlearning.com/showArticle.php?articleID=185303670

King, R. (2006, September 11). Social networks: Execs use them too. *BusinessWeek*. Retrieved September 11, 2006, from www.businessweek.com/print/technology/content/sep2006/tc20060911_414136.htm

Krathwohl, D. R. (2002). A revision of Bloom's taxonomy: An overview. *Theory into Practice, 41*(4), 212–218.

Kuropatwa, D. (2007). *Applied Math 40S wiki solutions manual: Front page*. Available: http://am40s.pbwiki.com

L

Laffey, J. (2004). Appropriation, mastery and resistance to technology in early childhood preservice teacher education. *Journal of Research on Technology in Education, 36*(4), 361–382.

Lakshman, N. (2006, October 2). Linux spreads its wings in India. *BusinessWeek*. Retrieved October 2, 2006 from www.businessweek.com/magazine/content/06_40/b4003069.htm?chan=search

Laptops for Learning Task Force. (2004). *Laptops for Learning final report and recommendations.* Retrieved November 20, 2006, from http://etc.usf.edu/L4L/

Lave, J. (1988). *Cognition in practice: Mind, mathematics, and culture in everyday life.* Cambridge, UK: Cambridge University Press.

Lave, J. & Wenger, E. (1991). *Situated learning: Legitimate peripheral participation.* Cambridge, UK: Cambridge University Press.

Leichtman Research Group. (2006). *Broadband Internet access & services in the home: Research study 2006.* Retrieved October 5, 2006, from www.leichtmanresearch.com/research/bband_home_brochure.pdf

LemonLINK. (2007). *About Project LemonLINK.* Available: www.lgsd.k12.ca.us/lemonlink/About.htm

Levin, D., & Arafeh, S. (2002). *The digital disconnect: The widening gap between Internet-savvy students and their schools.* Washington, DC: Pew Internet & American Life Project. Retrieved July 21, 2006, from www.pewinternet.org/pdfs/PIP_Schools_Internet_Report.pdf

Lewin, L. (1999). "Site reading" the World Wide Web. *Educational Leadership, 56*(5), 16–20.

Lindquist, J. (2004). The future of anytime, anywhere education. *THE Journal, 32*(4), 32–34.

M

Maccini, P., Gagnon, J. C., & Hughes, C. A. (2002). Technology-based practices for secondary students with learning disabilities. *Learning Disability Quarterly, 25*(4), 247–261.

Malone, J. A., Atweh, B., & Northfield, J. R. (Eds.). (1998). *Research and supervision in mathematics and science education.* Mahwah, NJ: Lawrence Erlbaum Associates.

Marsh, J. (2007). Available: www.shef.ac.uk/education/staff/academic/marshj.html

McLeod, S. (2006a). *Why blog as an administrator?* Available: http://scottmcleod.typepad.com/dangerouslyirrelevant/files/2006_dangerouslyirrelevant.org_Why_Blog_As_An_Administrator.pdf

McLeod, S. (2006b, September 27). *Posting student photos on the Web.* Retrieved October 5, 2006, from www.techlearning.com/blog/main/archives/2006/09/posting_student.php

McLeod, S. (2006c, February 22). *Should schools allow teachers to use non-school technology tools?* Available: www.schooltechleadershipblog.org/communication/

McNealy, S. (2006). *My voice: Top 10 reasons for not turning in my homework.* Available: www.sun.com/aboutsun/executives/mcnealy/myvoice.jsp

Meador, W. J. (2005, March 1). *Securing a school network.* Retrieved October 20, 2006, from www.techlearning.com/showArticle.php?articleID=60401696

Mereness, J. (2006, October 1). *Open source in South Korea.* Retrieved October 20, 2006 from www.techlearning.com/story/showArticle.php?articleID=193006191

Microsoft Corporation. (2006). *Explore the education competencies.* Retrieved October 20, 2006, from www.microsoft.com/education/competencies/default.mspx

Mindlin, A. (2006). *MySpace, refuge of the young, ages a bit.* Retrieved from www.nytimes.com/2006/10/09/technology/09drill.tml?ex=1187323200&en=77e57f9fc988c215&ei=5070

Mohr, K. A. J. (2004). English as an accelerated language: A call to action for reading teachers. *The Reading Teacher, 58*(1), 18–26.

Moodle. (2006). *Welcome to Moodle!* Retrieved October 20, 2006, from www.moodle.org

Munoz, M. (2006). *Apple tools create eager learners. Profiles in success: Corvallis Middle School.* Available: www.apple.com/education/profiles/corvallis/

N

National Center for Education Statistics (NCES). (2003). *Internet access in U.S. public schools and classrooms: 1994–2002.* Retrieved October 20, 2006, from http://nces.ed.gov/surveys/frss/publications/2004011/2.asp

National Center for Education Statistics (NCES). (n.d.). *NCES fast facts.* Retrieved July 23, 2006, from http://nces.ed.gov/fastfacts/

Naughton, D. (2006). Cooperative strategy training and oral interaction: Enhancing small group communication in the language classroom. *The Modern Language Journal, 90*(ii), 169–184.

NewMediaLiteracy.org. (2006). *Who we are.* Available: www.newmedialiteracy.org/about/

New Tech Foundation. (2006). *The New Tech Learning System.* Retrieved November 20, 2006, from www.newtechfoundation.org/initiatives_nth.html

Norris, C., Sullivan, T., Poirot, J., & Solloway, E. (2003). No access, no use, no impact: Snapshot surveys of educational technology in K–12. *Journal of Research on Technology in Education, 36*(1), 15–28.

North Central Regional Educational Laboratory (NCREL). (2003). *21st century skills: Literacy in the Digital Age.* Retrieved July 20, 2006, from www.ncrel.org/engauge/skills/skill21.htm

Noval, T. (2006). *Encouraging participation.* Available: www.techlearning.com/story/showArticle.jhtml?articleID=175007847

The Noyce Foundation. (2006). *The Noyce Foundation annual report.* Palo Alto, CA: Author.

O

Oakes, C. (2006, September 1). *How I became a WebHead*. Available: www.techlearning.com/story/showArticle.php?articleID=192201457

On Purpose Associates. (2001). *Brain-based learning*. Retrieved November 10, 2006, from www.funderstanding.com/brain_based_learning.cfm

Open Source Initiative. (2006). *The open source definition*. Retrieved August 10, 2006, from www.opensource.org

O'Reilly, T. (2005, September 30). *What is Web 2.0: Design patterns and business models for the next generation of software*. Retrieved July 20, 2006, from www.oreillynet.com/pub/a/oreilly/tim/news/2005/09/30/what-is-Web-20.html

P

Packett, B. (2007). *History according to Bob*. Available: www.summahistorica.com

Painter, D. D. (2004). *What do they need to know about cyber safety?* Retrieved August 1, 2004, from www.techlearning.com/story/showArticle.php?articleID=23903574

Palmeri, C. (2006, July 17). Tech toys for today's kids. *BusinessWeek*. Retrieved July 17, 2006, from www.businessweek.com/technology/content/jul2006/tc20060714_924286.htm

Partnership for 21st Century Skills. (2004). *Learning for the 21st century*. Retrieved December 10, 2006, from www.21stcenturyskills.org/images/stories/otherdocs/P21_Report.pdf

Partnership for 21st Century Skills. (2006). *Statement of principles: 21st century skills and the reauthorization of NCLB/ESEA*. Retrieved December 10, 2006, from www.21stcenturyskills.org/documents/NCLBMemoandPrinciples0630.pdf

Pawling, E. (1999). Modern languages and CD-ROM-based learning. *British Journal of Technology, 30*(2), 163–175.

Pelligrino, J. W. (2004). Designs for research on technology and assessment: Conflicting or complementary agendas? In B. Means & G. D. Haertel (Eds.), *Using technology evaluation to enhance student learning* (pp. 49–56). New York: Teachers College Press.

Peregoy, S. F., & Boyle O. F. (2005). *Reading, writing and learning in ESL: A resource book for K–12 teachers*. Boston: Pearson Education.

Pew Internet & American Life Project. (2006). *Bloggers: A portrait of the Internet's new storytellers*. Retrieved July 19, 2006, from www.pewInternet.org/pdfs/PIP Bloggers Report July 19 2006.pdf

Pierce, S. (2006). *Elementary level geography club*. National Council for Geographic Education, Curriculum and Instruction Committee. Available: www.ncge.org/resources/geoclub/geography_club_overview.pdf

Pink, D. (2006). *A whole new mind: Why right-brainers will rule the future*. New York: Penguin Books.

Poling, C. (2005). Blog on: Building communication and collaboration among staff and students. *Learning & Leading with Technology, 32*(6), 12–15.

Prensky, M. (2001, October). Digital natives, digital immigrants. *On the Horizon, 9*(5), 10–15. Available: www.marcprensky.com/writing/Prensky - Digital Natives, Digital Immigrants - Part1.pdf

Prensky, M. (2004). Proposal for educational software development sites: An open source tool to create the learning software we need. *On the Horizon, 12*(1) 41–44.

Project Tomorrow. (2006). *Our voices, our future: Student and teacher views on science, technology & education: National report on NetDay's 2005 Speak Up Event.* Irvine, CA: Author. Retrieved November 20, 2006, from www.netday.org/SPEAKUP/pdfs/ SpeakUpReport_05.pdf

Public Broadcasting Service (PBS). (2006). *School: The story of American public education.* Available: www.pbs.org/kcet/publicschool/

R

Roberts, M. M. (2006). Lessons for the future Internet: Learning from the past. *EDUCAUSE Review, 41*(4), 16–25. Retrieved December 10, 2006, from www.educause.edu/er/erm06/ erm0640.asp

Robertson, J. (2002, January 23). *How to evaluate a content management system.* Retrieved December 10, 2006, from http://steptwo.com.au/papers/kmc_evaluate/

Rockman, S. (2003, Fall). Learning from laptops. *Threshold, 24*–28. Retrieved December 15, 2006, from www.b-g.k12.ky.us/Tech/Laptops.pdf

Roth, W. M., & McGinn, M. K. (1998). *Legitimate peripheral participation in the education of researchers.* Retrieved December 15, 2006, from www.educ.uvic.ca/faculty/mroth/ teaching/580/lpp.pdf

Rovai, A. P. (2001). Building classroom community at a distance: A case study. *Educational Technology Research and Development (ETR&D), 49*(4), 33–48.

S

Sandholtz, J. H., Ringstaff, C., & Dwyer, D. C. (2000). The evolution of instruction in technology-rich classrooms. In *The Jossey-Bass Reader on Technology and Learning* (pp. 255–276). San Francisco: Jossey-Bass.

School 2.0. (2006). *Why is it called "School 2.0"?* Available: www.school2-0.org

Schrum, L. (1999). Technology professional development for teachers. *Educational Technology Research and Development (ETR&D), 47*(4), 83–90.

Schultz, L. (2005). *Bloom's taxonomy.* Retrieved August 1, 2006, from http://Web.odu.edu/educ/llschult/blooms_taxonomy.htm

Schwier, R. A. (2001). Catalysts, emphases and elements of virtual learning communities: Implications for research and practice. *The Quarterly Review of Distance Education, 2*(1), 5–18.

Seels, B., Campbell, S., & Talsma, V. (2003). Supporting excellence in technology through communities of learners. *Educational Technology Research and Development (ETR&D), 51*(1), 91–104.

Seelve, K. Q., & Bosman, J. (2006, August 9). Bloggers drive inquiry on how altered images saw print. *The New York Times.* Retrieved October 10, 2006, from www.nytimes.com/2006/08/09/technology/09photo.html

Shirky, C. (2003, April 24). *A group is its own worst enemy.* Address presented at the O'Reilly Emerging Technology Conference, Santa Clara, CA [Transcript]. Retrieved December 10, 2006, from www.shirky.com/writings/group_enemy.html

Short, R. A., Frye, B. J., King, J. R., & Homan, S. P. (1999). Connecting classrooms and early interventions. Reading Research and Instruction 38(4), 387–400.

Siemens, G. (2004, December 12). *Connectivism: A learning theory for the digital age.* Retrieved December 10, 2006, from www.elearnspace.org/Articles/connectivism.htm

Sloan, P., & Kaihla, P. (2006). Blogging for dollars. *Business 2.0 Magazine.* Retrieved December 15, 2006, from http://money.cnn.com/magazines/business2/business2_archive/2006/09/01/8384325/

Solomon, G. (2003, January 15). *Project-based learning: A primer.* Retrieved October 20, 2006, from www.techlearning.com/db_area/archives/TL/2003/01/project.php

Stanley, G. (2005). Interactive listening mazes. Retrieved from http://interactivelisteningmazes.blogspot.com

Staples, A., Pugach, M. C., & Himes, D. J. (2005). Rethinking the technology integration challenge: Cases from three urban elementary schools. *Journal of Research on Technology in Education, 37*(3), 285–311.

Steinberg, B. (2006, August 7). Back-to-school marketers test Web. *The Wall Street Journal Online.* Retrieved August 7, 2006, from http://online.wsj.com/article/SB115491307365928376.html

Stiggins, R. J. (1987). The design and development of performance assessments. *Educational Measurement: Issues and Practice, 6*, 33–42.

Strudler, N. B., & Grove, K. J. (2002). Integrating technology into teacher candidate's field experiences: A two-pronged approach. *Journal of Computing in Teacher Education, 19*(2), 33–39.

Sullivan, L. (2006). Blogs, wikis, forums sway consumer opinion, research shows. *Internet Week.* Retrieved August 15, 2006, from http://Internetweek.cmp.com/192201184

Swanson, H. L. & Hoskyn M. (1999). Definition X treatment interactions for students with learning disabilities. *The School Psychology Review, 28*(4), 644–58.

T

Taylor, S. (2006). *Tips for building an online community.* Available: www.techlearning.com/story/showArticle.jhtml?articleID=193401799

techLEARNING.com. (2006). *Survey results—Will Web 2.0 tools replace traditional suites?* Retrieved October 25, 2006, from www.techlearning.com/instantpoll/2006/0724.php

ThinkQuest. (2006). *Think together.* Oracle Education Foundation. Available: http://thinkquest.org

Thinkronize. (2006, October 23). *New research reveals that students' unauthorized redirection to commercial and pay sites is greatest concern to educators, with Internet pornography and predators also ranking high.* Available: www.thinkronize.com/press/PR/06_october23.html

Tinker, R. (2005). *Freeing educational applications.* Retrieved November 10, 2006, from www.concord.org/publications/newsletter/2005-spring/opensource.html

Tinker, R. (2006). *Open source educational applications.* Retrieved November 20, 2006, from www.concord.org/publications/files/perspective_open_source.pdf

Tosh, D. (2006). *Inside the mind of a Web 2.0 developer.* Available: www.techlearning.com/story/showArticle.php?articleID=192200020

Turner, S. D. (2006). *Broadband reality check II.* Washington, DC: Freepress.net. Available: www.freepress.net/docs/bbrc2-execsum.pdf

U

U.S. Department of Education. (1996). *National educational technology plan: Getting America's students ready for the 21st century.* Retrieved October 20, 2006, from www.ed.gov/about/offices/list/os/technology/plan/national/

U.S. Department of Education. (2001). *No child left behind* (Publication No. 107–110). [Online Version]. Retrieved October 20, 2006, from www.ed.gov/policy/elsec/leg/esea02/

U.S. Department of Education. (2004). *Toward a new Golden Age in American education: How the Internet, the law and today's students are revolutionizing expectations.* Washington, DC: Author.

U.S. Department of Education. (2005). *Executive summary of the national education technology plan.* Retrieved October 20, 2006, from www.ed.gov/about/offices/list/os/technology/plan/2004/site/theplan/edlite-thePlan.html

U.S. Department of Education. (2006). *Secretary Spellings announces partnership with states to improve accountability for limited English proficient students.* Available: www.ed.gov/news/pressreleases/2006/07/07272006.html

Utecht, J. (2006). *The thinking stick: Customization generation.* Retrieved September 25, 2006, from http://jeff.scofer.com/thinkingstick/?p=283

V

Vara, V. (2006, September 12). Offices co-opt consumer Web tools like "wikis" and social networking. *The Wall Street Journal Online*. Retrieved September 12, 2006, from http://online.wsj.com/article/SB115802778487360244.html

Villano, M. (2006a, April 19). *Beyond open source*. Retrieved April 19, 2006, from www.techlearning.com/showArticle.php?articleID=185300823

Villano, M. (2006b, May 1). *Indiana's open-source experiment*. Retrieved May 1, 2006, from www.techlearning.com/story/showArticle.php?articleID=186701271

Villano, M. (2006c, April 12). *Open arms for open source*. Retrieved April 12, 2006, from www.techlearning.com/story/showArticle.php?articleID=185300217

W

Warlick, D. (2006a). *About Blogmeister*. Retrieved October 10, 2006, from http://classblogmeister.com

Warlick, D. (2006b, September 11). *AUP 2.0*. Available: www.techlearning.com/blog/2006/09/aup_20.php

Warlick, D. (2006c, October). A day in the life of Web 2.0. *Technology & Learning, 27*(3). Retrieved October 20, 2006, from www.techlearning.com/showArticle.php?articleID=193200296

Warlick, D. (2006d, August 21). *Getting right down to it*. Retrieved August 21, 2006, from www.techlearning.com/blog/2006/08/getting_right_down_to_it.php

Warlick, D. (2006e, October 2). *The rise and fall of the hit—and the textbook industry*. Available: www.techlearning.com/blog/2006/10/the_rise_and_fall_of_the_hit_a.php

WebSiteOptimization.com. (2006). *Bandwidth report*. Retrieved July 31, 2006, from www.websiteoptimization.com/bw/

Weil, D. (2006). *The corporate blogging book: Absolutely everything you need to know to get it right*. New York: Penguin.

Wenger, E. (1998). *Communities of practice: Learning, meaning, and identity*. Cambridge, UK: Cambridge University Press.

Wenger, E. (2001). *Supporting communities of practice: A survey of community-oriented technologies*. Retrieved December 15, 2006, from www.ewenger.com/tech/executive_summary.htm

Whiting, R. (2006). *Case study: Using data mining to analyze student behavior*. Retrieved October 20, 2006, from www.schoolcio.com/showArticle.jhtml?articleID=193005274

Whitmell, T., & Killingsworth, B. (2006, October). Is it time to move our data and applications online? *Learning & Leading with Technology, 34*(2), 8–9. Available: www.iste.org/Content/NavigationMenu/Publications/LL/LLIssues/Volume_34_2006_2007_/October_No_2_2/34208w.pdf

Wiggins, G. (1993). Assessment: authenticity, context, and validity. *Phi Delta Kappan, 75*(November), 200–230.

Wikipedia. (2006a). *Blog.* Retrieved December 15, 2006, from http://en.wikipedia.org/wiki/Blog

Wikipedia. (2006b). *Podcast.* Retrieved August 20, 2006, from http://en.wikipedia.org/wiki/Podcasts

Williams, H. S., & Kingham, M. (2003). Infusion of technology into the curriculum. *Journal of Instructional Psychology, 30*(3), 178–184.

Woods, D. (2005, September 15). What is open source? Retrieved September 15, 2006, from www.onlamp.com/lpt/a/6111

X

Xu, Y., Gelfer, J., & Perkins, P. (2005). Using peer tutoring to increase social interactions in early schooling. *TESOL Quarterly, 39*(1), 83–106.

Z

Zha, S., Kelly, P., Park, M. K., & Fitzgerald, G. (2006). An investigation of communicative competence of ESL students using electronic discussion boards. *Journal of Research on Technology in Education, 38*(3), 349–367.

Zolli, A. (2006, September 25). Recognizing tomorrow's hot ideas today. *BusinessWeek.* Retrieved September 25, 2006, from www.businessweek.com/magazine/content/06_39/b4002405.htm

E

national educational technology standards

National Educational Technology Standards for Students (NETS•S)

The National Educational Technology Standards for students are divided into six broad categories. Standards within each category are to be introduced, reinforced, and mastered by students. Teachers can use these standards as guidelines for planning technology-based activities in which students achieve success in learning, communication, and life skills.

1. Creativity and Innovation

Students demonstrate creative thinking, construct knowledge, and develop innovative products and processes using technology. Students:

    a. apply existing knowledge to generate new ideas, products, or processes.

    b. create original works as a means of personal or group expression.

    c. use models and simulations to explore complex systems and issues.

    d. identify trends and forecast possibilities.

2. Communication and Collaboration

Students use digital media and environments to communicate and work collaboratively, including at a distance, to support individual learning and contribute to the learning of others. Students:

a. interact, collaborate, and publish with peers, experts, or others employing a variety of digital environments and media.

b. communicate information and ideas effectively to multiple audiences using a variety of media and formats.

c. develop cultural understanding and global awareness by engaging with learners of other cultures.

d. contribute to project teams to produce original works or solve problems.

3. Research and Information Fluency

Students apply digital tools to gather, evaluate, and use information. Students:

a. plan strategies to guide inquiry.

b. locate, organize, analyze, evaluate, synthesize, and ethically use information from a variety of sources and media.

c. evaluate and select information sources and digital tools based on the appropriateness to specific tasks.

d. process data and report results.

4. Critical Thinking, Problem Solving, and Decision Making

Students use critical-thinking skills to plan and conduct research, manage projects, solve problems, and make informed decisions using appropriate digital tools and resources. Students:

a. identify and define authentic problems and significant questions for investigation.

b. plan and manage activities to develop a solution or complete a project.

c. collect and analyze data to identify solutions and make informed decisions.

d. use multiple processes and diverse perspectives to explore alternative solutions.

5. Digital Citizenship

Students understand human, cultural, and societal issues related to technology and practice legal and ethical behavior. Students:

   a. advocate and practice the safe, legal, and responsible use of information and technology.

   b. exhibit a positive attitude toward using technology that supports collaboration, learning, and productivity.

   c. demonstrate personal responsibility for lifelong learning.

   d. exhibit leadership for digital citizenship.

6. Technology Operations and Concepts

Students demonstrate a sound understanding of technology concepts, systems, and operations. Students:

   a. understand and use technology systems.

   b. select and use applications effectively and productively.

   c. troubleshoot systems and applications.

   d. transfer current knowledge to the learning of new technologies.

National Educational Technology Standards for Teachers (NETS•T)

All classroom teachers should be prepared to meet the following standards and performance indicators.

I. Technology Operations and Concepts

Teachers demonstrate a sound understanding of technology operations and concepts. Teachers:

   A. demonstrate introductory knowledge, skills, and understanding of concepts related to technology (as described in the ISTE National Educational Technology Standards for Students).

   B. demonstrate continual growth in technology knowledge and skills to stay abreast of current and emerging technologies.

II. Planning and Designing Learning Environments and Experiences

Teachers plan and design effective learning environments and experiences supported by technology. Teachers:

A. design developmentally appropriate learning opportunities that apply technology-enhanced instructional strategies to support the diverse needs of learners.

B. apply current research on teaching and learning with technology when planning learning environments and experiences.

C. identify and locate technology resources and evaluate them for accuracy and suitability.

D. plan for the management of technology resources within the context of learning activities.

E. plan strategies to manage student learning in a technology-enhanced environment.

III. Teaching, Learning, and the Curriculum

Teachers implement curriculum plans that include methods and strategies for applying technology to maximize student learning. Teachers:

A. facilitate technology-enhanced experiences that address content standards and student technology standards.

B. use technology to support learner-centered strategies that address the diverse needs of students.

C. apply technology to develop students' higher-order skills and creativity.

D. manage student learning activities in a technology-enhanced environment.

IV. Assessment and Evaluation

Teachers apply technology to facilitate a variety of effective assessment and evaluation strategies. Teachers:

A. apply technology in assessing student learning of subject matter using a variety of assessment techniques.

B. use technology resources to collect and analyze data, interpret results, and communicate findings to improve instructional practice and maximize student learning.

C. apply multiple methods of evaluation to determine students' appropriate use of technology resources for learning, communication, and productivity.

V. Productivity and Professional Practice

Teachers use technology to enhance their productivity and professional practice. Teachers:

A. use technology resources to engage in ongoing professional development and lifelong learning.

B. continually evaluate and reflect on professional practice to make informed decisions regarding the use of technology in support of student learning.

C. apply technology to increase productivity.

D. use technology to communicate and collaborate with peers, parents, and the larger community in order to nurture student learning.

VI. Social, Ethical, Legal, and Human Issues

Teachers understand the social, ethical, legal, and human issues surrounding the use of technology in PK–12 schools and apply that understanding in practice. Teachers:

A. model and teach legal and ethical practice related to technology use.

B. apply technology resources to enable and empower learners with diverse backgrounds, characteristics, and abilities.

C. identify and use technology resources that affirm diversity.

D. promote safe and healthy use of technology resources.

E. facilitate equitable access to technology resources for all students.

National Educational Technology Standards for Administrators (NETS•A)

All school administrators should be prepared to meet the following standards and performance indicators. These standards are a national consensus among educational stakeholders regarding what best indicates effective school leadership for comprehensive and appropriate use of technology in schools.

I. **Leadership and Vision—Educational leaders inspire a shared vision for comprehensive integration of technology and foster an environment and culture conducive to the realization of that vision. Educational leaders:**

   A. facilitate the shared development by all stakeholders of a vision for technology use and widely communicate that vision.

   B. maintain an inclusive and cohesive process to develop, implement, and monitor a dynamic, long-range, and systemic technology plan to achieve the vision.

   C. foster and nurture a culture of responsible risk taking and advocate policies promoting continuous innovation with technology.

   D. use data in making leadership decisions.

   E. advocate for research-based effective practices in use of technology.

   F. advocate, on the state and national levels, for policies, programs, and funding opportunities that support implementation of the district technology plan.

II. **Learning and Teaching—Educational leaders ensure that curricular design, instructional strategies, and learning environments integrate appropriate technologies to maximize learning and teaching. Educational leaders:**

   A. identify, use, evaluate, and promote appropriate technologies to enhance and support instruction and standards-based curriculum leading to high levels of student achievement.

   B. facilitate and support collaborative technology-enriched learning environments conducive to innovation for improved learning.

   C. provide for learner-centered environments that use technology to meet the individual and diverse needs of learners.

D. facilitate the use of technologies to support and enhance instructional methods that develop higher-level thinking, decision-making, and problem-solving skills.

E. provide for and ensure that faculty and staff take advantage of quality professional learning opportunities for improved learning and teaching with technology.

III. **Productivity and Professional Practice—Educational leaders apply technology to enhance their professional practice and to increase their own productivity and that of others. Educational leaders:**

A. model the routine, intentional, and effective use of technology.

B. employ technology for communication and collaboration among colleagues, staff, parents, students, and the larger community.

C. create and participate in learning communities that stimulate, nurture, and support faculty and staff in using technology for improved productivity.

D. engage in sustained, job-related professional learning using technology resources.

E. maintain awareness of emerging technologies and their potential uses in education.

F. use technology to advance organizational improvement.

IV. **Support, Management, and Operations—Educational leaders ensure the integration of technology to support productive systems for learning and administration. Educational leaders:**

A. develop, implement, and monitor policies and guidelines to ensure compatibility of technologies.

B. implement and use integrated technology-based management and operations systems.

C. allocate financial and human resources to ensure complete and sustained implementation of the technology plan.

D. integrate strategic plans, technology plans, and other improvement plans and policies to align efforts and leverage resources.

E. implement procedures to drive continuous improvements of technology systems and to support technology-replacement cycles.

V. Assessment and Evaluation—Educational leaders use technology to plan and implement comprehensive systems of effective assessment and evaluation. Educational leaders:

A. use multiple methods to assess and evaluate appropriate uses of technology resources for learning, communication, and productivity.

B. use technology to collect and analyze data, interpret results, and communicate findings to improve instructional practice and student learning.

C. assess staff knowledge, skills, and performance in using technology and use results to facilitate quality professional development and to inform personnel decisions.

D. use technology to assess, evaluate, and manage administrative and operational systems.

VI. Social, Legal, and Ethical Issues—Educational leaders understand the social, legal, and ethical issues related to technology and model responsible decision making related to these issues. Educational leaders:

A. ensure equity of access to technology resources that enable and empower all learners and educators.

B. identify, communicate, model, and enforce social, legal, and ethical practices to promote responsible use of technology.

C. promote and enforce privacy, security, and online safety related to the use of technology.

D. promote and enforce environmentally safe and healthy practices in the use of technology.

E. participate in the development of policies that clearly enforce copyright law and assign ownership of intellectual property developed with district resources.

This material was originally produced as a project of the Technology Standards for School Administrators Collaborative.

index